OUR WORD IS OUR BOND

THE CULTURAL LIVES OF LAW

Edited by Austin Sarat

MARIANNE CONSTABLE

Our Word Is Our Bond

How Legal Speech Acts

STANFORD LAW BOOKS

An Imprint of Stanford University Press
Stanford, California

© Stanford University Press
Stanford, California

Library of Congress Cataloging-in-Publication Data

Constable, Marianne, author.
Our word is our bond : how legal speech acts / Marianne Constable.
    pages cm—(The cultural lives of law)
  Includes bibliographical references and index.
  ISBN 978-0-8047-7493-2 (cloth : alk. paper) —
  ISBN 978-0-8047-7494-9 (pbk. : alk. paper)
    1. Law—Language. 2. Sociological jurisprudence. I. Title.
II. Series: Cultural lives of law.
  K487.L36C658 2014
  340'.14–dc23
                                                    2013049863
ISBN 978-0-8047-9168-7 (electronic)

Typeset by Thompson Type in 10/14.5 Minion

Ought we not . . . to think of . . . the ground of possibility of all the sciences of man as closely as possible in correlation with our concern with language?

—Michel Foucault, *The Order of Things*, p. 285

Law is not necessarily just, but it does promise justice. We must look to the theory of law and justice to understand why that promise exists and under what conditions it may be fulfilled or abridged. The matter cannot be settled by definitional fiat.

—Philip Selznick, *The Moral Commonwealth*, pp. 443–444

Contents

Acknowledgments

I thank the many persons who have engaged in dialogue with me about law and language and the many institutions that have supported my work over the years. I also apologize to all whose insights about the matters of this book I have come to appreciate but fail to mention explicitly here or in my text.

At the University of California at Berkeley, I am continually reminded how much my current work owes to reading and thinking that began when I was a graduate student in the Jurisprudence and Social Policy program, working with Philippe Nonet. Since that time, Berkeley colleagues, including Frederick Dolan, Samera Esmeir, Felipe Gutterriez, Chris Kutz, David Lieberman, Ramona Naddaff, Sue Schweik, Leti Volpp, Nancy Weston, and especially Jonathan Simon, have contributed to my work here on law and language. I have been lucky to have students who ask great questions in my Rhetoric graduate seminars and undergraduate courses and to have colleagues at the Center for the Study of Law and Society and elsewhere on campus who have helped me to clarify my thoughts. The Undergraduate Research Apprentice Program has enabled me to work with a steady stream of dedicated undergraduates; among them Jesse Germinario, Maria Guerra, Rachel Stuart, Karin Vosgeritchian, and especially Juliana Stivanicevic were helpful on various aspects of this project. Graduate students, some of whom worked as research assistants, challenged me with excellent comments; among them were Sara Kendall, Katherine Lemons, Eugene McCarthy, Genevieve Painter, Chiara Ricciardone, K-Sue Park, and Megan Wachspress. Hamsa Murthy's examples helped me shape the book. The Zaffaroni Family Chair in Undergraduate Education, the Academic Senate Committee on Research, the Townsend Center for the Humanities, and a Humanities Research Fellowship supported my efforts in other ways.

The book manuscript has undergone various iterations, and I thank the following for careful comments on earlier drafts: Jennifer Culbert, Jeremy Elkins, Roy Kreitner, Shai Lavi, Katherine Lemons, Linda Ross Meyer, Justin Richland, Darien Schanske, Jonathan Simon, and Martha Umphrey. I discussed versions of what have become sections and chapters in many venues, sometimes even before realizing that they would contribute to the whole. Among persons and institutions outside Berkeley whom I would like to thank in particular for their willingness to engage with my work and for the rich discussions that followed their invitations are: Peter Brooks and participants in his Mellon seminar at Princeton University; Jennifer Culbert and her colleagues at Johns Hopkins University; Leif Dahlberg and participants at the Critical Legal Conference in Stockholm; Jill Frank and Erik Doxtader at the University of South Carolina's program on Social Advocacy and Ethical Life; Susan Sage Heinzelman of the Women's Studies Program at the University of Texas, Austin; Martin Krygier and his colleagues at the University of New South Wales; Shai Lavi and colleagues at Tel Aviv University; Nesam McMillan and her colleagues at Melbourne University, in Criminology and in the Law School; Austin Sarat of Amherst College and participants at the University of Alabama conference on Silence and Speech in American Law, as well as at the Northeast Law and Society retreat; Jack Sammons and colleagues at Mercer College of Law; Kim Scheppele and the many affiliates of the Law and Public Affairs Program at Princeton with whom she facilitated contact; Daniel Silver, John Beer, and others at the conference on the "Second Person" at the University of Chicago; Fiona Smith, Michael Freeman, and an impressive gathering of law and language scholars at London University; Jill Stauffer and Haverford College symposiasts; Simon Stern and his colleagues at the University of Toronto School of Law (where I first realized that I did indeed have a book); and Chris Tomlins and "law as . . ." conferees at UC Irvine. I thank Prof. Dr. Susanne Lepsius for providing an *Arbeitsplatz* and intellectual connections at the Faculty of Law at Ludwig-Maximilians-Universität. The Law & Society Association and the Association for the Study of Law, Culture and the Humanities annual meetings also provided me with invaluable interlocutors. As yet unmentioned yet deserving of thanks for inspiring me to pursue aspects of the project at particular moments are Danielle Allen, Mark Antaki, Roger Berkowitz, Peter Fitzpatrick, Jon Goldberg-Hiller, Nan Goodman, Jennet Kirkpatrick, Karen Knop, Beth Mertz, Stewart Motha, Jay Mootz, Kunal Parker,

Penny Pether, Sylvia Schafer, Susan Silbey, Susan Sterett, Helen Tartar, Barbara Welke, James Boyd White, and Steve Winter.

As befits a project that has been many years in the making, early incarnations of some of the material in this book have appeared in print elsewhere. Although I have rewritten most of it, I would be remiss if I did not mention that a discussion of Obama's oath and of Austin and *Hippolytus*, here presented as parts of the Introduction and Chapter Four, appeared in earlier form as "Our Word is Our Bond," in Austin Sarat, ed., *Speech and Silence in American Law*, Cambridge University Press, 2010, 18–38. Before I became fully aware of the need to supplement an Austinian account of law as speech act with an account of law as "imperfect" shared knowledge, as is done here, I published "Law as Claim to Justice" in Chris Tomlins, ed., *UC Irvine Law Review* (1:3, 2012): 631–640. A preliminary rethinking again involving Obama's oath appears in "Democratic Citizenship and Civil Political Conversation: What's Law Got to Do with It?" *Mercer Law Review* (63:3, 2012): 877–890. An overview of sorts regarding my views of law as language appears as "Speaking of the Imperfect: Law, Language and Justice," in Julen Etxabe and Monica Lopez, eds., *No Foundations: An International Journal of Law and Justice* (2012): 58–67. Finally, "Law as Language," forthcoming in *Critical Analysis of Law* (1:1, 2014), synthesizes material on law as language presented here and elaborates on some of the issues raised in the conclusion of this book.

In addition to the institutional support and funding sources mentioned above, I was granted a quarter at the UC Humanities Institute and a year at the Institute for Advanced Study at Princeton to work on other projects, for which I am grateful. I am also thankful for the institutional flexibility that allowed me to bump this book ahead of those projects!

The book would not be what it is without Kevin Wood, whose love confirms for me that even as our word is our bond, bonds and words exceed our speech acts. Finally, the book could not have been completed without the continuing encouragement and friendship of my grad school buddies, Lucy, Cathy and Mary, to whom this book is dedicated.

Obama's Oaths

The role of ordinary language in relation to the imperative of expression, is
that it is less in need of weeding than of nourishment.

—Stanley Cavell, "Passionate and Performative Utterances," in
Philosophy the Day after Tomorrow, p. 188

What is law? How is it related to language? For many, it is a truism that law is a
matter of language that cannot be captured by rules. For some, it is equally obvious that law may be unspoken and unwritten, that modern law is a matter of useless language or that attending mainly to words misses the violent reality of law.[1]
For others, by contrast, law is a matter of more or less effective if-then statements;
for many students, despite what some of their professors say, law is precisely a
matter of rules.[2]

This book investigates modern law's relation to language in the context of such
divergent views. To those who ask, "What is law?" the book argues that answers
today lie in exploring further law's relations to claiming and hearing. Claims
assert truths and demand recognition. Law, like language, may deceive or lie or
go wrong in its claims. Further, law may mishear and be misheard. Modern law
nevertheless shows great care for language. From the care that law accords to
language, this book shows, one learns about speech; reciprocally, through language and speech, one learns about law. Both language and law bind us; they
entangle and obligate us to one another and reveal the world to be one in which
"our word is our bond."

Obama's flubbed presidential oath shows some of the entanglements of language and the care that law takes around language. On January 20, 2009, Barack
Hussain Obama was sworn into office as President of the United States. Or was
he? Before Chief Justice Roberts, who himself had stumbled slightly over his
words, Obama swore that "I, Barack Hussain Obama, do solemnly swear that I

will *execute* the office of the President of the United States *faithfully*. I will to the best of my ability, preserve, protect and defend the Constitution. So help me God" (emphasis added).[3] A flurry of Internet activity about "oafs of office" followed the inauguration ceremony. On Wednesday, January 21, Obama again took the oath: "I do solemnly swear that I will *faithfully execute* the office of President of the United States . . ." (emphasis added).[4] A January 21 White House press release briefly explained: "We believe that the oath of office was administered effectively and that the President was sworn in appropriately yesterday. But the oath appears in the Constitution itself. And out of an abundance of caution, because there was one word out of sequence, Chief Justice Roberts administered the oath a second time."[5] The White House's "abundance of caution" over "one word out of sequence" in an oath that it nevertheless believed had been "administered effectively" enough that the President had been "sworn in appropriately" reveals the importance to lawyers—and Obama is nothing if not a lawyer's lawyer—of words.

The common or ordinary response, though, to the difference in wording between Obama's first and second oaths was that it did not matter. This response, as we shall see, reveals a carelessness about words. One can question whether the difference in wording actually warranted the retaking of the oath, and one can quibble about definitions of and distinctions among "legal," "ordinary," and "political" speech. (What indeed *is* the character of Obama's oath?) The point is that, despite the claims we often hear about the deplorable state of public discourse, language and speech are taken very seriously in some domains. Law appears to be such a domain. Is law distinct this way? One difficulty in addressing this question is that neither law nor language is straightforwardly and simply physical or mental or ideal. Law and language alike "straddl[e] the material and ideational divide" (in Justin Richland's words)[6] or are, like music, "ontological mutants" (in Jack Sammons's quotation of Lydia Goehr).[7]

One of the aims of this book, then, is to show that *law exists rhetorically*: Its claims often happen through words. What words are and how they claim—how they assert truth and demand recognition—is itself not easily said. The discussion of Obama's oath in this Introduction sets the stage by reminding readers of some of the ways that language ordinarily matters in modern law and legal action. The chapters that follow then draw on the work of many thinkers on language, including J. L. Austin, Stanley Cavell, Adolf Reinach, and Friedrich Nietzsche, to explore what words do, how claims work, and what law is.

One familiar way of thinking about how words matter in law involves the grammar and vocabulary of texts and utterances. Legal practice attends to matters of meaning, interpretation, and translation, and legal education grants prominence to issues of reading and writing. A second approach to thinking about how words matter in law focuses on the forms and conditions of utterance that are prescribed for inaugurations or for other legal acts such as marriages or criminal proceedings. As the chapters explain, what is commonly known as speech act theory maintains that law transforms states of affairs through ostensibly conventional performative acts involving utterances such as oaths and declarations. Unless particular forms, which may themselves be articulated in law, are met, acts such as inaugurations and marriages, or indictments, pleas, and convictions, are in some way flawed; they do not properly transform the states of affairs with which they are concerned. Third, language matters in and to law because it specifies and enables commitments and obligations. As later chapters show, such bonds depend on language, although not quite in the ways one might expect. They depend on the "we" that is revealed in the turn taking interactions of "I" and "you" in dialogue. Without the "we" to whom language and law appeal in their judgments and names for states of affairs in the world, judgments are unshared and obligations meaningless.

This is not to say, of course, that "we" are ever in perfect agreement with one another! Nor do the most perfect agreements accord perfectly with the world. Neither coherence nor correspondence theories capture what language—or law, for that matter—is. Rather, the book argues, imperfection and incompleteness are key to understanding law and language. A second aim of this book, then, is not only to show that words do things but to consider the implications of how *words go wrong*. On the one hand, words promise truth. They ostensibly show us the world as it is. On the other hand, they can be misspoken, misheard, misunderstood. They can be inappropriate or misappropriated, inaccurate or wrong, even downright dangerous. So too can law and legal claims. Taking language seriously thus highlights pathologies and promises of modern law that scholars who would give language short shrift may overlook. Modern Western law is increasingly formulated as "policy" that falls within the jurisdiction of empirical and/or rationalist social sciences. Expressed in particular sorts of disciplinary language, these knowledges largely take law to be a kind of problem solving that can be assessed in terms of its empirical impact and that is articulable in generalizable statements or rules. Rule following corresponds to the instrumental rule making that accompanies policy expertise. Policy claims, like other legal claims, though, are already embedded in particular practices of language that are necessarily imperfect or incomplete.[8] To use policy language to formulate ideal standards or rules against which to measure the empirical reality or adequacy of law is to take the power of such language for granted and to ignore the disciplinary constraints and background of practical knowledge that make all of the speech acts and events of law—including applications of rules—both possible and imperfect.

Attending carefully to language is important in law and for understanding law, but it is also crucial for another reason. Neglect or carelessness about language poses a worse danger to speech—whether one is concerned with political, democratic, or ordinary discourse—than do ignorance and lies. Falsehoods and deception, even ignorance, can be called out, challenged, and addressed, as indeed they often are in law and in education. But when speakers and hearers fail to notice what is being said and how, words lose their ability to show us our world. A third ambition of the book then is to suggest ways that we can *be more careful with speech*. Neither legal speech nor the attention paid to language in the humanities guarantees the quality, meaningfulness, efficacy, or justice of public discourse. To every example of carefully uttered appropriate speech correspond examples of carefully uttered euphemisms, formalisms, and obfuscations—traditional pathologies of law. Indeed, one could argue that "legalism" names precisely an overabundance of attention to language. Being careful about speech in the way that law is careful then allows one to be strategic—and even dishonest—in its use. The sort of carefulness that law displays around language use and speech can also help practitioners and critics of language and of law to contest opacity and dishonesty, however, as well as to challenge injustice.

Our Word Is Our Bond thus aims to refine the ways in which we think and talk about law and justice and also, in the name of law and justice, to enhance the appreciation with which we approach language and speech. It does not offer a theory of justice nor a "concept" of law as such. It shows, rather, how modern law is a matter of language and ultimately argues that justice today, however impossible to define and difficult to determine, depends on the relations we have with one another through language or on how legal speech—as claims and responses made in the name of the law—acts.

. . .

Let us return to the seemingly trivial incident of Obama's retaking the oath. Many claim that the words of the oath were an empty formality: Obama had become President at noon on January 20 anyway, they claim, even before his first oath, when George W. Bush left office. In any case, Obama retook the oath as it is articulated in the Constitution. For most, the story ends there. But it is one thing for schoolchildren to repeat their lessons properly; it is another for one of the most powerful men in the world to do so. Were it not for the second oath, might there have been grounds for claiming that President Obama had not been sworn in "appropriately," as the White House put it? That Chief Justice Roberts had not administered the oath "effectively"? That Obama was not actually President? Or that he need not "faithfully execute the office"?

The words as Obama first uttered them thus open up matters that are far from trivial.[9] They raise potential issues of appropriateness, of legitimacy, of obligation—grand matters usually associated with moral, political, and legal responsibility. Obama's repetition of the words in a different order in the second oath ostensibly resolves those issues. How could his words do these things? How do words raise, address, and resolve grand issues of responsibility? How do words do what they do? How do oaths and other examples of legal speech act? What are their implications for understanding how words and laws may or may not bind any one of us?

Media commentary following Obama's January 20 oath began with questions of *meaning*. Did word order make any difference to the substance of what Obama had said? Did the placement of "faithfully" *after* "will execute the oath of office of the United States" rather than *between* "will" and "execute" change the meaning of the words? Most, if not all, agreed that it did not. Some turned explicitly to rules of English grammar and usage. As English language and grammar textbooks and websites explain, the placement of an "adverb of manner" may occur either before the verb or at the end of the phrase it modifies. Although some commentators claimed that keeping "will execute" together, as Roberts and Obama had done, was preferable because it followed a rule against split infinitives, others pointed out—correctly—that "will" is a modal verb. No infinitive is split in the "will faithfully execute" language of the U.S. Constitution. At this point, discussion turned away from grammar and meaning and toward the issue of whether the precise language of Article II had to be followed.

No one pointed out that there is indeed a way in which the position of the adverb affected "the sense of the expression, i.e. the way in which it modifies that verb."[10] Both phrases—"will execute . . . faithfully" and "will faithfully execute"—do indicate that an executing act—drawing, for instance—is done in a manner in keeping with what the task (of drawing) ordinarily calls for. The adverb points to a style or manner of executing that relates the actual act of execution (drawing) to some prior understanding of what that act is. But that *someone* executes *something* allows one to distinguish two possible adverbial meanings. To say that some*thing* is "executed faithfully" implies that the thing executed—an artwork, perhaps—is a close copy. The adverb after the verb here focuses on the *object* of execution. Not executing something faithfully is to execute it, but not well; it is to do so *un*faithfully. By contrast, to say that some*one* "faithfully executes" something implies that the person executing does so with a particular sort of steadfastness or loyalty or commitment to the act. The focus is now on the attitude or manner of the *subject* doing the executing. To fail to faithfully execute something (if you will excuse the split infinitive) is for the person to act disloyally or faith*lessly*—and perhaps not even to carry out the act at all. (Someone) faithlessly executing is distinguishable from executing (something) unfaithfully.

These distinctions in meaning, which depend on emphasizing a grammatical subject or object, indeed hold in the case of Obama's oaths, unrecognized though they may have been. It makes sense to distinguish "executing an office faithfully/unfaithfully" from "faithfully/faithlessly executing an office." To execute an office is to perform a function; in so doing, one fulfills a post and carries out its duties. And one may both carry out one's *duties* (fulfill one's post, perform the functions of office) *faithfully* or to the letter AND *one* may *faithfully* or loyally carry out one's duties (fulfill one's post, perform the functions of office): loyally and to the letter; "faithfully execute" and "execute faithfully."

These are distinctions without a difference, however, if we rely on the blogosphere and even the White House. Such ostensibly grammatical niceties (like distinctions between content and form, it seems, or between the spirit and the letter of the law) fall away, whether for good or for ill, in practice. Americans expect their President *both* loyally and steadfastly to do his job *and* to do that job as specified by the letter of the Constitution.

And yet, if the words of the first oath mean the same as the words required by the Constitution or at least appear to do so to the American people, why did Obama take the second oath? If the issue of the difference in meaning between the two oaths is for all intents and purposes moot, then what is at stake in "one word out of sequence" that could justify readministering the oath?

The answer appears to be that if the grammar and meaning of Obama's first oath—or what linguists call its "syntax" and "semantics"—were unobjectionable, then the *form* of the utterance nevertheless was lacking. The very conventions or procedures that constitute the ceremony of inauguration as U.S. President were at stake. Even if previous Presidents had not always followed correct procedure (and it seems they did not),[11] the U.S. Constitution requires that a President take the oath before executing the office; hence, discussion of Article II. Being President, like having an agreement or being married, is a state of affairs brought about and warranted through legal procedures and legally articulated provisions. Lawyers and nonlawyers, outside as well as inside the White House, recognize that properly carrying out particular procedures—often involving the utterance of certain words in a particular way and in a particular context—brings about certain states of affairs. Conventions matter. Anyone who has encountered the requirements of modern law—deadlines, signatures, forms and formats—has experienced the ways that getting married, renewing a passport, registering a car, receiving mortgage authorization, or enrolling in public school may be stymied when particular procedural requirements are not met.

If requirements of form, whether these be conventional or articulated in written law, explain Obama's swearing of the second oath, though, form still does not explain why Presidents—or others—take oaths *at all*, a matter (like meaning) that remained unaddressed in public commentary. Suppose Obama had indeed become President at noon, irrespective of the language of Article II requiring him to take the oath "before" entering office and in the silence before the swearing of any oath. The swearing of the oath *still* does something. In solemnly swearing, President Obama explicitly commits himself to a particular way of executing the office and preserving and so forth the Constitution. Such a commitment could of course also be implied by the events leading up to the inauguration, but Obama's own explicit swearing of the oath publicly affirmed his acceptance of the obligations of office. He explicitly took on those obligations through his words at the moment that he swore the oath, rather than having them implicitly attributable to him on the basis of various events and actions surrounding his campaign and election. More than a mere expression, or even declaration, of an intention to faithfully execute the office, the oath *committed* him, like a promise, to doing so. Sworn to before the Chief Justice, the oath obligated or bound him in a particular way. It created a claim that he fulfill those obligations and, should he fail, a claim against him. Obama's oath thus attests to something often taken for granted: that one's word is one's bond. In giving his word, Obama both committed himself to others in a particular way and became President in a constitutionally established manner or form.

In other words, whether or not Americans perceived the difference in *meaning* between the first and second oaths (and it seems few did), Obama's swearing the oath a second time inaugurated him according to *form* or to the letter of the law and by its rules, while his very swearing of the oath at all produced an *obligation* that had previously been, at best, implicit. His uttering of the appropriate oath *transformed*—through his words, according to law—an earlier state of affairs in which questions could be raised as to his status and commitment as officeholder. The proper oath can be said to have *initiated* a state of affairs in which Obama was now indubitably President of the United States of America with all the obligations and responsibilities of office. Such transformation occurred in the name of the law: It was faithful to the language of law, it followed the procedures of Article II, and it appealed to and was warranted by the Constitution of the people whose President Obama had become.

Online discussion of Obama's oaths soon ended. Attention had focused on the sequence of words in the first oath in relation to the form of the oath that was mandated by constitutional law, rather than on the words' meaning or the oath's mattering. The flawed first oath raised potentially serious matters of politics—and of law and language. But perhaps due to the haste with which "out of an abundance of caution" the oath was readministered by the Chief Justice the next day (unrecorded this time by television cameras), public discussion never reached the more difficult question of how uttering sentences in the vocabulary and grammar of the English language according to conventional forms *matters*—how such utterances can initiate and transform states of affairs in the name of the law. Drawing on insights from both analytic and Continental philosophy of language and on particular works of literature, this book takes on precisely that question, locating it in the context of an exploration of words and law and how they bind us.

·   ·   ·

This book draws its examples primarily from contemporary U.S. law and reflects on ordinary English usages of "law," accepting all the qualifications that these parameters imply. The book's use of "law" is not limited to positive law or to the law of the state. Nor does it consist in a return or appeal to a natural law or justice that exists independently of human beings and their institutions and practices. The U.S. legal tradition and scholarship about it highlights the way that law is an idiom in which many different kinds of claims of justice and injustice have been made and may yet be made. Indeed, the book's own claims are actually compatible, in particular contexts, with all of the claims mentioned in this Introduction's first paragraph. The issue of course is: in what contexts? The contexts of claims matter. Particular claims are "suitable to some contexts and not to others," as Austin puts it:[12]

> It is essential to realize that "true" and "false," like "free" and "unfree," do not stand for anything simple at all; but only for a general dimension of being a right or proper thing to say as opposed to a wrong thing, in these circumstances, to this audience, for these purposes and with these intentions. (145)

For sociologists, the context of law and of claims about it is society; for political scientists, the state. Sociolegal work asks for whom laws are made and what interests they serve. Rhetoric asks analogous questions: to whom law appeals, what law says and how. But rhetoric also asks to whom sociolegal claims appeal, what they say and how. And when philosophy inquires into the foundations of law, rhetoric asks to whom foundations appeal and how.

Rhetorical questions of course need not be answered. They may sometimes be empty; they may also be obvious. Legal, sociolegal, and philosophical claims about law and claims to justice may also sometimes be taken for granted. A rhetorical investigation of those claims need not be a nihilistic disavowal of them, however. It may instead explore, as does this book, what claims are, how they assert truths and demand recognition, and in what ways they bind us. Rhetoric indeed point outs that language is not truth, but it recognizes that words, in particular contexts, may be true or false. So too, as this book's final chapter argues, law is not justice, but legal claims in particular contexts may be just or unjust. Further, just as particular utterances can be judged to be true or false only because language in some sense promises truth or to truly reveal the world, particular laws can be (judged to be) just or unjust only because law also in some sense claims justice. Even as legal positivism, the dominant scholarly account of law, disclaims or disavows the necessary justice of law, officials of positive law nevertheless insist—often crudely and through their actions—that they are carrying out their "duties," or obligations to which they are bound, in the *name* of law.

This book thus challenges the usual positivist approaches to law of law schools, sociolegal scholarship, and philosophy of law. (Elsewhere I refer to this as socio-legal positivism.)[13] All three latter fields in different ways minimize or circum-scribe the possibilities of legal speech and its relation to rules, action, community, and justice. Contemporary professional education acknowledges the primacy of reading and writing while often wrongly suggesting that law is a system of rules. Sociolegal research that makes a strong distinction between what it calls law-in-action and law-on-the-books fails to understand how legal speech acts. And the dominant philosophical view of law, which maintains that there is no necessary connection between law and justice, largely neglects the embeddedness of claims of law in shared practical knowledge of language. As we shall see, understanding claims of law to be performative and passionate utterances, or social acts that appeal implicitly to justice and that occur within the horizon of a world that is shown and yet not exhausted by our saying, offers an alternative to grasping law as a system of rules, as policy making or problem solving, in terms of empirical impact, as state authority or power, or even as fundamentally violent.

Underscoring law as language highlights what legal education, sociolegal study, and philosophy of law threaten to forget: that "our word is our bond." Through admittedly imperfect words or speech, and even when its explicit claims fail, law relates us to issues of justice. Through the gentle law of our language, this book shows, we know ourselves to be in a greater world of which we, however imperfectly, claim justice. Not every reader will need every lesson in this book, and language does not convey the complete story of law. But if this book accentu-ates aspects of law that are in some ways obvious and in other ways incomplete, it also does what we ask of language: It supplements accounts of law that are less obvious—and, one suspects, less true!

. . .

Chapter One shows that the White House's abundance of caution over one word out of sequence shares in current U.S. law's broader respect for and wariness about the potency of speech. Through statutory interpretation, First Amendment jurisprudence, intellectual property law, and criminal law, the United States does its best to master meanings and events of speech, in contexts ranging from ob-scenity and *Miranda* rights to evidence and perjury. Law structures what can be said in court and elsewhere, safeguarding some statements from particular interpretations and prohibiting others from being repeated or even presented.

Though all's well that ends well in Obama's reswearing of the oath, words cannot always be so easily taken back or redone. After reviewing some of the ways that U.S. law treats language and introducing J. L. Austin's account of speech acts, Chapter One argues that insofar as legal claims aim to persuade others, they are not only conventional or performative utterances, but also what Stanley Cavell calls "passionate utterances."[14] Despite the best efforts of legal actors and of law, unruly speech happens, even within law and as law sometimes acknowledges. Its own speech escapes its control in unpredictable ways as, for instance, when dicta become doctrine or mantras. In trying to master speech acts and events and in occasionally recognizing its inability to do so, U.S. law appears doubly indebted—or bound—to language. It manifests itself through speech, even as complete mastery of language exceeds its power.

The importance of words to law reveals itself not only in Obama's retaking the oath and in attempts to regulate language but, as Chapter Two notes, from the first day of law school. Turning to reason, writing and rhetoric, the 3 Rs of U.S. professional legal education, Chapter Two shows how even the simplest rules of grammatical legal writing raise big philosophical questions about intention, action, cause, and responsibility that are seldom addressed directly as such in school. The chapter develops the account of speech acts presented in Chapter One and introduces Friedrich Nietzsche's critique of grammar as metaphysics to argue that law and language alike are sites of judgment and of ascriptions of responsibility.[15] The argument proceeds through a close reading of the well-known torts case, *Palsgraf v. Long Island Railroad*.[16] The statement of facts in Justice Cardozo's *Palsgraf* opinion (which Wydick, in *Plain English for Lawyers*, celebrates as an example of good legal writing[17]), together with the rest of the opinion and Justice Andrews's dissent, shows the interplay of legal judgments and grammatical attributions of causal agency and responsibility.

Recall that the world of Obama's oath is a world of grammatical subjects and objects (persons and oaths, Presidents and offices), verbing and beverbed (swearing and being sworn, executing and being executed). So, too, in the English-language world more broadly, Chapter Two shows in the context of *Palsgraf*, somebody does something in a grammar of subjects and predicates that law would be hard pressed to do without. Legal writing instructions to "prefer the active voice" or to write in complete sentences with subjects and predicates reveal a world of "doers and deeds," as Nietzsche puts it, who can be held responsible for their acts. The "good legal writing" of Cardozo's statement of facts reveals a particular metaphysics, even as the *Palsgraf* opinions themselves are full of figures of speech and of ostensible deviations from rules. Read through Nietzsche and Austin, *Palsgraf* thus raises an issue common to both writing and law: the limits of rules. Law is no more a matter of rules than language is a matter of definitions and grammar. Stating facts, applying rules, and briefing cases may be pedagogically useful, but they far from exhaust what is involved in legal claims. Legal claims involve the shared use of words by speakers and hearers who together judge and name the happenings of their world in social acts that implicate past and future. Although occurring in the present, legal claims await their hearing and have the temporal structure of the future perfect. As Jacques Derrida points out: It *will have been* the case that a claim was made . . .[18] Once perfected or completed over time, acts or events of law and language alike become past perfect events of legal history.

Chapter Three examines the social character of skillful legal acts of speech more closely. Legal acts include not only inaugural oaths and legal opinions but also marriages, complaints, objections, appeals, and enactments. The first half of the chapter draws on Adolf Reinach's work to explain that, as social acts that must be heard by others to do what they do, legal acts are not simply causal.[19] The joint speaking and hearing, writing and reading, or expression and apprehension that occurs in a social act does not strictly cause the act; it *is* the act. Properly offered and apprehended by the judge who has the authority to sustain or overrule it, a trial lawyer's saying "I object" in court, for instance, *is* the objecting to what another has said. It does not cause the objection. Likewise, inaugurations or wedding ceremonies do not cause officeholders to take office nor cause couples to be married. They are the taking of office and the marrying. The joint expression and apprehension of particular legal/social acts transforms a state of affairs and initiates a new one: a presidency, a marriage, a need or an opportunity to respond to an objection or a complaint. Changes in states of affairs brought about *through* legal acts occur *in* the jointly performed social act of speaker and hearer and *upon* the completion of the social act. They are enabled through actors' shared knowledge.

The second half of Chapter Three shows how the shared knowledge of social acts that enables changes in states of affairs in the world belongs to "we" who partake in turn-taking claims of "I" and "you" in dialogue. You and I change places in dialogic social acts as "I" appeal to "you" to judge not simply as *I* do, but as "we" do, in the *name* of a particular and peculiar third party: our shared law. Ostensibly monological acts, such as enactments, are no exception to the dialogic character of language. Enactments that are "to be known," for instance, as "the Penal Code of California" require shared speech. Words bind those who share practical knowledge of speech, or who speak the same language or name and judge as *we* do, into various and overlapping "communities" whose members recognize and judge states of affairs through common, admittedly imperfect, practical knowledge of language. Those who speak a common tongue are bound to one another as community members speaking and living together in a manner that corresponds to grammatically "imperfect" or incomplete action. (The grammatical "aspect" of a verb refers to how a sentence expresses the temporality of a situation. An action can be viewed from outside, as a temporally completed whole or as "perfect": "*I spoke with you yesterday*" or "*Somebody sneezed.*" Temporality can also be expressed as an internal relation: "*While we were speaking,* somebody sneezed." The "imperfect" identifies a situation of continuous, habitual, or incomplete action [we were speaking] in which a particular action occurs [somebody sneezed].)[20]

In other words, law refers, on the one hand, to completed or perfected or perfectible acts or events (Chapter Two) and, on the other hand, to imperfect practical knowledge of a community's ways of living and speaking together (Chapter Three). Our continuous, habitual, routine, and interruptible shared ways of living are characterized by incompletely articulable understandings. Such imperfect knowledge forms a backdrop or context of law against which discrete social acts of law occur. Pierre Clastres might identify imperfect background law with the law of the chief who repeats "We are living this way, we have been living this way, we shall continue living this way"; such law resembles what Martin Krygier calls "tradition" or Robert Cover calls the *nomos* or normative world.[21] Law as social acts takes place in present active moments that are enabled by and also seem to interrupt law as a continuous and habitual way of living. In their future, legal acts may themselves become integrated into the ongoing background of how we live, or they may be distinguished, identified, and highlighted as the discrete events of which histories of law and community tell.

Chapters Two and Three together show that law, like language, is neither coincident with rules (Chapter Two) nor socially efficacious in quite the way empiricists would recognize (Chapter Three). The double aspect of law, as future perfect, dynamic social acts and as the imperfect practical knowledge required for those acts, offered in these chapters suggests that one can think about modern law in terms other than those of sociolegal studies or of legal positivism, without returning to an outmoded natural law that associates law with God or derives law from a "higher" morality.

Understanding law as both active events and practical knowledge this way does not mean that law is purely a matter of convention, though, as Chapter Four shows. Most would agree, generally speaking, to the conventional claim that promises should be kept. Criticizing Hippolytus's famous, "My tongue swore, but my mind did not," J. L. Austin for instance writes that "morality and accuracy alike are on the side of the plain saying that *our word is our bond*" (10). Yet from Euripides to Shoshana Felman, law and literature alike point out the injustice of keeping promises in a world where words and things go wrong.[22] They imply that "our word is our bond" is not as "plain" a saying as J. L. Austin suggests.

Chapter Four explores what an account of law that takes us to be speaking imperfectly with one another in joint social acts makes of "conventional" morality, such as the obligation to keep promises, the ur-example of speech act theory. The chapter ultimately shows how contract law, like tort and criminal law, responds to claims about a world, like the world presented in literature, in which not only promising, but also accident, deception, and wrongdoing, accompany our speaking and living with one another. Even as contract law fails to completely rectify breaches of promises, it nevertheless affirms, as do criminal and tort law, words that call for justice in a world that exceeds conventional claims and the mandates of our law. Law and language bind us not only through dialogic social acts and into imperfect communities (Chapter Three) but also to a larger world, Chapter Four argues, that exceeds both conventional moralities and articulations of positive law.

· · ·

Focusing on law as language allows one to see that positive law—whether taken to be official state law, social power or instrument, or system of rules—represents only one version of law, albeit the predominantly accepted scholarly one. It allows one to recognize that other conceptions of law—as custom, as tradition, as natural law, as belonging to all sorts of nonstate or nonnational collectives or groups—also offer imperfect and incomplete accounts of law.[23] It allows one to accept a critique of law as rules that is compatible with sociolegal studies (Chapter Two), while also drawing attention to the ways that sociolegal studies downplay legal speech and how it acts (Chapter Three). It allows one to see that law of whatever sort, like its language, is imperfect and incomplete and that if laws are or are said to be unjust, this can only be in a context in which justice is expected or claimed of them (Chapter Four).

Neither law nor justice is simply what lawyers and judges say nor even what officials and scholars more broadly claim they are. This does not mean that law or justice is completely independent of language in the ways that some would take an objective world to be. However inadequate our law and language to the world, we know our world and name our ways of living and being in it through law and language. Language is not like a window through which we look to an outside of which we are not part. Our speech is akin rather to the paths we walk as we make our way through the wider world. We know our world imperfectly *and* through the pathways we take. And law? What is law? That is the question to which the following chapters turn.

CHAPTER ONE

How to Do Things with Law

Law is a profession of words.

—David Mellinkoff, *The Language of Law*, p. vi

Like the White House's concern with Obama's oath, current U.S. law manifests broad respect for and simultaneous wariness about the potency of speech. As the Introduction notes, law regulates many areas and aspects of speech, not only through First Amendment jurisprudence but also, for instance, through criminal law, evidence law, and intellectual property law. Legal actions produce or review not only government documents but also private agreements, publications, and publicly displayed art. Law criminalizes some speech: forgery, fraud, libel, perjury. Civil and criminal procedures establish conditions of speech and expression, while also occasionally mandating that particular utterances be understood in particular ways.

Language cannot be bracketed as simply something that law regulates, however. Language permeates law. Lawyers use language to draft innumerable legal acts: complaints, wills, briefs, contracts, deeds, regulations, legislation. Not only lawyers, but also notaries, city clerks, regulatory officers, legislators, juries, civil servants, and the many others with whom, against whom, or on whose behalf these identifiably legal agents work, engage in recognizably legal acts involving speech: notarizing, notifying, petitioning, declaring, convicting, acquitting, bequeathing, amending, transferring. Formal legal declarations, such as jury instructions, verdicts, trial rulings, appellate decisions, local resolutions, administrative appointments, state and federal legislation, are prepared, announced, scrutinized, and challenged in legal actions that take place through language and must themselves accord with legally prescribed mandates and standards.

This chapter discusses the attention and care that U.S. law bestows on language and speech while foreshadowing themes to be developed in the next three chapters. The first section introduces the terminology of speech acts to show how U.S. law recognizes, beyond grammar and the meaning of words, the "actlike" or "performative" quality of speech. Legal claims in particular seem to correspond to the conventional acts and procedures that J. L. Austin identifies with the "illocutionary" aspect of utterances.[1] But, Section Two continues, insofar as legal claims seek to persuade others, they also appear to be "passionate utterances," in Stanley Cavell's terms.[2] The persuasive or passionate aspect of legal claims, like U.S. law's occasional acknowledgment of its own limitations as to speech and hearing, complicates accounts of law that would identify it strictly with conventional speech acts. Modern law is bound to language: It uses language, and language is not completely within its control. Attending to legal language thus supplements current accounts of law offered by empirical studies and by the legal positivism that predominates in contemporary philosophy of law, Section Three concludes. Law is not necessarily a matter of power or coercion, nor of higher morality or natural or divine justice, nor even of procedural fairness. Or rather, even when law is those things, it is also always a matter of language.

One. Speech Acts of Law: J. L. Austin

Most readers are familiar with some of the ways that vocabulary and grammar are implicated in legal disputes. Ross Charnock points to an English-language example of a dispute over words in which Justice Gray in 1893 held that tomatoes were vegetables for the purposes of the Tariff Act of 1883: "In the common language of the people [. . .] all these are vegetables, which are [. . .] like potatoes, carrots, parsnips, usually served at dinner with the fish or meats [. . .], and not, like fruits generally, as dessert" (*Nix v. Heddon*, 1893).[3]

In jurisprudential discussions today, the most famous example of disputes as to the meaning of words involves what counts as a "vehicle" in the context of a rule prohibiting vehicles in a park. H. L. A. Hart uses the hypothetical question of allowing "a toy motor car electrically propelled" into the park to discuss the indeterminacy of general standards that regulate conduct. "When the unenvisaged case does arise," he writes, "we confront the issues at stake and can then settle the question . . . In doing so we shall have rendered more determinate our initial aim, and shall accidentally have settled a question as to the meaning, for the purposes of this rule, of a general word."[4] The use of the future perfect ("shall have rendered . . . and . . . settled") implies the resolution or closure of a formerly open issue. Charnock notes that, in 1951, Chief Justice Goddard had considered a poultry shed to be a vehicle "within the meaning of §1 of the Road Traffic Act of 1930" (in *Garner v. Burr, KB*, 1951). Twenty years earlier, U.S. Justice Holmes had held that an aircraft was not a vehicle for the purpose of transportation across state lines (*McBoyle v. U.S.* 1931).[5] Such differences, as Lon Fuller points out, of course turn at least in part on the context of the dispute and on the purpose attributed to the statute or rule ostensibly controlling the case.[6]

Many cases make explicit the link between a determination of meaning and the purpose or context of the statute or rule under which the determination is made, even if they do not go so far as to explicitly acknowledge the strange retrospectivity suggested by Hart (and taken up in Chapter Two). A 2004 U.S. Supreme Court case, for instance, considers whether a Florida DUI (driving [a motor vehicle] under the influence of alcohol) offense counts as an "aggravated felony" for the purpose of deportation under the Immigration and Nationality Act (INA).[7] The Act defines aggravated felony to include "a crime of violence" for which the term of imprisonment is at least one year. The U.S. Code (Title 18, sec. 16) in turn defines a crime of violence as "an offense that has as an element the use . . . of physical force against the person or property of another." Did appellant Leocal's conviction of two DUI offenses for which he was serving time in prison constitute such an offense? An immigration judge and the Board of Immigration Appeals had ordered Leocal's deportation, and the Eleventh Circuit affirmed. On further appeal, though, the Supreme Court pointed out that the Florida statute does not require that an offender have any particular mental state (and that other DUI statutes require only proof of negligence). Insofar as *use* means "active employment," the Court argues, the Code implies that a "crime of violence" requires "active employment" of force. That someone "actively employs" physical force against another, reasons the Court, requires a higher degree of intent—or purpose—than does the negligent or accidental conduct required for conviction of DUI offenses. Purpose thus appears doubly relevant in this case of ascertaining whether a DUI conviction is an aggravated felony: It refers both to the reason for making the determination (deportation under the INA) and to the kind of "intent" or manner that is attributed to one who is convicted of DUI.

In another recent immigration-related case, the U.S. Supreme Court also considered an adverb of intent or purpose, "knowingly." Ignacio Flores-Figueroa had presented to his employer forged documents that, unknown to him, bore numbers assigned to real people. He was convicted not only of document fraud but of a federal felony, "aggravated identity theft," which carried with it an additional two-year sentence.[8] At issue was in part the identity-theft statute's requirement that an offender "knowingly transfers, possesses or uses, without lawful authority, a means of identification of another person." In overturning the additional charge, Justice Breyer argues that "it seems natural to read the statute's word 'knowingly' as applying" not only to the verbs in the text, but "to all the subsequently listed elements of the crime." He reasons that "if we say that someone knowingly ate a sandwich with cheese, we normally assume that the person knew both that he was eating a sandwich and that it contained cheese."

What "seems natural" and what "we normally assume" coincide for Breyer in this case but may leave one wondering about what "we" are to make of the legal meanings of "vehicles" and perhaps even of "vegetables." Interpretation of statutory language has generated its own literature and norms of the "natural" and "ordinary."[9] Words are to be given their "ordinary or natural meaning."[10] Effect should be given to every word of a statute—whenever possible. The assessment of possibility involves judgment of course.[11] Like rules of writing and of law (discussed in Chapter Two), ostensible rules of statutory interpretation may work as guidelines or as rules of thumb. They never completely determine the outcome of a case, however; nor do they guarantee acceptance of the interpretation or rationale contributing to the outcome or of the decision that announces it.

Neither do the meanings of words warrant that particular articulations will be taken as decisive or authoritative. For particular articulations to "count" as U.S. law or for particular rules or outcomes to "take," that is, not only must words be considered to suit their purpose in context, as already shown in discussion of the meaning of statutory language, but institutions must exist and particular conditions must be met. No matter how beautifully and adequately legislation is drafted, it does not officially become law until its enactment. No matter how well written and reasoned the opinion of a law student or law professor, such opinions remain "mock." Only under certain conditions, when presented by a judge within a particular jurisdiction, which is itself an institutional matter, are opinions taken to be law.[12]

The points of the preceding paragraph are not new. They are raised here because they serve as background against which to understand, first, the relevance of speech acts to law and, second, the way in which legal utterances are like other sorts of utterances. In depending for their success as law not only on the meaning of words but also on the circumstances in which they are spoken, utterances of law are like other kinds of speech. To hold, to dissent, to charge, to enact, to marry, to convict, are what J. L. Austin, followed by John Searle, Stanley Cavell, and others refer to as "speech acts."[13] All such utterances depend on the circumstances of their uttering. Even legal utterances that ostensibly state propositions succeed or fail in part on the basis of something other than their meaning or the truth or falsity of what they state. Assessments of findings, for instance, no less than assessments of other legal utterances, are not exhausted by the truth value of what they mean or state. A judgment may be based on a *false* finding, that is, but it is still a finding. Conversely, truths may fail to be found and relevant propositions may fail to be included as *findings*.

In Austin's formulation, performative speech acts include promising, warning, betting, declaring, appointing, and other utterances that are or are part of the doing of an action. Austin at first distinguishes performative utterances from constative utterances, which describe things or state propositions (3, 6). To utter "I promise I will come tomorrow" in the appropriate circumstances is "not to *describe* my doing of what I should be said in so uttering to be doing" or to describe my promising, according to Austin. Neither is it "to state that I am doing it." Rather "it is to do it" or to promise (6). Legal speech acts often do what they say in their doing. "I object," spoken in the appropriate circumstances, is not to describe my objecting or to state that I am objecting (nor is it to cause the objection, discussed further in Chapter Three). In proper context, it *is* objecting or the *act* of objection. And it can be put, and indeed here appears, in the explicit form of a first-person present indicative active sentence like "I hold . . ." or "We find . . ." (61–62).

As we shall see, the strong distinction between performative and constative utterances with which Austin begins breaks down, as he himself points out. Findings for instance both state propositions and, in being stated, formally find that something is the case. They are both constative and performative, in Austin's original formulation. The distinction is nevertheless pedagogically helpful because it highlights the difference between understanding utterances as static or nounlike sentences or statements or propositions and understanding utterances or uttering as dynamic or verblike acts or activities of language. Focusing on law as statements or propositions of facts or of rules, as some do, tends to draw attention away from law's performative or actlike character. Consider one way of teaching students to read (and brief) a standard first-year criminal-law case such as *Morissette v. United States* (see Appendix B).[14] The instructor asks, following identification of parties, procedural status, description of facts, and so forth, for the issue, rule, analysis, and conclusion in *Morissette*.[15] Morissette was convicted of conversion, under a federal statute, for gathering spent bomb casings from federal land. Apparently thinking they were abandoned property, he sold them. The Appellate Court affirmed Morissette's conviction. Having established these "facts," the class turns to the issues and the reasoning by which the Supreme Court reverses the appellate court's affirmation of the conviction. Students then read *Morissette* for its articulation of "rules": *that* wrongful intention is a requisite element of criminal liability; *that* in omitting reference to intention and referring to "knowing conversion" in its statute, Congress did not intend to create a new category of crime (unwitting conversion); and *that*, where intent is an element of a crime, trial court instructions raising a presumption of intention from the evidence are in error.

If the opinion is read *as it is written*, however, the Supreme Court in *Morissette* tells a story, which telling is itself a speech act, of the series of speech acts leading up to and comprising the announcement, again a speech act, of the Supreme Court judgment. The Court opinion reports (a speech act) that: under investigation, Morissette "voluntarily, promptly and candidly" told his story to investigators who nevertheless indicted him under a U.S. statute for "unlawfully, wilfully and knowingly steal[ing] and convert[ing] property of the United States." Indictment is of course a speech act. At trial, Morissette testified—another speech act—that he thought the casings were abandoned and that he had taken them "with no wrongful or criminal intent." The judge then instructed (speech act) the jury as to a presumption of intention in such a way that the trial court "convicted and sentenced" (speech acts) him. The Court of Appeals affirmed (speech act) the conviction on the basis of its interpretation (an act about speech, if not a speech act) of the statute that had been enacted (speech act) by Congress; one judge dissented (speech act). The Supreme Court now reverses (speech act) the Court of Appeals' decision.

In its opinion, the Supreme Court addresses the appellate court's interpretation of the statute, then the trial judge's instructions. The Court first points out that the Court of Appeals "construe[d] omission" (construal again being an act, this time based on an absence of speech) of criminal intent from the congressional statute as "dispensing with it." The Supreme Court by contrast turns to pronouncements (speech acts) of common-law commentators and state law to hold (speech act) that "where Congress borrows terms of art in which are accumulated the legal tradition and meaning of centuries of practice, it presumably knows and adopts the cluster of ideas . . . [A]bsence of contrary direction may be taken as satisfaction with widely accepted definitions . . ." The Supreme Court finds (speech act) "no grounds for inferring [as did the Court of Appeals in its ostensible speech act] any affirmative instruction [speech act] from Congress to eliminate intent from any offense with which this defendant was charged [another speech act]."

The Supreme Court then "read[s] the record" (like interpretation, at minimum an act about speech) for a theory of the case and finds (speech act) that the trial court "erred" in its speech act of "instructing" the jury as to "presumptive" intent. Such presumption allows the jury to make assumptions (a possible speech act? certainly an act of reasoning involving language) that conflict with the presumption of innocence. Given the trial evidence, the Court argues (speech act) that the jury could legitimately have concluded (speech act) otherwise . . .

You get the idea! The opinion itself becomes part of a series of speech acts that make claims about speech acts that claim to be, or to be in the name of, the law. As a speaking of law, the opinion is at least as much a story of claims about law as it is a set of statements of ostensibly timeless rules applied to propositions of fact.

Chapter Two will examine statements of facts and of rules further. Chapter Three will explore legal acts and how they work more carefully. Chapter Four will take up claims to justice in particular. For now, suffice it to say that speech acts, including legal speech acts, do what they do more or less well, depending on the conditions or context in which they are uttered. Of course, as Austin points out, like nonspeech acts, speech acts may "fail" as *acts*, in that they are susceptible to being done under duress, accidentally, owing to a mistake, or unintentionally (21) (see Chapter Two on intention). They are also susceptible to the kinds of "unhappiness" that afflict any kind of *speech*, such as being misheard and misunderstood (21–22) (see Chapter Three on hearing). But speech acts are also susceptible to "infelicities" particular to them, argues Austin. For a given speech act to be felicitous, he claims, there must exist an accepted procedure for the act (A.1) and the procedure must apply to the particular persons and situation (A.2). The utterance must be carried out correctly (B.1) and completely (B.2). Further, in a couple of conditions that Austin sets apart from the others by identifying them with Γ (or the Greek letter "gamma" or "C"), "where the procedure is designed for persons having certain thoughts or intentions, the persons in question must indeed have those thoughts" (Γ1) and "where subsequent conduct is part of the procedure, the persons must conduct themselves accordingly" (Γ2). (Again note, as shall be discussed further in Chapter Two, that in instances where Γ2 is relevant, Austin's speech act perfects or completes itself in the future.)

What do "felicity conditions" have to do with law? Many legal issues involving speech can be mapped onto them. The first four conditions, for instance, map onto practitioners' threshold questions as to whether a particular legal act, such as a contract, has occurred or whether particular documentary acts, such as deeds or birth certificates or wills, are valid and confirm or deny parties' claims. In a contract dispute over university labor relations, for instance, a lawyer may begin by investigating whether existing law governs this type of agreement (A). If so, which law (A.1)? Was this contract authorized by law (A2), and is the law that authorizes it applicable to these parties (A.2)? Are these parties (A.2) entitled to offer and accept in the terms that they have (B.1)? Did the contract occur before the appropriate authorities (A2)? Do these particular promises constitute an agreement (B)? Were the promises made correctly and completely (B.1 and 2)? What is one to make of a misunderstanding between the parties (Γ1)? What is to be done when the terms of the agreement become, or turn out to have been, impossible to carry out (Γ2)? In the case of a valid will, testamentary intent (Γ1) is expressed in particular language (A and B), and (in addition to signing and witnessing), there must be no subsequent repudiation (Γ2).

Comparable issues about the circumstances of speech acts arise in criminal procedure in the context of *Miranda* warnings and the right to remain silent, for instance.[16] On taking someone into custody, U.S. law enforcement officers have an obligation to warn the accused of the danger of speaking by issuing the now well-known *Miranda* warnings. For a defendant's speech to the police to be admissible as evidence at trial, the Supreme Court requires the warning. "Prior to any questioning," held the Supreme Court in 1966:

> the person must be warned that he has a right to remain silent, that any statement he does make may be used as evidence against him, and that he has a right to the presence of an attorney, either retained or appointed. The defendant may waive effectuation of these rights provided the waiver is made voluntarily, knowingly and intelligently. If, however, he indicates in any manner and at any stage of the process that he wishes to consult with an attorney before speaking there can be no questioning.

Likewise, if the individual is alone and indicates in any manner that he does not wish
to be interrogated, the police may not question him. (444–446)

Elsewhere I have shown in more detail how the Court, in the *Miranda* opinions
themselves, analyzes the speech situation of custodial interrogation.[17] The Court
in effect suggests that in the extraordinary circumstances of in-custody interrogation and of the proceedings that follow, legal officials may not properly be able
to apprehend the accused's words and "any statement" he or she makes, including those intended to be exculpatory, may be used against the accused. To establish conditions in which triers of fact can rely on what an accused has said as
testimony, then, the Court mandates the performance of a speech act of warning.
The court makes the police's warning of the danger of speaking a precondition
for introducing the accused's words as evidence at trial. A properly administered
and apprehended *Miranda* warning notifies the accused of a danger and ensures
that the accused enters the danger knowingly. It also offers the accused an opportunity to avoid the danger of speaking by remaining silent or to enter into it
more carefully with a lawyer.

The *Miranda* opinions themselves and the cases that immediately followed it
inquired into the constitutionality of requiring the warning or, in Austin's terms,
into the existence of an accepted procedure for the decision (A.1). The question,
after *Dickerson* settles that *Miranda* is a "constitutional rule," becomes what the
now-accepted *Miranda* ruling requires (A.1 or A.2).[18] Does a particular utterance made in given conditions constitute proper enough expression of a warning
(A.2)? Under precisely which conditions must warning be given (A.2)? By whom
and to whom (A2)? What are the proper conditions of waiver (A.2) and the forms
that waiver can take (B.1)? At what moment must warning and waiver occur
(A.2, B.2)? Has the speech act of warning or waiver been completed in such a way
that a particular state of affairs ensues (B.2)? And how long do these states, and
the opportunity to respond to the previous speech act, last (B.2)? Sociolinguists
may also inquire into an addressee's understanding of the warning (Γ1) and of
officials' and defendants' conduct following a particular utterance (Γ2).[19]

Distinguishing between situations in which conventions or procedures do not
exist or in which conventions are not accepted (A1) and situations in which existing conventions are inappropriate to the particular case (A2) may be difficult,
Austin notes. Further, some speech acts may be flawed in more than one way.
Specifying the infelicity may not matter, though. When the captain of a team

says, "I pick George," and George says, "I'm not playing," for instance, the upshot is the same whether one identifies the infelicity to be a lack of conventions for selecting among nonplayers (A1) or to be the inappropriateness of George under existing conventions (A2). Austin (who cotaught at least one seminar with H. L. A. Hart[20]) suggests that law tends to characterize otherwise ambiguous situations as new, rather than claiming the nonexistence or nonacceptance of rules:

> The law abounds in such difficult decisions—in which, of course, it becomes more or less arbitrary whether we regard ourselves as deciding (A.1) that a convention does not exist or as deciding (A.2) that the circumstances are not appropriate for the invocation of a convention which undoubtedly does exist: either way, we shall tend to be bound by the "precedent" we set. Lawyers usually prefer the latter course, as being to apply rather than to make law. (32)

Consider Austin's comments in relation to gay marriage in the United States. Sixteen states now allow same-sex marriage, but some states and congressional laws do not recognize such marriages. In the past, states banned gay relationships or did not have rules for recognizing gay marriages. Today, as gay marriage cases move to the Supreme Court, the issues can be framed as whether laws or conventions recognizing same-sex marriage cases are properly law (A1) or as whether existing and accepted rules for marriage apply to gay couples (A2). A U.S. Ninth Circuit Court panel held that a California law banning same-sex marriage violates equal protection and due process for gays and is not good law (A1). A U.S. First Circuit Court recently also held that a federal statute improperly denied benefits to same-sex couples married under Massachusetts's Defense of Marriage Act (A2). The shift in public attitudes toward domestic partnerships more broadly and of some state laws toward acceptance of gay relationships (it is usually no longer considered defamation to call someone "gay" in many states) raises questions as to the "existence" and "acceptability" of what were hitherto conventions and also as to their applicability to "new" cases.

Austin's gamma conditions, too, are relevant to law. Issues about the infelicity of oaths and promises (discussed further in Chapter Four) often concern "having certain thoughts" at the time of an utterance (Γ_1), and their alleged breach often involves analysis of "subsequent conduct" (Γ_2). Consider an example offered by historian Lucy Salyer.[21] In 1881, a German immigrant, Frederick Wusterbarth, swore an oath of allegiance to the United States, thereby becoming a naturalized citizen. Thirty-seven years later, corresponding with anti-German sentiment during World War I, the U.S. government strained to articulate a basis for stripping Wusterbarth—who had refused to donate money to the Red Cross—of his citizenship. Wusterbarth had indeed met the conditions of citizenship in the 1880s and had explicitly renounced his German allegiance when he swore "true faith and allegiance" to the United States (A and B). Not finding enough of a problem in Wusterbarth's conduct subsequent to the oath to justify denaturaliza-tion (Γ_2), the government turned to new knowledges of the "unconscious mind" to show that "the person in question," as Austin put it, did not have "certain thoughts or intentions" at the time of the oath (Γ_1). As Salyer explains, judges au-thorizing naturalization maintained that the longer one was a citizen, the more one's love for one's adopted country should grow. If it did not, argued the court, "the conclusion is irresistible, that at the time he took the oath of renunciation, he did so with a mental reservation."[22]

The point here is that in moving beyond matters of the meaning of ostensible statements or enactments of law to considering what Austin would call their "fe-licity conditions," law recognizes that speech *acts*. Legal practitioners concern themselves not only with the *meaning* of utterances or propositions in context that is, but also with the manner of an *act* of utterance, asking under what condi-tions and how it was authorized and performed and as a way of doing what. In attending to such matters, legal practitioners contrast favorably to much socio-legal scholarship and even to some legal doctrinal scholarship. Recall *Miranda*. As previously mentioned, a felicitous *Miranda* warning warns an accused of a danger and offers the accused a choice between remaining silent, entering into the danger more carefully with a lawyer, or braving the extraordinary speech situation of in-custody interrogation alone. An accused who remains silent in effect accepts the acknowledgment that these are not conditions conducive to his or her status as a legal subject speaking to and being heard by representatives of his or her law. An accused who asks for a lawyer in effect concedes that the cir-cumstances are adequate for speech, provided that a representative (to whom the accused in yet another speech act grants the power to speak and act on his or her behalf) is present. And, finally, an accused who waives the right to remain silent accepts that conditions of interrogation are appropriate for speech and allows police to continue their questioning.

Such an interpretation, focusing as it does on the *Miranda* warning as one in a sequence of speech acts analogous to offers that may be accepted, for instance, draws attention to the way that warning and waivers or other responses to the warning are made. It differs from two other common scholarly approaches to *Miranda* that display limited understanding of how speech acts or of what performative speech acts, such as warnings, actually do in their saying. Rather than considering what is done in the speech act of warning, as the *Miranda* Court had done, legal-doctrinal approaches assessed *Miranda* largely in terms of legal reasoning and constitutional fit. Sociolegal approaches, by contrast, have analyzed the *effects* or impact of the *Miranda* ruling and warnings on prosecution and conviction rates. The former approach considers the validity and soundness of arguments for the *Miranda* decision's constitutionality. On the surface, it focuses on propositions of law that can be analogized to constative utterances. The 2000 *Dickerson* case, which, as already mentioned, holds that *Miranda* is indeed a "constitutional rule," at least provisionally lays this dispute to rest. (Meanwhile it also enables new issues about speech acts of warning and waiver to arise, as we'll see in later chapters.) The sociolegal approach focuses neither on the validity or soundness of the Court's argument for the warning nor (often) on what is done *in* warning or what the warning says and does but rather on what happens *by* warning or on the warning's effects on evidence and on institutions that, unlike the accused, are not the direct addressees or apprehenders of the warning. As distinct from legal practitioners and others concerned with the manner of warning and waiver, legal scholars who stick to narrowly formal doctrinal issues and sociolegal scholars who are concerned only with the effects of *Miranda* on prosecution rates, no less than the philosophers Austin criticized fifty years ago, appear unaware of the significance of what Austin comes to call, as we shall see, the "illocutionary" aspect of speech or of what is done in saying as such!

In the course of his lectures, as mentioned, Austin comes to recognize that all sensible utterances actually involve both meaning and action, both constative and performative elements. Partway through the lectures, he argues explicitly that, despite the constative-performative distinction with which he began, understanding speech is not a matter of classifying *sentences* or statements. His own preliminary distinction between constative and performative utterances, as sentences that describe and that do, breaks down. After distinguishing between *sentences* that state, describe, or report and can ostensibly be assessed in terms of the truth of what they mean and sentences that do what they do in being said; that is, Austin argues that *both* constative and performative sentences do or perform things in being uttered. Reporting, stating, and describing are themselves speech acts and, he suggests, ritual or conventional ones at that. Conversely, even performative utterances can be assessed for their truth: A warning, for instance, may caution falsely about a nonexistent danger. Remember the little boy who cried, "Wolf!"?

In what he characterizes as a fresh start, then, Austin points out that all (sensible) speech acts or utterances can be said to do at least three different sorts of things. They say something *locutionarily* in a vocabulary and grammar, such as presenting relevant data or naming a danger.[23] They do something *illocutionarily in* being said, such as finding or warning. And they do something *perlocutionarily by* being said, such as confounding scholars or affecting conviction rates. Austin usually presents these as three different aspects of a given event of the issuing of an utterance, although he sometimes seems to present them as discrete acts. In any case, though, as Austin puts it, we are actually concerned with nothing short of the "total speech act in the total speech situation" (148), a matter that will be illustrated further by *Palsgraf v. Long Island Railroad* in Chapter Two.

In sum, speech act analysis offers an alternative to understanding law as either doctrinal and propositional or fundamentally a matter of empirical impact or even social pressure. Speech acts allow one to emphasize, as does much law in practice, that the significance of utterances is not simply in either reporting true-or-false propositions or in their effects. The *Miranda* warning is one example. Evidence law concerning hearsay offers another. Hearsay involves the report by a witness of the utterance of another. It is a "statement, other than one made by the declarant while testifying at the trial or hearing, offered in evidence to prove the truth of the matter asserted."[24] Such evidence is generally not admitted because the original utterance's reliability cannot be tested through cross-examination or assessment of the demeanor of its speaker under oath. A witness cannot testify that "Defendant X told me he borrowed the lawnmower" as evidence of the truth that X borrowed the lawnmower. But the witness can testify that "X told me that he borrowed the lawnmower" as evidence that, for instance, X is capable of speech or was within earshot. Though hearsay is not necessarily admissible to show the truth of what was said, then, hearsay is admissible to show that utterance occurred. The list of exceptions to the rule excluding hearsay evidence is actually quite long and intricate. "Excited utterances," for example, are not excluded, insofar as statements "relating to a startling event or condition, made while the declarant was under the stress of excitement that it caused" are considered sufficiently "reliable." When documents are no longer available or when the original speaker of an utterance has died or the speaker is otherwise unavailable for cross-examination, too, a witness's report as to what was read or heard may be admissible as to the "truth of the matter."

Like criminal law and evidence law, First Amendment jurisprudence also manifests a sense of speech as not simply a matter of meaning and truth but as a kind of action.[25] The First Amendment's protection of speech does not extend to criminal acts of speech, such as perjury and bribery, mislabeling a bottle, or misstating one's income. In perjury law, false utterance is a criminal *act* not because the falsity of the statement is evidence of a crime but because the *stating* of the falsity (that is material to a legal proceeding and so forth) is criminal. Some First Amendment jurisprudence indeed valorizes meaning in "protecting" speech, when it identifies the governmental restrictions on speech to which courts accord "strict scrutiny" as "content"-based, for example. The acknowledgment of content-neutral "time, place, and manner" regulations to which the Supreme Court allows greater leeway, however, attests to its recognition that conditions or circumstances of speech acts matter.

That utterances are both meaningful and done, or both constative and performative in Austin's original formulation, makes them difficult to grasp. Consider, for example, Supreme Court Justice Antonin Scalia's classification of "statements" as "testimonial" or "nontestimonial."[26] The Confrontation Clause of the Sixth Amendment gives an accused the right to confront those testifying against him or her. In cases involving the right of a defendant to confront or cross-examine witnesses, Scalia argues:

> *Statements* are nontestimonial [and hence admissible] when made in the course of police interrogation under circumstances objectively indicating that the primary purpose of the interrogation is to enable police assistance to meet an ongoing emergency. They are testimonial [and hence inadmissible] when the circumstances objectively indicate that there is no such ongoing emergency, and that the primary purpose of the interrogation is to establish or prove past events potentially relevant to later criminal prosecution. (*Davis v. Washington*, 547 U.S. 813, at 820, italics added)

At stake in *Davis* (2006) is the decision that "nontestimonial statements," such as those made to a 911 operator, are admissible at trial without their speaker being available for cross-examination, although "testimonial" ones, such as those made to police after an emergency has passed or to police interrogators when oneself or one's spouse is a suspect, as in *Crawford v. Washington* (2004), are inadmissible.

Scalia recognizes that meaning or content alone cannot distinguish testimonial from nontestimonial statements. Despite a textualist jurisprudence, which ostensibly turns to "tradition" to find the "plain meaning" of a text and rejects purposive statutory and constitutional interpretation, he perceives that statements do different things. In a manner that parallels his approach to judicial decision making, he then categorizes statements on the basis of the situation in which they *first* appear, according to the purpose for which, at that time, they are to be used. Although he sees that repetition of a call for help in a different speech situation may do something other than when it is first uttered, he does not reclassify it as an act of testimony when presented at a hearing.

In other words, Scalia seems to think that because a statement to a 911 operator (perlocutionarily, in Austin's terms) enables assistance in an emergency, the repetition of the statement is not and never will be (illocutionarily) a testimonial act. (Such 911 statements are hearsay, although they generally fall within the "present sense expression" or "excited utterance" exceptions to the hearsay rule and are admissible.) Two years before *Davis*, Scalia had already rejected another option for determining admissibility: letting judges decide based on their own assessments of reliability. Rejecting in *Crawford* the "reliability" framework of *Ohio v. Roberts* (448 U.S. 56, 1980), he turned instead to what the Framers would have made of the Confrontation Clause. In *Crawford*, he held that the statements of a wife who made incriminating statements about her husband to police concerning the stabbing of another man were testimonial acts of bearing witness and inadmissible under the Confrontation Clause. Relying on *Webster's Dictionary*, Scalia claimed that, "An accuser who makes a formal statement to government officers bears testimony in a sense that a person who makes a casual remark to an acquaintance does not." He aligned the wife's constative utterance with the testimony of an "accuser" making a "formal statement," quoting *Webster's*, to the effect that testimony is "'a solemn declaration or affirmation made for the purpose of establishing or proving some fact,'" although the accusatory (illocutionary) aspect of the utterance would emerge only in the course of proceedings against the husband.

In *Davis*, Scalia loses further sight of the character of bearing witness as an *act*, when he in effect argues, more or less by definition, that particular kinds of *statements* "cause the declarant to be a 'witness' within the meaning of the Confrontation Clause." Taking testimony to be the nounlike object produced at the moment of occurrence of verblike acts of accusing, declaring, or affirming, but not of calling for help, Scalia slips further into his understanding of adjectivally "testimonial" utterances not as dynamic speech but as "solemn" and constative statements, which a 911 call is not. The concurring justices in *Crawford*, Rehnquist and O'Connor, argued against this distinction between testimonial and nontestimonial statements, pointing out that "we have never drawn [such] a distinction." (Both had left the Court by the time *Davis* was decided.) For the purpose of admissibility as evidence, they claimed, testimonial evidence refers to sworn statements. The common law had treated all unsworn statements as nontestimonial (hearsay and hence inadmissible, unless subject to a rule of exception), they pointed out. Rejecting both "reliability" as the test for admissibility and "solemnity" as the identifier of testimony, they recalled a part of *Webster's* definition of testimony that Scalia did not cite: "Such affirmation in judicial proceedings, may be verbal or written, but must be under oath."

The difficulty the Court has disentangling testimonial from nontestimonial statements epitomizes the difficulties one has maintaining distinctions between constative and performative utterances. The discounting of the relevance of the sworn oath for identifying testimony or acts of bearing witness and the significance Scalia accords instead to the "solemnity" of statements shows, moreover, how not only words, such as "testimony," but also acts, such as swearing, themselves shift meaning and act differently at different times. Swearing, or giving one's word, formerly warranted or guaranteed solemnity and reliability in ways that it is no longer thought to do. (Scalia's move away from the oath is not the same as allowing as an alternative to it the "affirmation," which, since the seventeenth century, has been accorded to those whose religious faith prevents them from conscientiously swearing an oath and which the U.S. Constitution allows to presidential office holders.)[27] Scalia's rejection of testimony as a sworn statement epitomizes a modern view in which neither gods nor oaths hold the significance they once had (see Chapter Four).

Despite their disagreements, Scalia and the rest of the justices clearly agree that accuracy and reliability as well as the conditions or manner in which an utterance bears witness are relevant to its admissibility as evidence and its use as testimony. The difficulties that courts and others have separating propositional content from acts of speech parallel the difficulties that Austin encounters in trying to sustain his original distinction between constative and performative utterances and that he will later encounter in distinguishing illocutionary from perlocutionary acts. For the time being, though, it is enough to note that law looks beyond vocabulary and grammar to ascertain what utterances are, say, and do. U.S. law recognizes that the significance and felicitousness of speech somehow lies as much in what speech does and how it does it as in its propositional content measured against standards of accuracy or of reliability.

Two. Hearing Claims: Stanley Cavell

Even as Austin draws attention beyond the propositional content of sentences to the actlike quality or dynamism of speech, he also draws attention to the ways in which speech acts may go wrong. Here again, Austinian insights correspond to practical legal concerns. Much law appears designed precisely to prevent the unhappiness or infelicitousness of speech, especially legal speech. Law establishes procedures and conditions for many different types of speech, from commercial speech to political speech, from courtroom speech to voting. Through civil and criminal procedure, it authorizes particular speakers to speak in a particular order or at particular times and places in particular ways . It explicitly allows for changes in its own speech acts: Legal acts may reverse or suspend judgments; hold statutes unconstitutional or amend them; and revoke, amend, dismiss, overrule, and otherwise qualify and establish limits and deadlines for earlier utterances.

Noting the existence of procedures for legal speech acts draws attention to their conventionality, as per an ostensibly Austinian account of performative legal speech. Noting the conditions under which these acts occur, however, also draws attention to the limits of that account.[28] For legal acts must not only be spoken under particular conditions; they must also be heard in particular ways. Law pays as much attention to *hearing* and the hearer (or reading and the reader) of speech as it does to its speaking and speaker, even if legal scholars do not always pay as much attention to sound as they might.[29] An Austinian account that suggests that legal speech acts are simply more or less successful performances that can be put in a first-person present indicative active form and can be assessed by conventions or procedures of *speaking* (or writing) does not go far enough in recognizing the role of the hearer. This section thus argues that legal acts resemble what Stanley Cavell would call "passionate" utterances. Not only are there different kinds of hearing, but the dependence of an act on its being heard by another opens it up to unconventional interpretations and possibilities.[30]

Law may appear to consist largely of conventional utterances, that is, but an act of law that is not heard or apprehended makes little sense. In chains of claims and counterclaims, U.S. law must hear and be heard. Hearing as well as claiming falls within the purview of law. Law manifests a concern, of course, for standing or for what is popularly called "voice" and for its own proper jurisdiction or, literally, speaking of law.[31] It attends equally, though, to witnessing and notice, for instance, to warrant that utterances (including writings) are properly apprehended or heard. Speech matters only when there are listeners; publication, when there are readers. The traditional significance of a hearing as the occasion in which a legal subject receives an audience should not be underestimated. *Audi et alteram partem*, or "hear the other side," not only informs current legal processes but emanates from Greek and Roman traditions.[32] If legal acts fail to be properly heard or apprehended, they are illegitimate or invalid. Subsequent legal acts may acknowledge this explicitly, refusing to recognize them, qualifying purported decisions or agreements, or even insisting, through legal fictions, that no act occurred.

As officials and other legal participants apprehend, respond to, and engage with the claims of others, they are challenged and persuaded by those whom they would in turn persuade. In legal speech acts of all sorts, the "I claim . . ." of an official or of others is designed equally as an "I persuade you . . ." It appeals not only by convention to formal authority and to rules, but also in more unruly ways to right and justice. In courts, legislatures, and town halls, as well as outside of them, unconventional appeals are made, successfully and unsuccessfully, strategically and sincerely, falsely and felicitously, even when formal law and legal conventions are not, or do not turn out to be, on their side. But they cannot be made at all unless they are heard.

The very appellation of law as a system of "justice" in which "justices" hear reinforces a sense that participating in legal proceedings involves not only conventions of formal or positive state law but also an audience before a hearer, after which the hearer declares that and how "justice" be done. The arrangements and orality of medieval English criminal trials never let participants forget that law must be heard to do justice. The claims of legal officials, however conventional at some level, no less than the claims of those who challenge law, defend themselves against it, and work to change it are in this sense Cavellian "passionate" utterances.[33]

In his friendly-amendment-cum-radical-critique of Austin, that is, Cavell argues that there exist sensible utterances that are neither constative nor performative. Utterances such as insults and seductions, writes Cavell, are neither constative nor performative: They do not claim to describe or report, but neither do they make the same sense as a performative utterance when put in first-person present indicative active form. "I insult you" or "I seduce you"—or even "I persuade you"—does not do what it says in the same way as the explicit performative "I promise . . ." or "I hold . . ." or "I urge . . ." does. Austin's later focus on illocutionary acts over perlocutionary acts privileges speaking and speaker over hearing and hearer or the "I" over the "you," Cavell writes. Although the performative utterances that Austin later aligns with illocutionary acts need not take particular grammatical form, they can, in principle, be expressed in first-person present indicative active form. "Watch out" becomes "I warn you that the bull is about to charge." "Done" may be "I accept your wager." Their "focus," both Cavell and Austin agree, is on the "I" who speaks. "Passionate utterances," by contrast, depend more on "you," Cavell writes. They require a hearer who is attuned to what the speaker is doing in a particular way, as much as they need a speaker with designs on an addressee.

Cavell makes a strong distinction between performative and passionate utterance, contrasting the "offer of participation in the order of law" of the performative utterance to the invitation into the "disorders of desire" of the passionate one (185). For Cavell, passionate utterance requires imagination; performative utterance does not: It requires knowledge of convention. When performative acts fail, they are "characteristically reparable," he writes, insofar as one can turn to proper procedure. (Recall Obama's retaking of the oath in keeping with Article II.) "I do not, except in special circumstances, wonder how I might make a promise or a gift, or apologize, or render a verdict," Cavell writes (173). Passionate utterances, though, Cavell continues, "make room for, and reward imagination and virtuosity, unequally distributed capacities among the species. . . . To persuade you may well take considerable thought, to insinuate as much as to console may require tact, to seduce or to confuse you may take talent" (173).

Cavell's strong distinction between performance and passion, convention and improvisation, law and desire, will be discussed again (in Chapters Three and Four). Contra Cavell, and as James Boyd White has long reminded us, the claims of participants made within the ostensible "order" of law are replete with imagination and virtuosity, however much positive law may wish to circumscribe or sublimate the disorderly desires that belong to its realm.[34] For now, it is enough to point out that, rhetorically speaking, law involves passionate utterance. Even as legal acts seem to epitomize conventional offers and demands or even mandates and imperatives to participate in the "order of law," law also seeks to persuade "you" and is persuadable by "you." It allows for its own contestation or *agon*. Legal acts are directed toward hearers, without whom they could not be persuasive or be the claims they are. As claims, asserting and demanding, they are born of desire, and they seek to move you. Although they may not ultimately be persuasive, legal utterances respond to particular and changeable states of affairs (or to changes in recognition of states of affairs[35]) by making claims on their hearers to acknowledge their truth or their right, or to acknowledge what Chapter Four will return to as the (un)fairness or (in)justice that they assert or demand of the situation.

Perjury law reveals the importance of hearing and possibilities of variations in it. While perjury is a criminal act, courts take what Lawrence Solan and Peter Tiersma call a more "literal" approach to perjury than to crimes, such as bribery or conspiracy, that occur outside legal proceedings.[36] Perjury law, they explain, is not meant to punish untruth as such but to protect the integrity of legal proceedings (213). Prototypical lying, they argue, both conveys false information and causes hearers to believe something false (232). By contrast, misleading, yet literally true, sworn responses to questions are not necessarily perjured. Solan and Tiersma offer the following example: Q: Do you have a Chevy? A: I have a Ford (when the respondent has both a Chevy and a Ford) (214).

Solan and Tiersma argue that a literal truth defense to perjury is problematic. They suggest that, by taking the question that is asked into account, one instead ascertain whether an answer is "responsive." The Ford example is unresponsive. It is the questioning lawyer's job to ensure that a witness gives "relevant and relatively complete responses . . . that we should be able to interpret . . . accordingly. Were it not so, the entire questioning process would collapse," they argue. "But who do we blame when . . . the witness intentionally gives an unresponsive answer to create a false impression of responsiveness? Do we let . . . creditors go uncompensated because their lawyer's trial skills were not sufficiently honed, or do we prosecute the witness for perjury to discourage deceitful conduct?" (220). If you are asked why you were not at work yesterday, and you answer "I was sick," although you did not get sick until after spending all day at the beach drinking beer, for instance, Solan and Tiersma point out that nothing in the answer alerts the questioner to the possibility that the answer, although literally true, is unresponsive (219–220). They would distinguish between situations where it should be evident that an answer is unresponsive, in which case the lawyer should probe further, as in the Ford/Chevy example, and answers where a questioner cannot tell that an answer is unresponsive, in which case a jury should decide whether the reply communicates something false in light of the question and whether the defendant believed it to be false (221).

I introduce perjury to illustrate different ways of hearing and to suggest the narrowness of both literal assessment of a single proposition and assessment of an utterance in relation to the single question that it is meant to address. Either way, the court limits what it hears. The radical alternative would be for it to expand its inquiry into potential deception in a speech situation whose context includes not only the interaction between lawyer and witness but also the very "fact" about which the witness is ostensibly testifying. Rather than expanding inquiry about the utterance to the "totality" of its circumstances, which circumstances are themselves at issue and by definition currently (insofar as they are being litigated) elude its grasp, the court retreats in perjury cases to a narrowly circumscribed set of elements (oath, intent, falsity, materiality to outcome)[37] whose assessment lies within the terms of what courts can hear and competently ascertain. (Note as an aside for now that, whatever the problems that intention or will raises for philosophers and others, courts and legislatures seldom consider narrow inquiry into criminal intent to be outside their competence or that of the jury! Both the immigration cases and the *Morissette* case previously mentioned show how courts indeed classify various kinds of intent. At the same time, though, courts refuse, as indeed they must, to enter into the grander issues of law, language, and knowledge that are implicated by the very introduction of intention and will. If legislatures resemble philosophers of law interested in parsing out, as course descriptions would have it, various moral and political foundations of law, courts are like students who build on the particular foundations that most suit their predilections. It takes a rhetorician like Nietzsche to ask what it means to presume that there are foundations at all or, as in Chapters Two and Four, to interrogate assumptions about intention.)

While courts retreat to narrowly circumscribed elements in assessing perjury, another kind of hearing is involved in cases of misprision of felony or concealment of knowledge of a crime to which one has not necessarily assented. In misprision cases, the issue of the difference between a failure to report knowledge and active concealment of it shows an expansion of hearing to take in not only the conditions surrounding particular speech acts but also the conditions surrounding even the silences out of which speech may come.[38] Likewise, in contract law, differences between omission and neglect may become an issue.[39] Hearing may include silences when a particular case attempts "to reconcile two . . . elements, morality and law, by binding parties to what is implied by their silence as well as by their speech."[40]

Courts both limit and sometimes suggest the limits of the abilities of those participating in the legal process to hear speech and silence. Motions *in limine* preempt the inclusion, or occasionally exclusion, of evidence that may unduly affect a jury.[41] The formal *Miranda* warning, however problematically it may be executed and responses to it interpreted, constitutes an acknowledgment, noted in the first section of this chapter, that police and trial courts may not be properly able to apprehend an accused's utterances. If in perjury law, courts restrict themselves to what they can know, then in obscenity law, U.S. law cannot even say what it knows. Recall Justice Potter Stewart's acknowledgment that he might not be able to intelligently define obscenity, but "I know it when I see it."

Obscenity law returns us to and unsettles any strong distinctions between the seemingly articulate and conventional performative utterances of orderly law and the passionate utterances that, as Cavell puts it, invite one into "improvisation into the disorders of desire." Over the years the tests for what is obscene have changed. In 1957, the Supreme Court clarified that First Amendment protection did not extend to material that the "average person" judged was of "prurient interest." This meant that obscenity could be lawfully prohibited. In the Fanny Hill case (1966) about a 1760 book, *Memoirs of a Lady of Pleasure*, the Supreme Court overturned a Massachusetts court that had held the book obscene, finding that, although the work appealed to a prurient interest in sex and was patently offensive, it was not "utterly without socially-redeeming value."[42] Today, leaving obscenity to be judged according to local community standards brings expressions "designed to incite lustful thoughts" within the conventional order of law, even as regulation of expression appears to be in tension with the tendency to "free" speech from regulation or to establish a realm of unruly desire independent of the order of law.

If law struggles to control or prohibit speech that would titillate hearers or viewers, it is also conversely the case that law's own speech sometimes escapes its control. Controversies over the ability and effectiveness of judicial instructions to a jury to disregard formally inadmissible evidence raise precisely this issue.[43] The marshaling of "dicta" exemplifies the long-term unpredictability within law of speech. Consider how the possibility of a tiered approach to judicial review that the 1938 Court explicitly mentioned was "unnecessary to consider" in the now famous footnote 4 of *U.S. v. Carolene Products* (see also Chapter Three) has since become the established framework within which all advocates and judges concerned with Fourteenth Amendment issues must contend.[44] Even the strategic use of utterances thought of as dicta play on possibilities that future cases will allow such utterances to be heard differently in the future.

Legal reasoning and evidence law, perjury law, contracts and Constitutional law all show the importance of hearing, while suggesting that U.S. law is susceptible to incapacities of speech and limitations of hearing that it cannot escape and sometimes acknowledges. In such recognition, law manifests a sense both of the complexities of speech acts and events and of some of its own limits as speaker and hearer of law and of language. It offers claimants opportunities to challenge it, even as it strives to control the terms and conditions within which such challenges occur. Despite the law's best efforts to control speech though, events of unruly speech happen. Persons speak in ways that law forbids and challenge not only law's formal legal claims but also its ability to manage language. False shouts of "fire" metaphorically and sometimes literally plague crowded theaters.[45] Even as modern law is bound to speech and hearing, language exceeds law. Formal or official law fails to have the final word. Law relies on language that is spoken and heard in ways that are sometimes beyond it.

Three. Modern Law and Language

Sections One and Two suggest that U.S. law is both fearful and hopeful about speech. Its practitioners speak and "ad-vocate"; its officials are constituted as hearers; and its theorists valorize reason and argument. U.S. law also treads carefully around speech acts, recognizing them as dynamic events that occur inside and outside of court, testing and contesting not only the meaning but also the force and authority of utterances, and circumscribing or limiting their unpredictability. Law also acknowledges or recognizes some of its own limitations around speaking and hearing. At stake in law's treatment of speech today then is the possibility that something—language? or a law of language perhaps?—lies at least in part beyond the reach of the long arm of positive law and its empirical realities. After explaining what is meant by positive law, this section argues that attending to law as language, as the following chapters do, enhances contemporary understanding of law.

"Positive law" refers to the system of human-made law that we now usually associate with the state, its institutions, and, as Max Weber put it, its monopoly over legitimate violence. Official or formal law today is often said to constitute a "system." Almost every criminology and political science textbook presents law as a "legal system," identifying the domestic legal system with the state and its institutions.[46] Legal positivist H. L. A. Hart argues, in his renowned *The Concept of Law*, that a "union of primary and secondary rules" in which there is no necessary connection between law and justice is at the center of "a legal system."[47]

One notes that human-made systems of positive law have not always exhausted conceptions of law, however. Positive law has not always been the exclusive or at least the predominant system of law that legal-philosophical and sociolegal scholarship takes it to be. To point this out is not to call for a return to a natural law that affirms God or morality or reason as the source of law and that represents the traditional alternative to legal positivism in the philosophy of law. Rather, it is to recognize that even so-called positive law systems, whether of institutions or rules, domestic or international, are not discrete. Legal orders overlap and interact.

In the past, one held simultaneous relations and obligations to ecclesiastical, feudal, and monarchic legal orders. Still today, legal and community memberships are not limited to single or only state membership. In North America, indigenous persons and members of First Nations belong to nonstate communities of law.[48] The religious pluralism of India, the aboriginal laws of Australia, and family law in Israel show persons to be beholden to more than one law.[49] Studies of colonial and postcolonial law show the permeability of state law and show how elements associated with a state function interactively with nonstate law in an environment that cannot fully be distinguished from law.[50] What with public and private international law, immigration law, treaties, and transnational private agreements, one is hard pressed to delineate a determinate closed system of domestic or of state law, much less a set of discrete or noninterdependent entities to whom a given body of law exclusively belongs.[51] Even as states depend on one another and on other entities for recognition, though, many English speakers, including scholars who write about law, identify law with the official doctrines or rules and formal and informal practices of states.

Different disciplines approach and treat in various ways the relation of the state to entities and elements other than itself and the dependence of state law on something other than rules. They offer theories of sovereignty or analyses of political power or of social control, for instance, to account for the significance, functioning, and limitations of positive or state law.[52] The chapters that follow explain law in terms of language, in a way that both justifies the inclusion, as law, of what we take to be positive law and also points to the incompleteness of legal positivist accounts of law. H. L. A. Hart once considered "modern municipal legal systems" to be "central clear instances to which the expression 'law' and 'legal system' have undisputed application," maintaining that "international law and primitive law . . . have certain features of the central case but lack others."[53] The turn to language, to which Hart is to a certain degree sympathetic, inverts the centrality of the case for state law as law and revives issues of the relations of law and justice to which legal positivism gives short shrift.[54]

The turn to language in the next chapters not only displaces the claims of the state to exclusive jurisdiction (or authority to "speak law") but also allows one to understand more fully how law works inside and outside the state. Ultimately, one sees how legal acts happen in and through language that appeals to overlapping communities of speakers whose language reveals their world. Contemporary law, these chapters will show, involves judgments and claims that are social acts and manifest themselves in imperfect interactions of speech. Such basic insights supplement contemporary scholarship of and about law.[55] Sociolegal studies sometimes point out for instance that things need to happen to a court's utterance for it to become an effective rule.[56] They offer the by-now unsurprising insight that "rules" of positive law, including the rulings of judges, are not in themselves as efficacious at setting policy or solving disputes as some may wish or believe or as law students are sometimes taught. Indeed, such studies show, rules and rulings alone do not have "impact." The lack of impact of an official utterance means that legal utterances are not simple matters of cause and effect. As these studies suggest, if one is to understand how utterances can come to have impact or how rules emerge, then one must attend to how texts circulate, to how language is used in interactions and institutions, and to what responses are to such use. The "efficacy" of legal speech requires that particular institutional conditions or, to translate into the language of speech acts, felicity conditions be met.

Attending to language sheds light not only on the workings of law but also on the powers and constraints of official actors and on the constitution of communities. In their acts of law, legal officials appeal to hearers who share their knowledge or understanding of language. To be understood, they must defer in some way to the responses and speech of those with whom they would speak or of those whom they would rule. As Chapter Three will show, even grammatically neutral or impersonal legal enactments, addressed "to whom it may concern," for instance, presume a "we" who can hear and "know," when they begin "This act shall be known as . . ."[57]

Those who share such common language are strictly identical neither with officials who accept the law, nor with citizens who generally obey it, nor even with the conjunction of the two, despite what Hart implies when he considers law to be a system of primary and secondary rules, in which primary rules are the rules that citizens generally obey, determined by secondary rules that officials generally accept.[58] Rather, as we shall see, speakers and hearers constitute communities who already share practices of language and, indeed, of law. Their sharing and knowledges are variable and incomplete. Through their language and law, however, they judge the world in common, or at least in common enough ways that they can speak with one another and live together and challenge one another's claims.[59] In claiming, they participate in legal and social acts; they share practical knowledge of speech and action that one might associate with tradition.[60]

"Tradition" is of course as vexed a term as "community." A "community" that shares practical knowledge of language does not mean that all agree. As Wittgenstein puts it: "It is what human beings *say* that is true and false, and they agree in the *language* they use. That is not agreement in opinions but in form of life."[61] Attending to language thus brings to the fore a potential disjunct between the laws or rules of the state and the urge toward their positive articulation and codification, on the one hand, and the imperfect or incomplete laws and traditions of language and of so-called communities on the other. The practical law or knowledge of a community or even a citizenry need not coincide with its own articulated rules or with state law.[62] As sociolegal studies point out, many nonstate communities invoke and act in accordance with unstated norms or laws.[63] The permeable and overlapping identities of legal actors or claimants whose primary affiliations are not to the state and whose appeal to law is not necessarily to that of positive state law suggest a multiplicity of memberships even in a global age. Persons invoking foreign law in conflict cases or private international law, for instance, relate both to the foreign law and to the law of the state in which the issue of jurisdiction (again, the speaking of law) arises.[64] That claims such as those made in the name of nonstate law are largely unsuccessful in the terms of official state and interstate law should not lead us to ignore that there are many sorts of nonofficial laws in whose names community members engage and to which they appeal, both among themselves and in dealing with other laws.[65] The claims against the state of such collectivities and of those who belong to them point not to the power of law to enforce itself or to have an impact, but to the ways that law manifests itself through claims made of and with others.

Language is inextricable from claims of membership and jurisdiction, even within states. States require language tests for citizenship. Irrespective of state citizenship, that foreign language speakers may not understand claims made in English has implications for state law. Nonforeigners who understand English but cannot grasp more formal or complex aspects of legal speech because of the particularities of their educations or experiences, also present special issues in law. Claims about language preservation, education, and translation are legal claims, often made in other languages.

Insofar as studies of law and society themselves make claims about law, they too can be said to belong to language "communities" that use words to assert truths and to demand recognition of those truths as "their own." Such claims "belong" to the field in which they are spoken or claimed.[66] Despite some strands of legal realism that would dismiss legal language in the name of a radical distinction between "law-in-action" and "law-on-the-books," sociolegal studies cannot completely disregard language nor unmoor it from their own claims about law. Marc Galanter's now-classic (1974) "Why the 'Haves' Come Out Ahead: Speculations on the Limits of Legal Change" may at first seem an unlikely article on which to draw to show how sociolegal studies reinforce the importance of speech acts and language in law.[67] "Haves" does not explicitly deal with language, but points precisely to the relevance of legal actors' speech capacities and incapacities to "the way the system works" (97).

"Haves" begins by inviting the reader to think of the legal "system" as composed of four elements: rules, courts, lawyers, and parties. It concludes by warning that one ought not expect judicial declarations or decisions to have "rule-changing" impact. Aiming to reverse the usual analyses that "start at the rules end and work down through the institutional facilities to see what effect the rules have on the parties," Galanter sets out to "think about the different kinds of parties and the effect these differences might have on the way the system works" (97). Galanter makes clear that he views adjudication not in terms of speech acts at all, but in terms of rules (an issue which will be addressed further in Chapter Two): "Courts devise interstitial rules, combine diverse rules, and apply old rules to new situations" (96). The only reference to speech in his assumptions comes in the recognition of "higher" agencies "*announcing* (making, interpreting) rules," while "lower" agencies are "*assigned*" the "responsibility of enforcing (implementing, applying) these rules" (96, emphasis added).

Describing the opportunities and limitations of parties of different sorts to formulate and respond to legal "claims" (97), Galanter links issues of access to justice explicitly to factors of socioeconomic and sociolegal power. He distinguishes between "repeat players" (RPs) and "one shotters" (OSs); RPs are "larger units" with smaller "stakes in any given case" than OSs (98). He does not equate RPs simply with "haves (in terms of power, wealth and status)" nor "OSs with 'have-nots,'" though. RPs may be alcoholic derelicts or government; OS criminal defendants may be wealthy, he writes. But the categories of RP and OS on the one hand, and of "have" and "have-not" on the other, overlap. As Galanter puts it:

> What this analysis does is to define a position of advantage in the configuration of contending parties and indicate how those with other advantages tend to occupy this position of advantage and to have their other advantages reinforced and augmented thereby. This position of advantage is one of the ways in which a legal system formally neutral as between "haves" and "have-nots" may perpetuate and augment the advantages of the former. (103–104)

The relationships, community building, knowledge, access, education, and skills that reinforce the "position of advantage" of the haves in Galanter's analysis require language. The "advance intelligence" of RPs allows them to "structure the next transaction and build a record" (98). Acts of "transaction" and "record" clearly involve language when carried out by "the insurance company, the prosecutor, the finance company" and "the taxpayer and the welfare client," for instance, or by "the professional criminal" (97). Further, the RP "*writes* the form contract, requires the security deposit, and the like" (98, emphasis added). When RPs "develop expertise and have ready access to specialists," Galanter writes, they do not only "enjoy economies of scale and have low start up costs for any case" (98). They also get help "in routine negotiations," presumably carried out through language, and are able to "trade" and "bargain" over time, on the basis of their "reputation" (99), a matter of language, while OSs have no opportunity to keep in the good books of others. RPs' informal relations include the "receptivity" of those they deal with regularly to the "version of the conflict *told* by" RPs as nonstrangers (99, note 9, emphasis added). Receptivity may extend to clerks' "scheduling" (in words) in ways amenable to them (99, note 9). The RP's "accumulated expertise enables him" to "play for rules" not only in litigation but also in lobbying for legislation "persuasively" through claims (100). By "virtue of experience and expertise" RPs are able to *tell*, on *hearing* or *reading* them, what rules matter. Resources of "knowledge, attentiveness, and expert services," as well as money, according to Galanter, allow RPs to "invest in rules" favorable to them (103).

To Galanter, features of the legal system appear as devices "for maintaining the partial dissociation of everyday practices from . . . authoritative and normative commitments" (147) and "articulate the legal system to the discontinuities of culture and social structure" (148). His article concludes that "rule changes which relate directly to the strategic position of parties by facilitating organization [and] increasing the supply of legal services (where these in turn provide a focus for articulating and organizing common interests)" are, along with reallocation of costs and the organization of the legal profession, among the "most powerful" ways of contributing to "redistributive social change" (150). Even as the "advantages" and "articulations"[68] with which Galanter is concerned are embedded in language, though, the article never explicitly acknowledges a role for language in the "strategies" he names, nor in the "legal system," in "everyday practices," in "normative commitments," or in "culture and social structure."

The point here is not simply to extend the way that some sociolegal scholarship can go about its work.[69] The point rather is to show that issues of modern law and justice are matters of language or of speech and hearing through and through. Galanter's article shows how knowledges and uses of language are implicated in even the most carefully delineated accounts of the powerful structures of contemporary U.S. federal and state institutions. That persons and groups differ in their abilities to engage with and in their relations to official law is a matter of speech, which is why lawyers and practitioners of law are schooled in reading and writing. Issues of access to justice, like questions about whether foreign-language speakers or others understand the *Miranda* warning, whether corporate campaign contributions should be limited or hearsay should be admitted, are matters of language. This does not mean that they should all be First Amendment issues. What it means is that the First Amendment is only one of many areas in which law and language interact and that attending to issues of language, broadly understood, is crucial to understanding law and to conditions of participation and engagement in our public sphere.

Finally, the recognition that law is a matter of language tempers both the romanticism and utopianism associated with aspirations or ideals of law and the harshness of apparently wholesale critiques of law. Both law and language can go wrong. Both are susceptible to misuse. In situations of privilege or power, law indeed appears as an idiom in which privilege and power are asserted as well as contested. But the imperfections of language and its potential to deceive do not prevent us from, at least occasionally, expressing ourselves to one another in a good-enough manner. So too, the imperfections and misuse of law do not prevent it from occasionally saying and doing what it claims well enough. The chapters that follow explore just how law does so.

· · ·

In sum, in recognizing that speech acts and in trying to master events of speech while occasionally acknowledging the limitations of its mastery, U.S. law shows its indebtedness to a "law" (if we can call it that) of language that is in some sense beyond it. Our often garrulous and sometimes successful, sometimes unhappy, positive law is not a sovereign law, nor can it be. Not only is it challenged by many other laws, as sociolegal studies point out, but it is beholden to speech. Hence the "abundance of caution" that modern law—and lawyers in the White House—conventionally display around words!

CHAPTER TWO

Learning by the Rules

"Reason" in language: oh what a deceitful old woman! I fear we are not getting rid of God because we still believe in grammar . . .

—Nietzsche, *Twilight of the Idols*, "'Reason' in Philosophy," section 5

In *Plain English for Lawyers*, an elegant and pithy little book that rivals Strunk
and White's *Elements of Style*, Richard Wydick writes that "good legal writing
should not differ, without good reason, from ordinary well-written English."[1] He
offers Benjamin Cardozo's "statement of facts" in *Palsgraf v. Long Island Railroad* as an example of good writing. This well-known tort (or accident) case was
decided by New York's highest court in 1928 and has now become an old chestnut of American legal education.[2] What is "ordinary well-written English"? And
what is good reason to deviate from it? This chapter shows in part how the commitments of law and legal education to grammar and reason, such as those of
Wydick, very nicely reveal what Friedrich Nietzsche would consider the metaphysics of modern law. Metaphysics refers to the philosophy of reality, or to the
first principles that ostensibly lie beyond physics (*phusis*) or matter.

From the beginning of law school, as Elizabeth Mertz shows, would-be practitioners are exposed through language and dialogue to a form of reasoning
that is associated with "thinking like a lawyer." Students become "strategists of
speech."[3] As they are tutored in a particular way of reading and speaking, it becomes natural to them "to accept that the facts emerging from the nested authoritative levels of discourse in legal settings will be the basis for definitive legal
findings" (110). The legal language that students learn converts "every possible
event or conflict into a shared rhetoric . . . [that] . . . generates an appearance of
neutrality" in which sociocultural specificity drains away (132), she argues. The
"politics" enacted in what Mertz calls the "metalinguistic structure of the law

school classroom" resembles that of the courtroom, she writes, in which politics is "concealed through the fiction that this discourse is 'legal' rather than 'political'" (134). Encouraged to "separate their inner opinions and feelings from the discursively defined legal personae they are learning to embody," students inhabit and speak an "I" that, Mertz argues, is not "their own self" (135). They "begin to speak as players in a legal drama" (135). They come to speak, one might say, in the name of the law.

Speaking in the name of the law extends far beyond legal dramas of classroom and courtroom. It characterizes the activities of more than students, professors, lawyers, and judges. Chapter Three attends further to the "I" and the "we" of legal discourse. Chapter Two meanwhile shows that not only legal writing and reason, but even "well-written" and "plain English" privileges particular conceptions of reality. English grammar divides facts and findings about the "real" world into deeds and doers in control of their doings. Language advocates error, as Nietzsche puts it, in law as elsewhere. At a grammatical level, "complete" sentences in which subjects predicate follow the illusory model of a God in charge of His creation: God creates, humanity acts, authors write, subjects predicate, and nouns verb! Although in actuality "accountability is lacking," as Nietzsche writes, language attributes responsibility to subjects for what they do.[4] The imposition of grammatical and linguistic constructions on a world of becoming secures "truth" by compartmentalizing and rendering things static. Indeed, throughout Western history, Nietzsche continues, we have imagined entire true worlds—heaven, the noumenal world, the so-called ideal versus real world—in static and universal terms and have used these worlds and their truths as standards by which to judge *this* world as lacking.[5] At the same time as words offer standards, though, they are unable to capture a world that is perpetually in flux, Nietzsche writes. For him, words represent only the dead leaves of his "painted thoughts."[6]

Wydick's selection of Cardozo's statement of facts in *Palsgraf* as an example of "good legal writing," as we shall see, shows in part the hold that an understanding of the world as static and as divisible into subjects and objects who act and are acted on has on us and in our law. The language of the *Palsgraf* opinions (see Appendix C) show how law appears to be a system of universal or at least atemporal rules or standards that are differentiated from and applied to facts, even as the existence of law itself is considered a matter of fact. *Palsgraf* also opens up another account of law and language, though. In saying and doing things besides stating facts and applying rules, the *Palsgraf* opinions show law to consist at least in part of acts and events that are attributed to a singular moment but that actually happen over time and may become matters of legal histories.

As all who have taken first-year torts will recall, Justice Cardozo's majority opinion is famous for its redefinition of negligence and cause in tort or accident law.[7] "Negligence" generally refers to a failure of a duty to take care. "Tort law" emerged in the nineteenth century to refer to civil or private actions or lawsuits concerning breaches or failures of noncontractual duties. Criminal actions, as contrasted to civil ones, concern a breach of duty to society. Criminal charges accusing a defendant of wrongdoing are brought in the name of the state or the people; a guilty verdict leads to punishment for wrongdoing. Civil complaints, by contrast, are generally brought by private parties and allege a defendant's liability for harm done to the plaintiff. Conviction in a civil suit results not in punishing the defendant as such but in the defendant's making restitution for causing harms to the plaintiff. In overturning the state's intermediate court and finding that the Long Island Railroad was not liable for Helen Palsgraf's injuries, Cardozo engaged in conventional legal analysis while ushering in a new way of talking about liability for accidents. In particular, he limited liability to foreseeable risks, thereby rejecting both the contemporary understanding of negligence and dissenting Justice Andrews's attempt to extend liability to all the harms that result from—or are "proximately caused" by—a wrongful act. Both civil and criminal law, with their particular commitments to cause and intention, this chapter suggests, partake in the metaphysics that Friedrich Nietzsche identifies with "the error" of reason.

Section One presents Cardozo's and Andrews's characterizations of the case. Their statements of facts correspond not only to the attributions of action, cause, and responsibility made in the later arguments of their opinions but also to those predicated in the grammar of the English language. In announcing the facts of the situation as they do, the ordinary well-written English of these statements of facts, Section One shows, treats otherwise undifferentiated happenings as events and as acts of willing or intending subjects who, as Nietzsche points out, can thereby be held responsible for what they do. Section Two turns to characterizations of specifically legal happenings. Treating claims of law in writings and opinions such as those of Cardozo and Andrews as simply stating facts and applying rules misrepresents judicial acts of judgment and dissent. Presuming that laws are rules or that they are fundamentally the statements of judges and lawyers fails to acknowledge many other kinds of legal speech and legal actors. Not only through rules but through rhetoric, Section Three argues, claims of law and of language happen over time. Legal claimants assert and contest judgments and understandings of responsibility and make demands in the name of their law. Recognizing language and law alike to be sites of judgment that raise issues of agency and action and attribute cause and responsibility transforms legal writing—the constantly underfoot, yet somewhat-neglected stepchild of legal education—into a consort worthy of philosophy.

One. Good Legal Writing: *Palsgraf*

In his first chapter, Wydick explains what distinguishes the "plain English" writing style of the following passage from that found in most legal writing:

> Plaintiff was standing on a platform of defendant's railroad after buying a ticket to go to Rockaway Beach. A train stopped at the station, bound for another place. Two men ran forward to catch it. One of the men reached the platform of the car without mishap, though the train was already moving. The other man, carrying a package, jumped aboard the car, but seemed unsteady as if about to fall. A guard on the car, who had held the door open, reached forward to help him in, and another guard on the platform pushed him from behind. In this act, the package was dislodged, and fell upon the rails. It was a package of small size, about fifteen inches long, and was covered by a newspaper. In fact it contained fireworks, but there was nothing in its appearance to give notice of its contents. The fireworks when they fell exploded. The shock of the explosion threw down some scales at the other end of the platform many feet away. The scales struck the plaintiff, causing injuries for which she sues.

Wydick points to the "economy of words" in the passage; the choice of contemporary concrete words; the arrangement of subjects and verbs, and of verbs and objects, so as to leave no ambiguities as to who did what to whom; the use of simple and active verb forms; and the varied length of sentences that contain only one main thought (5–6). He shows that legal writing need not be wordy, indirect, passive, or tortuous. By following a few rules of English usage or what Wydick calls "elements of plain English style" (6)—"omit surplus words" (7); "prefer the active voice" (27); "use base verbs, not nominalizations" (23); and the like—Wydick suggests that one can write concise legal prose that will be understandable to clients, lawyers, and judges. He maintains, as do legal writing instructors generally, that "in short, good legal writing is plain English" (5).[8]

Consider now dissenting Justice Andrews's description of the same case:

> Assisting a passenger to board a train, the defendant's servant negligently knocked a package from his arms. It fell between the platform and the cars. Of its contents the servant knew and could know nothing. A violent explosion followed. The concussion broke some scales standing a considerable distance away. In falling they injured the plaintiff, an intending passenger.

Note the economy of Andrews's words. His description of this Rube Goldberg machine of a case uses fifty-eight words to Cardozo's 181, leaves out arguably irrelevant information such as where the train was bound or that there were two men. All of Andrews's sentences and verb clauses are active. Cardozo's description contains numerous passive constructions (plaintiff was standing, train was moving, package was dislodged and was covered). Five short active sentences link Andrews's "defendant's servant"'s act of "negligently knock[ing]" to the scales' active "injur[ing]" of the passenger.

Is Andrews's statement any less ordinary or well written than Cardozo's? Doesn't it fit Wydick's rules equally well if not better? Why wasn't it selected as an example of good legal writing? Is it less good? Is it less legal? And what about the rest of Cardozo's opinion? Does Cardozo have a good reason for a sentence like: "If no hazard was apparent to the eye of ordinary vigilance, an act innocent and harmless, at least to outward seeming, with reference to her, did not take to itself the quality of a tort because it happened to be a wrong, though apparently not one involving the risk of bodily insecurity, with reference to someone else"? Or a reason for: "There is room for argument that a distinction is to be drawn according to the diversity of interests invaded by the act, as where conduct negligent in that it threatens an insignificant invasion of an interest in property results in an unforeseeable invasion of an interest of another order, as, e.g., one of bodily security"?

Wydick indeed notes that "In general, . . . Justice Cardozo's writing style is too ornate for modern tastes."[9] In a footnote, he suggests examining the opinions of former U.S. Supreme Court Justice Lewis E. Powell or U.S. Circuit Judge Richard Posner as examples of "modern plain English style." The point of this chapter, though, is not to focus on the ornateness of Cardozo's style elsewhere nor to find a more modern plain style; it is, rather, to ask what the selection of this particular statement of facts as an example of good legal writing can tell us about law and writing.

Recall that a complete sentence includes a subject and a predicate or a noun that verbs. The subjects of active sentences predicate: Authors write, agents act, gods create, humans sin. The (grammatical) subjects of passive sentences, by contrast, are acted on: Books are written, balls are kicked, worlds are created, mistakes made, and packages dislodged. Most but not all of the sentences comprising Cardozo's description of the circumstances of the *Palsgraf* case are active: Train stopped, two men ran, one reached the train, the other jumped, one guard reached the man, another pushed, package fell, package contained fireworks, fireworks exploded, shock threw scales, scales struck plaintiff. Andrews's description is also full of active sentences: Servant knocked package, package fell, servant knew nothing, explosion followed, concussion broke scales, scales injured plaintiff. If complete sentences reveal a world grammatically divided into doers and their doing or deeds, then legal writing instructions to prefer the active voice reveal a preference for subjects who act over subjects who are acted on. Indeed, such a preference characterizes modern English writing more broadly.

Nietzsche points out that insofar as human beings act rather than being acted on and packages fall rather than being dislodged, we model our thought on "God creates." By grammatical preference, we establish subjects who are, like God as First Cause or Creator, in some sense in charge of and identifiable with their acts. In language, acts follow as the effects of subjects in control of what they do. Language thereby establishes the conditions whereby subjects can be held responsible for what they cause or do. Language "advocates" error, Nietzsche writes.[10] Criminal law epitomizes this so-called error when it associates gradations of intent with the levels of seriousness of a crime. But in tort law, too (despite some common understandings of "accidents" as events for which one cannot be held responsible), liability is a matter of establishing that a subject's act—and not another kind of event or a mere happening—caused the harm, as we shall see.

Writing instructors often point out that the word choice in a statement of facts leads a reader into a view of the issues. Andrews, whose dissent ultimately favors Palsgraf, opens and closes his statement of facts by referring twice to "passengers" who are grammatical objects of assistance and of injury. Cardozo by contrast begins and ends with an impersonal "plaintiff," whom he never calls a "passenger," although—in more words than Andrews's adjective "intending," which makes her an active subject—she is modified by having bought a ticket to go to Rockaway Beach. Cardozo's "plaintiff" at the beginning of the paragraph passively "was standing." In the paragraph's final sentence, "plaintiff" is the grammatical object of striking scales that cause her injury. Only in a dependent clause does she sue.

Cardozo's word choice keeps Palsgraf as plaintiff at a distance from both the action at issue and from the defendant who, in Cardozo's writing, is not identified as, but owns, the railroad. Cardozo's "guards" are not explicitly linked to the nameless "defendant" to whom the railroad belongs, to which the platform belongs, on which the plaintiff was standing. The guards act on a man whose package passively "was dislodged." In contrast, Andrews offers a linked chain of acts and events that begin with the railroad's servants' action. Andrews's "defendant's servant" negligently knocks the package, which in turn actively falls. In its brevity, Andrews's "a violent explosion followed" has an immediacy to it, which Cardozo's slightly more labored "the fireworks when they fell exploded"—with its separation of subject from predicate—does not. And while Andrews acknowledges that the scales stand a considerable distance away (from where the package falls) compared to Cardozo's specification that the scales are "at the other end of the platform many feet away" (from where the shock of the explosion happens), Andrews's scales injure Palsgraf directly. Andrews writes that "they injured the plaintiff," where "injuring" is directly predicated of the scales. Cardozo inserts an extra step or cause; he writes that the scales "struck the plaintiff, causing injury," implying that the grammatical object *injury* followed, as noun or state of affairs or production, an event of scales "causing."

So far, we have ventured only into what law students learn when they are taught to present the facts of a case both accurately and in a manner that will favor the party they represent. Justices Cardozo and Andrews represent not parties, though, but law. The primary issue of the railroad's liability joins and divides Cardozo and Andrews, no less than it joins and divides the Long Island Railroad and Helen Palsgraf. The justices' depictions of the "facts" through grammar and word choice suggest varying distance from the parties and also map onto their assessments of cause and responsibility and their judgments in the case. Both justices engage in conventional "legal reasoning" or argument, citing precedents, offering hypotheticals to which they compare past cases and the current one, and employing logic, yet their styles differ. As the mouthpiece of the Court's four-to-three majority opinion, Cardozo writes in a manner that suggests omniscience and authority in his argument and in his statement of facts. Andrews does not describe the package about which he says the defendant's servant could and did know nothing, for instance. Cardozo by contrast describes the package precisely, as "of small size, about fifteen inches long, and . . . covered by a newspaper" before indicating what "in fact" the package contained: fireworks.

Cardozo opens the argument following his statement of facts with a declarative sentence, Andrews with a query. Cardozo argues through earlier cases and definitions of negligence that plaintiff Palsgraf has no grounds for suing the railroad because the guards had no duty to her. A different conclusion, he argues, in the reductio ad absurdum of his next paragraph, involves "us"—the Court—"and swiftly too, in a range of contradictions . . . Life will have to be made over, and human nature transformed" if the Court is to hold persons responsible for all the unintended consequences of their actions or, in Cardozo's words, "before prevision so extravagant can be accepted as the norm of conduct, the customary standard to which behavior must conform." The unintentional wrong, he continues, "is defined in terms of the natural or probable," which he equates with the foreseeable.

In other words, Cardozo maintains that liability—or responsibility—corresponds to obligation or duty defined in terms of foreseeable risk. The Long Island Railroad (abbreviated as "Railroad" below) cannot be liable to Palsgraf for the harms caused by its breach of a conventionally understood moral duty to her, Cardozo maintains, because it has no moral duty to her to begin with. There is no moral duty to Palsgraf because no harm to her could have been foreseen in the guard's (admitted act of) helping a man with a package aboard. Cardozo can thus be understood (at least) two ways: as maintaining a classic—moral—position in which responsibility is correlative to obligation or duty, and also as initiating a utilitarian approach to duty, by defining it in terms of the predictability of harm.

Andrews disputes both points. He broadens the scope of classic responsibility beyond the party to whom the duty is owed, to include all the results of an act. Because the knocking of the package was a careless or negligent act, he argues, the Railroad is liable for the harms that are caused by its employee's wrongful act. The Long Island Railroad is liable, Andrews argues, because liability extends to all harms caused by a wrong.

Cardozo and Andrews couch the arguments in their opinions differently. Cardozo uses quotations and citations of authority to identify his claims with what appears to be the only law possible. The law of New York State ostensibly articulates "the norm of conduct, the customary standard to which behavior must conform." Cardozo uses passive sentences and negations that lend themselves to an oppositional or polar logic of what is and what is not. The conduct of the de-

fendant's guard "was not a wrong in its relation to the plaintiff"; it was "not negligent at all" in relation to her. "Negligence in the abstract . . . is surely not a tort."
Because "there is no tort to be redressed, . . . there is no occasion to consider what
damage might be recovered . . ." He concludes what appears to be a purely conceptual logic by finding no rule of recovery that applies to Palsgraf.

Cardozo characterizes opposing arguments—but not his own—as built on
words' shifting meanings. Andrews by contrast accepts that words—and more—
are at stake. In what some might consider a suggestive or ornamental style, he acknowledges with various flourishes alternative approaches, offers what he admits
are only rough definitions of negligence and proximate cause, and draws attention to points at which one might take issue with his reasoning. "The proposition
is this," he writes, or "it seems to me."

Cardozo barely uses first-person pronouns. When he does, they occur in the
plural as "we, the Court" who are faced with this case or who speak the law. Andrews's first person sometimes refers to the Court that hears the case, occasionally contracts to "I" who "think," but also extends to "we" the readers, who are
concerned with protecting our society from danger and who share with Andrews
"the language of the street." Like Cardozo, Andrews also uses the terms *natural*
and *probable*, but not to define (or as Cardozo does, to deny) the "wrongfulness" or foreseeability of the railroad's act in relation to the plaintiff or injury but
rather to describe the causal relation between Palsgraf's injury and the act of the
Long Island Railroad's employee.

Andrews begins by asking whether Palsgraf may recover. The answer, he
writes, making room for opinions other than his own, "*depends* upon our theory as to the nature of negligence" (emphasis added). He continues with questions: whether negligence is relative to particular persons (as Cardozo argues)
and whether the "doer" of an unreasonable act is liable for all of its "proximate
consequences." This dispute "is not *just* a matter of words" (emphasis added), he
insists, as he takes up the two issues in turn.

First, the claim in tort law that a defendant's duty must be owed to the plaintiff for the plaintiff to recover is, Andrews writes, "I think" too narrow. Appealing to ordinary English for a conception of "wrong," he argues that driving down
Broadway at a reckless speed is a wrongful act "not only to those who happen to
be within the radius of danger but to all who might have been there—a wrong
to the public at large." "Such is the language of the street. Such the language of
the courts . . . Such again and again their language . . ." Andrews's claims about

the language of "wrong" link "we" who drive down Broadway recklessly, to the courts and to Mr. Justice Holmes in particular, to "each one of us" who have a duty to protect society from unnecessary danger, with which the paragraph ends. Andrews then affirms an earlier case that states the law "as it should be and as it is": "The act being wrongful the doer was liable for its proximate results." "If this be so," Andrews concludes in regard to his first issue, then Palsgraf's claim is after all for a breach or failure of duty to herself. In other words, "harm to some one being the natural result of the [wrongful] act, not only that one alone, but all those in fact injured may complain" and Palsgraf's claim is not—as Cardozo suggests—derivative of the claims, unpursued, of the man whose package was jostled.

Cardozo's response to Andrews's first point is that Andrews confuses tort and crime. As Andrews acknowledges, a crime requires "intent" to do wrong. Concern with "intent" draws attention beyond the preference in law and legal writing for active subjects, to the use of adverbs to describe the manner in which actors undertake or carry out their actions. (There are also adverbs of time and place.) If, in ordinary English, adverbs or expressions modifying verbs are "called for, or even in order" when actions are done "in some *special* way or circumstances, different from those in which such an act is naturally done (and of course both the normal and the abnormal differ according to what verb in particular is in question),"[11] then the plethora of adverbs used in law, even as legal writers are urged to use them discriminately and to favor "strong verbs" instead, indeed testifies to law's realm as one of "trouble cases."[12] In criminal law, liability often rides on whether acts are done knowingly (recall *Morissette* and the immigration cases of Chapter One), intentionally, deliberately, willingly, voluntarily, freely, spontaneously, involuntarily, accidentally, mistakenly, maliciously, inadvertently, unwillingly, and so forth. (See Section 7 of the California Penal Code in Appendix D.)

In other words, adverbs and intentions describe and modify actions and verbs. They correspond to subjects' responsibility or accountability. Like a ball that is kicked, a passive subject—a defendant undergoing an epileptic seizure, for instance—is not in control of his or her bodily acts. Such a passive subject acts only "involuntarily" and is excused from criminal liability. Criminal law distinguishes not only between acts that are done intentionally, for which one is fully responsible, and acts done involuntarily, for which one is excused, but also among kinds of intention and sorts of acts to which different sorts of responsibility accrue. It breaks up some acts into planning and executing. It clusters others. Breaking and entering to commit further offense, for instance, becomes burglary. Killing leads to different verdicts and sentences depending on whether one acted maliciously, deliberately, knowingly, or carelessly. Killing is also justified insofar as one acted defensively rather than to kill.

If intention modifies an act, it also attributes coherence to the doer of the deed, to the "I" or the "ego" responsible for it. It provides the hook needed for attributing responsibility, judging liability, meting out punishment. A passive subject who is acted on is an object without intention and, as already mentioned, is excused. An active subject who has good reason for acting is justified in the action. When Nietzsche writes that he fears we are not getting rid of God because we still believe in grammar, he reminds us how (German and English) grammar models itself on a Creator-Subject who need only act or will—or speak—to seamlessly predicate or create an object-world. Of course other grammars are possible.[13] But in English, to attribute acts or verbal predicates to human subjects is to presume a capacity for intentional action that appears grounded in a subject's will or ability to choose or to determine action. Indeed, writes Nietzsche, we were granted free will *so that* we could be found guilty.[14]

Compare the "freedom to act" belonging to persons to the "caused behavior" of animals—or even the caused behavior of human beings. In classical natural law, a person chooses to act rightly or wrongly in a free act of the "will" or by intending, which in effect constitutes an act before the act. That a "sinner" freely wills or chooses to do wrong justifies holding the person responsible for the action. If no choice or intention were possible, responsibility and punishment would not make sense. Today we dismiss animal trials with a laugh.[15] We treat juvenile subjects differently than mature adults. This too is compatible with retributive (ex post) accounts of punishment that maintain that punishment must be proportional to the wrongfulness of an act and that presume that acting requires a particular capacity to choose or will or intend to do right or wrong that animals and youths—and in the past, slaves—do not have.[16]

Even in deterministic accounts of human behavior that discount free will, the "subject" serves as a locus for understanding—and moderating or controlling—behavior. In such accounts, conduct results from or is caused by social, economic, biological factors. Broad social and economic measures sometimes address what are taken to be general causes of criminal behavior, such as poverty or unemployment. Meanwhile punishment—or socialization or training—seeks to recalibrate the ways that crime-prone individuals take factors, such as what they gain or risk in committing crimes, into account. "Purposive" rather than "willed" behavior characterizes individuals who, in deterministic accounts, are still attributed some capacity for deciding what to do. In these sorts of accounts, individual behavior, rather than being freely chosen or unconstrainedly willed, now ostensibly refers back to preexisting external causes that motivate the individual to behave a particular way as means to his or her end. Behavior follows the individual's anticipation (or calculation) of effects (pleasurable or painful, advantageous or costly), which calculation is considered to be the individual's doing.

The subject who behaves on the basis of outside forces and effects differs from the subject of natural law who wills or chooses right or wrong action. The former must be deterred from future behaviors while the latter is to be punished (guilty, in debt) for past actions. To be distinguished from both are passive subjects already mentioned who, under the sway of a disease, for instance, are incapable of controlling movement and thus of acting or of behaving. Like disorganized "psyches" who know not what they do, passive subjects again are in effect objects that cannot be held responsible for results that they produce or cause.[17] Although the will of the subject of natural law may no longer serve as the origin of free action then, causal explanations of individual behavior posit an analogous capacity in empirically determined subjects who ordinarily predicate or control what they do. That capacity remains of central concern in the criminal law. Its character is precisely what is at stake in debates about the proper aims of punishment; retribution, deterrence, rehabilitation, and even incapacitation depend on what sort of capacity or control one attributes to subjects.

In sum, criminal conviction requires a subject who intends to act and acts accordingly. Lack of capacity to form intent—or to know what one is doing—suggests an inability to be guilty or not guilty; it justifies a finding of not guilty by reason of insanity. If, in law, there is to be *nulla poena sine crimen; nullum crimem sine lege* (no punishment without a crime, no crime without a law), then in legal writing, too, with its preference for active sentences, there is no sentence without the conviction of a subject who predicates! That there are crimes of intent such as conspiracy also reveals the importance that law accords to subjects who act on the basis of their capacity to will or to intend. That criminalizing acts of omission, such as breaches of duties to rescue, sits uneasily with the law attests further to the entanglement of act and intention: no act, so no intention?

As we saw in *Morissette*, no criminal intention (*mens rea*), no criminal act; so, no conviction.[18] In the absence of criminal acts, ostensibly punitive measures correspond to preventive detention or incapacitation.

Although tort law, like other areas of civil (or private) law, concerns itself not with the punishment of intentionally wrong acts but with restitution for carelessly caused harms, plain English shows tort law too to be a site in which attributions of responsibility occur. The English language presumes that subjects predicate and that nouns verb. Judgments of liability do not attach to any noun whatsoever, though, but only to subjects capable of acting. Tort law, with its concern for the difference between action and causal event, reminds us of the particular responsibility of acting subjects. Negligence law is a little like a parent whose child has just dropped a vase. The parent tells the child, "Because it broke, you'll have to pay for it from your allowance." The child protests, "But I didn't mean to!" and the parent replies, "You should have meant *not* to!" In other words, in tort law, "accidents" are neither intentional nor by chance. Liability attaches to subjects who have a duty to care.[19] Their liability for acting negligently turns on the way a harm was caused. If criminal law is concerned with the many ways in which one wills or intends one's acts, then accident law is concerned with another adverbial issue: the many ways in which acts fail or at least cause unintended effects. One distinguishes in law, as Austin points out of "ordinary language," between acting "accidentally," "by mistake," "inadvertently," and so forth.[20]

Because Cardozo and Andrews both acknowledge that *Palsgraf* involves unintended harm, that case concerns what the guard's act of pushing has to do with the harm to Palsgraf. Just as free will serves as an imaginary cause through which to hold persons accountable in criminal law, according to Nietzsche, so too in tort law, attributing causes to events makes the strange familiar while providing a sense of control. Did a particular act cause the harm? And should the guard have meant not to? Andrews focuses on the first question; Cardozo, on the second.

Cardozo claims that investigation into cause in *Palsgraf* is unnecessary. According to him, a tort plaintiff like Palsgraf can recover only when the unintended harm results from an act that "as to him had possibilities of danger so many and so apparent as to entitle him to be protected against the doing of it though the harm was unintended." As we have seen, the pusher had no duty to Palsgraf, according to Cardozo, insofar as no perceptible risk to Palsgraf lay in the pushing of the passenger with the package. Irrespective of the wrongfulness of the push vis-à-vis that other passenger, then, he argues, the cause of Palsgraf's injury is irrelevant. Tort liability here is still fundamentally a matter of breaching one's duty or moral obligation. Unforeseeable harm involves no breach of duty to the one harmed. It is the unfortunate result of a cause or an event that on its own (without the breach of a duty to the one harmed) cannot warrant investigation into cause, much less entitle recovery. In other words, Cardozo maintains that, for Palsgraf to recover, "negligently" must modify not the guard's act of knocking the package as such, but an act (or breach) of the guard (or the Long Island Railroad) vis-à-vis Palsgraf. (If the Railroad had had a duty to secure objects that could fall on waiting passengers, for instance, its failure to secure the scales might have been negligent toward Palsgraf.)

In Andrews's statement of facts, by contrast, the guard has already been deemed to have acted "negligently" (or breached a duty to care) in knocking the package. However unintentionally the guard injured Palsgraf, Andrews insists, the guard was a subject presumably capable of intention and of acting in accordance with duty. According to Andrews, the Railroad is responsible for all harms resulting from or caused by its guard's negligence. Andrews's second issue is thus that of cause and effect: Was the harm, however unintended, caused by the negligent act? For Cardozo, no such question arises: The act (and the guard) is not negligent in relation to this plaintiff. The event of her being harmed constitutes an event for which no human agent or legal party is responsible.

The language and grammar of Cardozo's statement of facts now explains itself further. As we have seen, Andrews's statement explicitly asserts the negligence of the defendant's servant's action and links that act, through a rough chain of grammatical objects and grammatically active subjects, to Palsgraf's injury. Cardozo's statement dwells longer on the package, emphasizing in the course of three passive constructions its opaqueness. The package's grammatical passivity separates the action that goes on alongside the "stopped" and "already moving" train and the event that happens "at the other end of the platform many feet away." The covered package stymies or blocks the view of the most vigilant eye, even that of the omniscient observer that Cardozo himself seems to be. "There was nothing in its appearance to give notice," writes Cardozo *after* describing what the package did "in fact" contain. Foreseeability, according to Cardozo, circumscribes an actor's liability. Foreseeability and liability also stop here, at the package, about which the defendant's servant could and did know nothing. Even in their statements of facts, Cardozo's and Andrews's differing uses of a gram-

mar of active and passive subjects and predicates correspond to their analyses of
the dispute.

At the same time, they share the logic or rhetoric of responsibility that characterizes the metaphysics of law and language. Andrews ultimately maintains
that a subject who acts wrongly is liable for as many of the consequences of his
or her act that convenience, public policy, a rough sense of justice, expedience,
common sense, practical politics, fair judgment and—one could add—the active
grammar of his statement of facts, variously dictate! In the colorfully written argument addressing his second issue, whether the defendant's servant's act caused
the unintentional harm to Palsgraf, Andrews acknowledges that attributing
cause—and proximate cause in particular—is a matter of "not logic" but "judgment," in which there are "no fixed rules" but only "hints." Here Andrews' skep-
ticism—or realism—superficially resembles Nietzsche's own critique of cause as
a human creation or invention designed to make us feel better about a world that
exceeds our mastery.[21]

Claiming that "philosophical doctrines" of cause do not help us and that
"analogy is of little aid" in defining "proximate cause," Andrews turns to metaphor. "You may speak of a chain, or if you please, a net" of causes, he writes. He
three times refers to a "stream" to explain the difficulties of identifying cause.
First, he argues, if we negligently build the foundations of a dam that breaks and
injures property "down stream," we are liable for the consequences proximately
caused by our negligence, even if they are "unusual, unexpected, unforeseen and
unforseeable." But this does not tell us what *proximate cause* means. Second, he
writes of a spring, joined by tributary after tributary, that reaches the ocean. Although for a time the sources—or causes—of the river may be distinguished, "at
last, inevitably no trace of separation remains." Finally, he mentions a case in
which "we" asked whether "a stream of events" was deflected or "forced into new
and unexpected channels" by an ostensible proximate cause. This, he argues, "is
rather rhetoric than law. There is in truth little to guide us [as to what is proximate cause] other than common sense."

Andrews's common sense offers him a number of possible factors to indicate
proximate cause; none is definitive. There are various possible proximate causes:
those "but for" which the result would not have followed, cause–result combina-
tions that admit of no intervening cause, and causes from which the result is
ordinarily expected to follow. Eventually, he claims to settle on "the factor which
must determine the case before us": "what might ordinarily be expected to follow

the fire or the explosion." But rather than simply honing in on ordinary expectations, he also invokes other meanings of proximate cause. He argues that, "except for the explosion," Palsgraf would not have been injured and that the only intervening cause between the explosion and injury was the weighing machine. "There was no remoteness in time, little in space," he writes, referring to the relation between explosion and injury. Ordinary expectations join other indicators of proximate cause: Injury followed explosion in "a natural and continuous sequence" and "injury in some form was most probable."

It is important to note that despite Cardozo's and Andrews's disagreements, accountability must attach, for both, to an *action*—whether the negligent act of the servant (for Andrews) or the would-be failure of duty in the pushing done by the guard (for Cardozo)—and hence to a subject. It cannot be accorded to *events* as such. Thus Andrews traces the explosion that causes the injury back to the defendant's act, while Cardozo argues that Palsgraf's injury does not result from an act, or at least from what in relation to her can be considered an act, insofar as acts correspond to duties for which subjects are responsible. The dispute between Cardozo and Andrews confirms the difficulty Andrews says we have in isolating causes. It also shows how accountability—despite Cardozo's claim that "the law of causation is foreign to this case"—is ultimately a matter, in Andrews's words, of tracing "the effect of an act to the end"—or rather back to a beginning or to a willing subject.

In other words, Cardozo depicts the guard's act of pushing as ending with what his statement of facts presents as the passive event of the dislodging of the package. Because the effects of the act end before reaching Palsgraf, there is no need to inquire further into the guard's or Railroad's responsibility. By contrast, despite Andrews's acknowledgment of the impossibility of isolating causes, his statement of facts links the explosion that he will identify as the proximate cause of Palsgraf's injury both backward and forward through active sentences to the servant's knocking of the package and to Palsgraf's injury.

The variety of possible descriptions of a happening as an act and as an event stems in part from the indeterminacy of the beginning and end, and sources and causes, of happenings, as Andrews discusses. As we have seen, the "guard pushed the man from behind" ostensibly refers to the same act or event as the "assisting of a passenger" that Andrews attributes to the Railroad's servant as an act. That the servant "negligently knocked the package" redescribes and emphasizes another aspect of what is ostensibly the same act of pushing or helping. In writing that "in the act of pushing, the package [passively] was dislodged," Cardozo implies that what Andrews calls "negligently knocking" was incidental to the act. Distinguishing a deed from a doer and attributing intentionality to the doer circumscribes an act; it identifies the act as a particular sort of event that can be distinguished from other sorts of events for which no human subject is responsible. In a scientific age, former "acts" of God become caused events or disasters against which humans insure themselves. Note too in this context the difficulty some have grasping the "actor network theory" of Bruno Latour, which attributes agency to nonhuman "actants."[22] Michel Foucault's account of power that is not "held" or "exercised" by a sovereign and Martin Heidegger's things that show themselves likewise challenge our grammatical habits.[23] Or consider, in a lighter vein, the words of a defendant on the stand in a *New Yorker* cartoon: "I took aim, pulled the trigger, and then, suddenly, shots rang out."[24]

Compare now Cardozo's passive "the package was dislodged" to an active "the guard dislodged the package" or even "the man dropped the package." Compare the active "the guard knocked the package" to Andrews's adverbially descriptive "the servant negligently knocked the package" and to the simple "the package fell." All are complete sentences. They avoid base nominalizations. They keep relations between subject, verb, and object clear.[25] Yet neither rules of grammar nor elements of style determine which if any of these sentences to use. That happenings can be characterized in different ways—as acts, as events, as causes of or as results of other acts and events to which they are more and less immediately related—shows how language and grammar presuppose and entail attributions of responsibility and assignments of cause which, as Andrews points out, are in large part matters of judgment and, as Cardozo shows, are matters about which law claims to be decisive. Conversely, of course, assignments of cause and attributions of responsibility also predispose careful legal writers to make particular choices of language and grammar. The point here, though, is that language is being used in the moment of attribution itself.

Something happens. Its characterization makes a difference. If the happening is characterized as an *act*, someone appears responsible for it: Grammatically, a subject with agency predicates. Thus: The guard pushed the man with the package; the guards caused the fireworks to explode; the Railroad's servants negligently, or in some other way that modifies the "normal" doing of the act, injured

Palsgraf. If a happening is characterized as an *event*, it appears to be caused, although tracing its origin, much less allocating responsibility for it to a human subject, may be difficult: The scales struck Palsgraf, the exploding fireworks caused the scales to fall, the package fell. One must then look backwards to find the particular kind of cause that we have come to associate with responsibility or liability or accountability at all. If a happening is described *in the passive voice*, one appears loath to assign cause or responsibility: Palsgraf was injured, the package was dislodged, its contents were covered. The English language offers many, yet particular, possibilities for understanding the world. There is no rule as to which description of a happening to choose, though preferring or choosing a particular description—as one must, in writing and speaking—brings with it particular understandings of that situation and of responsibility in the world. Or, as H. L. A. Hart once put it,

> sentences of the form "He did it" have been traditionally regarded as primarily descriptive whereas their principal function is what I venture to call *ascriptive*, being quite literally to ascribe responsibility for actions much as the principal function of sentences of the form "This is his" is to ascribe rights in property.[26]

The descriptive language used to characterize happenings reveals a world of responsibility and of law, Section One has shown. Cardozo's and Andrews's statements of facts fit the opinions of which they are part yet do not correspond simply—as only either true or false—to happenings in the world. A preference for one statement of facts over another is neither simply a matter of truth and accuracy nor an additional matter of the plainness or correctness of its grammar and the ordinariness of its English. Through their language, statements of facts select and highlight particular aspects of the world. They characterize the happenings that they describe in ways that already presume particular possibilities of judgments or relations of responsibility for deeds done in that world. Indeed a "*factum*" in Latin is a thing done or a deed; an accident is for we moderns a fact, rather than a happening that befalls by chance. The appropriateness of a statement of facts depends on what a speaker is doing or on the acts in which the speaker is engaged. In J. L. Austin's words, "There are various *degrees and dimensions* of success in making statements: the statements fit the facts always more or less loosely, in different ways on different occasions for different intents and purposes."[27] Cardozo, announcing the Court's judgment in favor of the Railroad, and Andrews, dissenting from that judgment, present the *Palsgraf* facts accordingly. Both of the justices' statements of facts narrate, accurately and in plain English, what happened. As the next section will show, their statements nevertheless support different opinions and the opposing judgments expressed in their speech acts of announcing the judgment or holding and of dissenting from it.

Two. Reasons and Rhetorics: Cardozo and Andrews

Understanding the *Palsgraf* opinions as themselves acts of speech shows law itself to consist at least in part of dynamic events. Attending not only to the metaphysics revealed in grammar, but also to the ways that law acts, Section Two shows law, like language, to be more than a static system of rules or even of their applications.

Cardozo's majority opinion and Andrews's dissent can each be described both as acts and as events of different sorts. Cardozo *announces* the decision of the Court; he *dismisses* the complaint; he *reverses* the appellate court; he *rules* that one is reliable only for foreseeable harms; he *holds* that the Long Island Railroad is not liable. He *affirms* that the scope of legal liability for negligence extends only to those to whom one has a moral duty. He *applies* a rule that associates duty with foreseeable risk. He *ushers in* a new era of accident law. He *reinforces* the conditions of capitalism. And so forth.[28] His opinion can be used to exemplify good legal writing or to illustrate an ornate and antiquated style. It can be broken down into distinct argumentative stages and into sequences of discrete acts: Cardozo states, questions, cites, refers, hypothesizes, illustrates, answers, argues, and responds (as does Andrews).

Here Austin's distinctions again prove useful. Announcing, dismissing, reversing, holding, ruling (and dissenting) are, in Austin's terms, *illocutionary* speech acts like promising or warning or announcing.[29] Illocutionary acts correspond to what Austin at first called "performative utterances," now expanded to include the reporting, stating, or describing done in what Austin at first called "constative utterances." Cardozo performs the dismissing of the complaint *in* speaking or writing. His utterance could also be converted into what Austin points to as an explicit performative grammar that is in first-person present indicative active form: "We, the Court, hereby dismiss . . ." The dismissal happens in the moment of its being uttered or issued and transforms, in its being issued, the state of affairs or status of Palsgraf's complaint. Dismissal happens *in*, not only as a result of or *by*, the act of dismissing, as the double meaning of the noun *dismissal* indicates. When Cardozo "dismisses," that is, he verbs. The noun "dismissal" may refer to the grammatical object of the (verbal) act of dismissing—what results from dismissing—or it may be the gerund or activity, action or act itself of dismissing. So, too, Andrews dissents in his dissent. *Dissent* as dissenting is the act in which he engages; *dissent* as the nounlike dissenting opinion is the object that results from the act. Likewise, a complaint may be an act or an object, as may reversal, holding, and so forth.

However one describes Cardozo's announcement, the existence of a standard, formally recognized or authorized text establishes for most purposes *what* Cardozo says. The text of Cardozo's opinion informs us of what J. L. Austin would call Cardozo's "locutionary act." (I am here treating Cardozo's written opinion as what Cardozo says. Chapters Three and Four discuss writing as a particular sort of saying; Chapter Four also takes up in part a criticism that Austin pays short shrift to the physicality of speaking or of uttering sounds.) Quoting the text of Cardozo's opinion directly is one way of describing Cardozo's locutionary act or what he said: *Cardozo writes, "Plaintiff was standing . . . should be reversed, and the complaint dismissed, with costs in all courts."* Indirect report is another way of doing so: *Cardozo writes that Palsgraf was standing . . . and that the complaint should be dismissed, with costs.*

Cardozo's and Andrews's utterances do not explicitly announce themselves, although they could, as acting or performing. They do not say, "We hold . . . ," or "so ordered," or "I hereby dissent . . ." Their character as illocutionary acts of holding and of dissenting is indicated, rather, by reading them in context. The Court's illocutionary act of reversing the lower court judgments, for instance, appears in the modality of "should" at the end of the majority opinion. "The judgment of the Appellate Division and that of the Trial Term should be reversed, and the complaint dismissed," concludes Cardozo. Andrews uses the same sort of locution: "The judgment appealed from should be affirmed, with costs." The concurrences of the other justices, although in the present indicative active, do not appear in the first-person "We concur" either. Rather, "Pound, Lehman, and Kellogg, J. J., concur . . ."

The justices' illocutionary acts—of announcing, holding, ruling, reversing, dismissing, dissenting, and concurring—are identifiable as such, not because the justices say explicitly that they reverse or dissent then. Rather the justices' actions are inferred from their words in the broader context of who and what they are—justices of New York's high court—and what is conventionally expected of justices following the hearing of an appeal. By virtue of role and circumstance, Cardozo and Andrews, as justices of the New York high court who have heard the Long Island Railroad's appeal in Palsgraf's case, are warranted in presenting their opinions as the law of the State of New York. Not just anyone anywhere, as Chapter One pointed out, however faultless their knowledge and application of legal rules and their expression thereof through the application of rules of ordinary English, can engage in an act of legal judgment or dissent.

Institutions, deliberately and otherwise, establish the norms and procedures or conventions that make it possible for legal acts to work and for legal claims to have the authority that they do. Like Austin's felicity conditions, those conventions are taught to others and may change over time. Federal and state judicial opinions, for instance, are subject to changing conventions.[30] Unanimity among U.S. Supreme Court justices was once the norm for high court cases, with single dissents accompanying majority opinions next most common. Over the course of the twentieth century, the announcement of a judgment as a plurality opinion accompanied by multiple dissents has increased. As Robert Post points out, 84 percent of the Supreme Court's opinions were unanimous in the 1921–1928 terms; only 27 percent were unanimous during the 1993–1998 terms. Changes in the character of Supreme Court opinions, he shows, track a shift in the Court from a "court of last resort" to a "ministry of justice," as well as a change in the "implicit norms" of Supreme Court decision making:

> Justices of the Taft Court [in the 1920s] felt presumptively obligated to join Court opinions, even if they disagreed with their content, so as to preserve the influence and prestige of the Court. No such norm is apparent among modern Justices. This revolution in the practice of dissent in part reflects a shift in the Court's jurisprudential understanding of the nature of law, from a grid of fixed and certain principles designed for the settlement of disputes, to the site of ongoing processes of adjustment and statesmanship designed to achieve social purposes.[31]

Like statements of facts then, opinions may also be subject to assessment related to the ways in which they are written. In the twenty-first century, as the Supreme Court has tried to achieve broader consensus through majority rather than plurality opinions, for instance, lower court judges for whom these opinions are authoritative have criticized Court opinions for becoming vaguer and offering less useful guidance.[32]

So far, we have seen that Cardozo's *Palsgraf* opinion can be reported as a locutionary act and characterized as an illocutionary act that can be assessed in terms of particular conventions. It can also be described in terms of its effects, such as changing the course of tort law. Unlike dismissing, reversing, and announcing, changing the course of tort law is not performed as such by Cardozo; he cannot *in* speaking change the direction of tort law ("I hereby change the course of tort law" will not work). Change may follow or result rather *from* announcement and reception of his opinion; it may occur *by* his or its speaking. As a more-or-less contingent effect of what was said, changing history is, again in Austin's terms, a *perlocutionary* act. As when someone double-books him- or herself (perlocutionarily) by promising (illocutionarily) to be in two different places at a particular time, the act of changing history, like the act of double-booking, is not ordinarily done through saying "I double-book myself" or "I change history." (One could conceivably double-book oneself deliberately this way. But that it is necessary to point out that double-booking could be done deliberately suggests that it does not normally happen this way.) One can of course *describe* what one is doing while one does it through such utterances, in the same way as one can say "I run" while running. But insofar as change in the course of tort law happened, it was caused *by* Cardozo's ruling; it did not happen *in* his ruling nor by his performing the change. Locutionary meaning, illocutionary force, and perlocutionary effect again appear as different aspects of the same utterance or speech event, together comprising the Austinian "total speech act in a total speech situation."

As from the *Morissette* opinion (discussed in Chapter One), so too from Cardozo's *Palsgraf* opinion, one can extract statements of rules. As in *Morissette*, the speech situation in *Palsgraf* is not best described as an application of rules to facts though. In the first place, although one must admittedly be cautious in drawing inferences from what is not said, neither Cardozo nor Andrews claims to be establishing rules. To read *Palsgraf* as a matter of rules is to approach Cardozo's majority opinion with a *presumption* of law as rules, as indeed many readers do. But this is to confuse a student briefing a case for its rules with the judge who decides it. To read *Palsgraf* as the application of rules likewise transforms what Cardozo says and does beyond his statement of facts into relatively narrow matters of legal reasoning whose assessment focuses on the accuracy and consistency of doctrinal claims. Its skills are those of debate. Such a view limits assessment of legal judgment to the accuracy of fact, the validity of claims, and the soundness of reasoning, skills that are necessary but not exhaustive of what is needed in law and in life. The value of an opinion according to this approach lies in its logical relations and in the accord of its premises with statutory or constitutional or common law texts. Although in principle this category of texts is an expansive one, the interpretation of texts is often narrowed so that the text can function as a standard against which to measure ostensible rules or principles from which judgments are to ensue. Circumscribing texts and opinions this way may accord with the implicit norms of briefing a case, in which students learn some of the conventions of lawyering, but it is only a part of the claiming and arguing that lawyers do and an inapt description of judging.

Furthermore, to read Cardozo's opinion as applying legal rules to facts presumes that facts and rules are straightforward givens, not subject to prior issues about what count as facts or about judgments inherent in language about action, cause, and responsibility. It disregards the ways in which Cardozo's "statement of facts" is itself not simply a matter of rules but of judgment, *already* relating words and world in particular ways, as Section One showed. It is to adopt the view of Ward Farnsworth's "toolkit" for legal study, in which "the consequences of a rule [as opposed to a standard] are triggered once we settle the facts (164)."[33] Identifying rules contributes as much to one's characterization of facts as characterizing facts contributes to one's application of rules, however. Consider how a justice might characterize the *Palsgraf* facts so as to justify recovery under Cardozo's "rules." Or how a justice might do so in such a way as to deny Palsgraf recovery under Andrews's "rules." (Distinguishing standards from rules, as does Farnsworth, like distinguishing values from facts, does not get us out of the chicken-or-the-egg conundrum of "which comes first: the rule-or-the-facts?" insofar as standards or values are, like rules, also taken to be empirical matters or facts of subjective commitment.[34])

Finally, reading opinions as applications of rules ignores that rules eventually run out. If there exists no ultimate rule for establishing or judging a statement of facts beyond what fits the circumstances (where accuracy is but one dimension of fit), then there likewise exists no ultimate rule for selecting and applying legal rules. No rule can definitively establish how to apply rules or how to make exceptions to rules for applying rules. The ability to read Cardozo's majority opinion as a matter of rules, like Wydick's selection of a judicial statement of facts as an example of good legal writing, testifies to a propensity to identify law with authoritative statements and propositional truths.

Giving up the strict equivalence of statements of fact with true propositions and of judgments or judicial outcomes with applications of rules does not require one to give up on the articulation or presence of law or of judgments of responsibility. Rather it allows one, first, to take seriously varieties of legal speech or claims and, second, to credit legal utterances, such as Andrews's claim that he too speaks in the name of the law, that might otherwise be given short shrift.

Cardozo of course speaks in the name of the law of New York when, drawing on precedent and following norms of judicial reasoning, he announces the decision of the majority of the Court. He implies that counterexamples to the Court's ruling can be distinguished and that the law has ever been only so. He appeals beyond formal doctrinal sources to, for instance, "the norm of conduct, the customary standard to which behavior must conform." Yet he distances himself from claims such as Andrews's about the "instability" and "shifting meanings" of words. No uncertain or risky judgments admitting room for disagreement or multiple points of view in this majority opinion! Rather than presenting his opinion—as does Andrews—as a matter of considered choice or preference that he hopes his readership will share, Cardozo, as spokesperson of "the law" whose "point of view" his judgment epitomizes, offers an argument that appears to follow without question from legal precedents, rules of logic, and laws of human nature. Far from being uncertain, the latter "cannot be made over," Cardozo writes. Cardozo's majority opinion thus lends itself to being read for clear-cut propositions and statements of rules in a way that Andrews's dissent does not.

Andrews too, however, appeals to and writes in the name of law. He presents his dissent, in the moment of its utterance, as making claims of law. A claim, recall, both asserts and demands. Andrews cites precedents for a "law as it should be and as it is" that diverges from Cardozo's understanding of New York law. In the name of law, Andrews cites an "illustration given in an unpublished manuscript by a distinguished and helpful writer on the law of torts" that is clearly not the formal or enacted positive law of New York. Making room for differences of opinion as to negligence and proximate cause, Andrews's dissent suggests the possibility, within New York State, of another law than New York's positive law. He suggests the openness of law to contestation within its own terms when, for instance, he introduces into his argument such figurative elements as "the fact" of wrongful injury hidden "behind [a] cloud of words." Insofar as he maintains that causes can never be completely distinguished, he also implies that the judicial task of assigning responsibility for the effects of acts requires an impossible judgment. The Court "must" judge, he writes, in the face of an absence of certainty and a lack of definitions or rules for identifying cause. Appealing to "common sense" and to the "general understanding of mankind," "we" who must judge, according to Andrews, ultimately "draw a wavering line . . . as best we can."

That Andrews's dissenting opinion in *Palsgraf* does not manifest itself as stating rules or as declaring the positive—enacted—law of New York does not prevent his claims from being spoken in the name of law. Rather Andrews's dissent shows that the name of the law extends beyond claims recognized by positive law and by a positivist legal system as true assertions and as its own law.

In other words, Cardozo's statement of facts exemplifies good legal writing not because it corresponds most closely and concisely with reality, as Section One showed, nor because it is determined by or determines rules as such. The rest of Cardozo's opinion may exemplify good legal judgment, but it does not do so only insofar as it gets "the rules" right. Rather it presents its decision, including the statement of facts, in accordance with the particular authoritative conventions of New York State law. Cardozo presents his reasoning in *Palsgraf* as a conceptual logic that contrasts, as we have seen, with Andrews's portrayal of judging as the happening of a variety of acts and claims that are ultimately almost randomly made in the context of fallible human understandings. Andrews clearly makes much of rhetoric. But Cardozo's presentation of the Court's decision as inexorable also involves masterful acts of speech that draw on implicit norms of opinion writing and on the grammar and possibilities of the English tongue that implicate a particular metaphysics. To ignore the rhetorical aspect of Cardozo's opinion reinforces tendencies to conceive of law narrowly as simply statements of rules or as rules' "natural" application.

Understanding that facts (Section One) and rules (Section Two) exist rhetorically, as we saw, does not require giving up law. Neither does giving up the equivalence of judicial decision making with the application of rules require one to throw out all the rules. Rules may be steps for learning law; they must not to be mistaken for it, though. As Dreyfus and Dreyfus point out, rules are needed for beginners of a practice, as yet unable to recognize or judge situations, to be able to act.[35]

Competent actors, too, may use rules in hard cases. But experts adept at recognizing or judging situations no longer need or use rules. Think of the difference here between the expert or native speaker and the beginning or even intermediate foreign language speaker. Nietzsche, with his great fascination for learning and for learning to learn, writes, "For me they were steps, I have climbed up upon them—therefore I had to pass over them. But they thought I wanted to settle down on them."[36] Neither rules of law nor statements of rules are steps on which to settle.

Settling on law as rules, in other words, offers as limited an understanding of law as definitions and grammar offer of language. Legal educators may claim, as Ward Farnsworth puts it, that "most laws—whether made by legislatures, courts, agencies, or anyone else can be understood as if-then statements. Usually they are commands enforced by penalties if they aren't obeyed" (164) or that "rules tell people in advance what consequences will follow from their acts" (171).[37] This is not enough, however. Most laws and legal speech acts are not if-then statements, much less efficacious commands, even if, in Farnsworth's words, they "can be understood" that way.

Formulations of law as statements of rules do sometimes indicate that an act is a result or consequence of a checklist of conditions: *Once* xyz *occurs, then* abc *follows or exists.* Much of the Internal Revenue Code that informs tax practice appears this way, but legal propositions are not necessarily hypothetical statements. An apparent statement of a rule, rather than establishing xyz as the *pre*condition for abc, that is, may equally well name xyz as *being* abc or abc as *being* xyz.[38] Statements of rules are often formulated descriptively in the indicative mode, naming what is done.[39] When xyz occurs, this *is* a dissent or a complaint or a promise. In such a performative act's occurring, or being said in a particular way, some state of affairs will indeed have been transformed or initiated *in* the act's being done or the utterance's being said, not simply causally or as the effect of a completed sentence. Even valid enactments, the ostensible epitome of positivist statements of rules declare, "Thus shall it be," without in their declarations producing or causing obedience. Causal accounts, like accounts of law as atemporal or logical systems of rules, Chapter Three will show, offer only a limited or partial understanding of how claims of law and language do things.

Three. Future Perfect Realities: Derrida's "Fabulous Retroactivity"

The first two sections of this chapter have shown that though some may construe the *Palsgraf* decision as rule following or even as rule creating, the announcement of the decision is a complex rhetorical act in which the Court's judgment appears as an authoritative application of rules to facts because of the way that it is written and the conventions and institutions surrounding that writing. Both Cardozo's holding and Andrews's dissent consist of and appeal to much more than statements of facts and applications of rules. They occur, it appears, as speech acts that can be expressed in the first-person present indicative active form that J. L. Austin associates with an explicit performative formula. Section Three now shows, further, how legal acts, as performative acts that make claims in the name of law, extend beyond the present moment of their utterance and appeal beyond speaker and speaking, revealing their situatedness in a broader world.

The felicity of a speech act depends in part, as Austin points out in condition B1, on its being carried out completely. The adverb implies that it occurs over a period of time. The act nevertheless appears to take place in a singular "present," at a so-called moment of utterance. Although one often attributes a date or a year to an act, the specification of the moment in which it takes place, like the appropriateness of a statement of facts, varies on different occasions for different intents and purposes.

Today we attribute Cardozo's (announcement of the) *Palsgraf* ruling to a particular year. In 1928, Cardozo's announcement of the ruling established, despite our own questions about its continued relevance, what was *henceforth to be* the holding of the case. For the purpose of any related pending cases during 1928, the moment of Cardozo's ruling corresponds more specifically to a month and day. And like the moment of inauguration of a U.S. President or of marriage, that moment, whether it is characterized as taking place in a given year, on a given day, or at a given hour, marks the initiation of a more enduring state of affairs.

A peculiar temporality characterizes the moment of a speech act that simultaneously marks the completion of a ceremonial utterance, which occurs over a period of time, the "present" in which the Austinian explicit performative speech act occurs, and the "now" that (hereby) initiates a more enduring state of affairs. Taking place at least in some sense in a present, the utterance cannot be (said to be) the act it is until it is or has been completed. The need for completion means that the act is "imperfect" in a grammatical sense. It is ongoing and incomplete in its own present doing. Austin's Γ2 condition acknowledges that there are speech acts for which "subsequent conduct" or "uptake" is necessary to its felicity. Jacques Derrida points to a "fabulous retroactivity" in the signing of the U.S. Declaration of Independence by representatives of the very people whom the declarative act ostensibly brings into existence.[40] For Derrida, the event of a founding declaration "is only in truth possible thanks to the inadequation to it-self of a present"; the "proper tense" for the founding declaration of a people that will have given to itself the power or right to sign, he writes, is the future perfect.

The future perfect offers a way of thinking about the temporal structure not only of signed founding declarations but of speech acts and of legal acts and even legal events more broadly. Recall (from Chapter One, Section One) that Hart, too, writes that in deciding questions that arise as to the applicability of (a state-ment of) a rule to a particular instance, one "shall have rendered more determi-nate our initial aim" and "shall . . . have settled" questions as to the meaning of the rule. Such a structure resembles that of common law precedent also.[41] At the moment of its holding, a decision such as *Palsgraf* may *become* precedent. It *is* precedent though only for future cases. Before these future cases arise, it is not clear that any such cases will emerge nor what sort of precedent has been set. At the moment of the *Palsgraf* decision or at the time of its announcement, *Palsgraf* is not yet, and indeed may not ever turn out to be, precedent. It serves as prec-edent only after an appropriately related case arises, at which point it *will have become* precedent.

The peculiar temporality of legal decisions characterizes other acts and events. News media covered the October 1995 protest in Washington, D.C., known as the Million Man March, extensively at the time, describing it and pondering its antecedents, strategy, and implications. When asked about the significance of the gathering, one march supporter said, "The real test of the success of this march is going to be what the people do when they get home."[42] The question, in other words, could only be answerable in the future. And indeed, the Million Man March that was designed to draw attention to national issues of concern to African American males and to build black community in a domestic U.S. context is now associated with spurring the Million Woman March and with the formulation of various "Million Marches," including the 2011 "March of One Million" in Cairo's Tahrir Square—all "significances" of the event that could not have been known at the time, but constitute what the Million Man March has since come to be!

In other words, performative speech acts and events that correspond to pres-ent indicative active sentences are only completed over time or "perfected" in a future. In the future, they may be relegated to a past as discrete acts or events or be recalled as having occurred and having been completed or perfected in the past. They become history: *In 1928, Cardozo decided . . .* or *In 1928, Palsgraf was decided . . .* or *The Million Man March occurred in 1995.* Their status as completed acts or events that transform states of affairs may be revisited, however. Many today argue that developments in tort law have superseded Cardozo's approach in *Palsgraf.*

Be that as it may, direct and sometimes indirect quotation of speech is not generally relegated to the past. Speech is not considered perfected or complete in the ways that nonspeech acts and events can be. Even today, *Cardozo argues in* Palsgraf . . . and *Andrews claims . . .* , in the present tense, that is. Already in 1928, *the guards knocked the package* and *the fireworks fell* in the past, however. In other words, one refers to the memorialization of speech acts in writings in the present imperfect (or continuous or progressive): *Cardozo holds . . .* even though *Palsgraf* has been superseded. An act that occurs in the present may become a past act then, but the text in which it occurs says and continues to say, imperfectly and in its own present, the same thing.[43]

The peculiar temporality of speech acts suggests that law like language is not a simple matter of what exists in a present that passes. Its saying endures, even if the states of affairs that it brings about do not. Nor is law or a legal act simply a matter of an utterance's future effects. The present articulation of a legal speech act is necessarily incomplete in that it awaits a future to become what it is or will have been. The assessment of the success of an act, however, cannot be simply in terms of future impact, for the accomplishment of the act or performance can be distinguished from its fulfillment. Criminal law distinguishes the act of "solicitation," whose accomplishment involves one person asking something illicit or illegal of another, for instance, from that of "conspiracy," which implicates both parties in the fulfillment of the request or solicitation. The accomplishment of legal acts, such as objecting or demanding, can also be distinguished from further acts of their fulfillment or from whether the objection is sustained or the demand met. Fulfillment may be in part a matter of causal effectiveness; accomplishment itself is not.

The same applies to claiming, the crucial legal speech act. Many actors make different claims in the name of the law. Some speakers, such as a presiding judge or a consulting attorney, claim to know the law and to speak with authority. Others, such as plaintiffs or defendants, claim that law is on their side. Still others, interest groups and legislators, claim to know what law should be. Legal claims may thus be made on behalf of an official "system of law," as when Cardozo announces the Court's decision. They may also counter some aspect of that law from within its own institutions, as in Andrews's dissent or when an electorate places a referendum on a ballot. Claims are made against current states of affairs—legal and otherwise—when parties bring suit against one another, when they challenge statutes or appeal decisions. One can stretch the legal "claim" to cover questions asked in the name of the law, such as those addressed to a witness on the stand, insofar as they assert a speaker's right to single the witness out in this way, and they demand recognition of the utterance as having legal authority. Claims of law or in the name of law are made not only in assertions of rules or demands of rights, then, but in objections, interrogations, cross-examinations, declarations, testimony, complaints, depositions, and so forth. Claims of law are legal acts; legal acts are legal claims.

Many claims made in the name of law do not necessarily *exist* as positive law at the moment they are made; neither are they necessarily effective nor do they necessarily produce future results. What specifically legal claims have in common then is not that at the moment of their utterance—whether spoken on behalf of, against, or even oblivious to what counts as current positive law—they exist as or even appeal to recognized positive law (although they may do so). Rather, as we shall see in Chapter Three, at the moment of their being spoken they appeal to a "law" that they affirm as a speaker's and hearer's jointly owned law to demand the recognition that belongs to what they assert. (Even unspoken words, it will later appear, have the potential to do so. The acts of state officials, that is, make claims in the name of positive law even when no words are spoken.) The utterance of legal claims initiates new states of affairs without necessarily producing results.

Legal claims may or may not ultimately be persuasive. Insofar as they aim in part to persuade, though, legal claims and acts done in the name of positive or nonpositive law both await their future and participate in some sense in a past or in a continuing tradition of knowledge. That the *Palsgraf* holding *is* the law does not follow as an effect of the decision or announcement, although it depends on conventions or knowledge of the past. A state of affairs is transformed in the announcement of the *Palsgraf* decision and holding, yet future apprehension, recognition and even—paradoxically—continued acceptance of *Palsgraf* as law remains to be seen. Neither Cardozo nor Andrews atomistically "declares" what the law is, nor does either justice "make" law afresh.[44]

Speaking in a particular way then *is* the holding. Speaking in a particular way is dissenting or the dissent, complaining or a complaint. Despite a grammar that characterizes a dissent or complaint (noun) as the object of dissenting/complaining (verb), dissent*ing* or complain*ing* does not follow as effect of speaking. Speech neither simply constitutes a cause of dissent or complaint nor simply produces them as results. Dissenting or complaining happens *in* their speaking. Even if rules of civil procedure establish the consequences or effects of what a particular utterance does, they also *name*, however imperfectly, what complaining as complaint properly *is* as well as the conditions of the new state of affairs that complain*ing* brings about: a complaint has been or will have been made.

Understanding words and their uses corresponds to a common knowledge of naming on the part of speakers and hearers. Those who share a common language judge the world in similar ways. They inhabit in some sense what Robert Cover calls a *nomos* or meaning-making community.[45] While officials and others may disagree with one another (Chapter One), the "law" to which and the language through which they appeal refers to their incompletely articulated common understanding of the way of living to which their differing claims relate.

Again, this is not to say that all who make claims in the name of some law will have recognizable (or "cognizable") claims, or even the standing to make claims, under any given regime of positive law. Far from it. Positive or state law selects and winnows the claims that it formally recognizes. Recall that the accomplishment of an act of claiming—as an assertion and a demand—is to be distinguished from the fulfillment of its demand or confirmation of its assertions. That there are claims made in the name of the law that are not recognized as law by formal or state law or that may not even ask for recognition as positive law challenges any easy equivalence of positive state law with law. Claims of law show how legal speech acts involve more than what a positivist account of law as a system of statements of rules and their application suggests. Recall Andrews's dissent, a legal speech act that makes a claim in the name of the law of New York, which was not and apparently will not ever become positive law. If Andrews's dissent in the name of the law is not positive law, it nevertheless occurs as a legal claim within a context of ostensibly positive law that enables contestation in the name of law.

Again, this does not mean that either the positive law or Andrews's dissent is just. Neither positivist nor nonpositivist legal claims need be just. Indeed speech acts done in the name of law may be—and some would argue always are—spoken strategically, hypocritically, prudentially, even unfairly. But insofar as claims are spoken in the name of some law, they assert the truth of which they speak and they demand from those to whom they are spoken recognition as belonging to the shared law in the name of which the claim is made. The chapters that follow ultimately argue that in appealing to shared law, such claims raise issues of justice, whether or not they affirm or contest positive law and whether or not they *are* just.

For now, the point is that, like Cardozo's holding and Andrews's dissent, legal claims or speech acts are simultaneously matters of fact and of law. The assertions and demands of claims are matters the truth of which one is able to judge and the justice of which may become an issue. Determining their truth and justice involves cognitive knowledge of what exists and practical knowledge of language. Assessing the "fact" and "value" of an act such as Cardozo's holding is as much about verifying the particular conditions surrounding Cardozo's announcement as it is about the correspondence of the state of affairs named in the holding to post-1928 New York law. Being able to judge such conditions and states is a matter of language and of time. Even an ostensibly nonlegal claim that someone, having been convicted or acquitted, is *really* guilty," for instance, turns in part on the active and proper use of a language of "reality" and "guilt." Claiming that Cardozo's act of holding happened and that the holding is New York State law requires knowledge of speech and of the world that is shared among those who speak the same tongue. Such speaking, as the next chapter shows, involves dialogue with others over time.

· · ·

In sum, *Palsgraf* exemplifies good legal writing not because Cardozo follows rules in his statement of facts. Rather, we are able to see how speaking or writing and judging, of facts and of law, correspond because Cardozo's opinion exemplifies good writing. Language and law correspond in their division of the world into doers and deeds, actions and events, facts and law. Law and language alike reveal themselves to be sites of judgments and of attributions of cause and responsibility, whose claims themselves take place as acts and events that our law and language locate in time.

CHAPTER THREE

Legal Acts as Social Acts

Certainly, then, ordinary language is not the *last* word: in principle it can everywhere be supplemented and improved upon and superseded. Only remember: it *is* the *first* word.

—J. L. Austin, "A Plea for Excuses," *Philosophical Papers*, p. 185

The most sustained alternative to understanding law as a matter of rules currently comes from interdisciplinary law-and-society or sociolegal scholarship. Sociolegal studies associate the binding of law with social power or force that produces empirical impacts or effects. To their credit, such studies draw attention to dynamic practices of law or to ways that law is transacted. Insofar as they adopt a strict legal realist distinction between law-on-the-books and law-in-action, however, they dismiss legal speech too quickly. Insofar as sociolegal studies treat legal language as fundamentally a matter of cause or of impact, they distort law.[1] This chapter argues that the bond of law is indeed social, although not in the ways that much sociolegal scholarship accepts. Rather, we are bound to law, and law binds us today through shared language. The chapter shows how our bonds manifest themselves through dialogic acts or interactions in which we make claims, however imperfectly, of one another.

As social acts, that is, legal acts need to be heard or apprehended or registered by a second person to happen. Participants in social acts engage with one another as "I" who speak and "you" who hear. The formal enactments of law today seldom address themselves explicitly to "you," of course. Statutes and ordinances use passive and third-person constructions in what appear to be definitions and propositions. Enactments like this are not commands as we ordinarily understand them nor as John Austin's *Province of Jurisprudence Determined* defines them. They neither take the form of explicit commands requiring a particular other or others to act nor of if-then statements or hypothetical imperatives. They often do not even seem to be the utterances of particularly forceful speakers. Even, or perhaps especially, those who would identify law with the power of a violent state admit that the formally valid enactments of officialdom are not always implemented and may be neither powerful nor efficacious. Ostensibly addressed "to whom it may concern," today's legal enactments on their face declare what "is," "may be," or "shall be." The California criminal code, for instance, opens with "This Act shall be known as THE PENAL CODE OF CALIFORNIA" (1). It maintains that "Words used in this code in the present tense include the future as well as the present" (7) and goes on to define its terms, categorizing crimes and what "shall be" their punishment. (Excerpts from the Code appear in Appendix D.)

Despite the apparent impersonality of its language, an act such as the Penal Code requires a subject for it to "be known"; the subject must know the language of the act. Other legal acts, such as complaint, testament, inauguration, conviction, or marriage, also occur in and through being spoken or written. They too rely on a shared practical knowledge of language that constitutes "you" and "I" as "we," this chapter shows. As social acts and speech events, legal acts depend on dialogue.

Sections One and Two emphasize that a legal speech act is not, strictly speaking, *caused* by its speaking subject. Rather, social acts of complaining, bequeathing, inaugurating, convicting, and marrying require *joint* speaking and hearing (or writing and reading, or expression and apprehension). Joint speaking and hearing do not cause, but together *are*, what the (singular) social act *is*. The first section draws on Adolf Reinach's account of social acts as requiring hearers for their completion to supplement J. L. Austin's account of speech acts.[2] The second section uses marriage as an example to show how social acts of law transform situations, appealing to shared understandings (of the marriage act, for instance) to initiate particular states of affairs (such as being married, rather than single or divorced) in which new names (such as "husband" and "wife") become appropriate. Empirical force does not bind us to the use of these names and judgments. But neither are names strictly matters of convention: New uses of names may be initiated, and names may be reappropriated.[3]

Section Three discusses the dialogical character of speech and of even ostensibly monological legal acts. Even the most conventional or performative utterances of law involve a hearing "you" and a speaking "I" who understand one another's language and how to speak with one another. In dialogue, persons take turns being "you" and "I," initiating new states of affairs and opening up and closing down possibilities of response, without determining them. Law refers both to the imperfect practical knowledge of law and language to which speaker-hearers appeal and to the social acts or speech events that are enabled by and may become part of such knowledge, Section Four argues. Legal acts appeal in a particular way to "you," Section Five continues; the utterances of I-who-speak are designed to recall to you-who-hear who "we"—who share practices of speech and hearing, or of language and of law—are. Insofar as legal claims are persuasive acts "designed" to "make demands on you," they are what Stanley Cavell calls "passionate utterances." They express their desires as the assertions and demands of claims made in the name of an ostensible third party "our" law.

In the context of a *Miranda* warning, for instance, one can distinguish between social acts or speech acts that occur in the dialogue between official and accused and the shared knowledge of language that must be present for the exchange to occur. So, too, one can distinguish at least two dimensions of law as language. First, future perfect social acts or claims like the warning occur as present indicative or imperative speech, initiate a future, and can be recounted as past. Second, shared practical knowledge corresponds to the ways that, like official and accused, we are continuously, habitually, and incompletely speaking a language such as English when we make claims of one another. Such practical knowledge corresponds, in a grammatical sense, to the "imperfect." In grammar, the "imperfect" refers not to the tense or mood of a verb but to the aspect of a sentence indicating incomplete, continual, ongoing, habitual, routine, or interruptible action. Compare the imperfect, *we were speaking*, with the past perfect, *we spoke* or *we agreed*. Even while persons in dialogue are bound to one another through simultaneously passionate and performative speech acts, this chapter concludes, they are speaking or making claims of one another imperfectly. They do so as members of communities who apprehend one another to various degrees, who sometimes disagree, and whose practical knowledge of law and language is never completely articulated or articulable in the speech acts or events of their law.

One. Speech Act as Social Act: Adolf Reinach

That legal acts are social acts, dependent not only on speakers following particular conventions but also on the apprehension of responsive hearers, qualifies what is sometimes taken to be an Austinian account of legal speech acts. Insofar as Austin is taken to focus on the admittedly dynamic activity of speaking or uttering, rather than on the joint act of the speaker and hearer together, his account may suggest to some that speech acts are caused by speakers (or even that their success is to be gauged by a speaker's intentions) within a context that is determined by social conventions of speech. Acts of law cannot be performed by speakers alone, however, nor are they simply conventional.

Indeed, well before J. L. Austin introduced "performative utterances" or "speech acts," Adolf Reinach identified acts such as promises as "social acts" or acts that are in need of being heard or that happen only in being apprehended.[4] (I follow John F. Crosby's translation of Reinach's *vernehmen* as "apprehend" and use "the term 'hear' in a broad sense." As Crosby points out, this enables one to speak of hearing even when ears are not involved, as when one apprehends by reading something.[5]) Social acts generally include Austinian speech acts: promising, apologizing, commanding, requesting, informing, and more. They include the many explicitly legal acts encountered so far: enacting, indicting, objecting, instructing, sentencing, appealing, holding, announcing, concurring, dissenting, dismissing, and so forth. All of these acts, in need of being heard by another, differ from experiences and acts, such as feeling sorry or miserable or intending to say or deciding to do something, that need not express themselves to others. Social acts "do not have in words and the like their accidental, additional expression, but . . . are performed in the very act of speaking . . . [Further] it is characteristic [of social acts] that *they announce themselves to another* through words or some similar forms of expression" (36, emphasis added).

Reinach's "social acts" resemble Austin's illocutionary acts. Insofar as social acts need to be heard, though, they exclude some seemingly illocutionary acts, especially (but not exclusively) members of the family of acts that Austin calls "expositive." Acts of inferring, assessing, presuming, deducing, interpreting, and concluding, for instance, may be carried out without being announced or heard. Many acts of reasoning are not social acts as such. The association of legal acts with the Reinachian requirement that successful social acts need to be heard thus qualifies the association of law with the list of performative speech acts or utterances in Austin's twelfth lecture. Deduction, for instance, one activity of legal reasoning, is not a social act. "I deduce xyz," even said aloud to another, is not a social act of deduction. Saying it may indeed clarify to another one's reasons or argument or what one is doing or thinking, perhaps even as one does or thinks it, but it is a *social* act only insofar as it is an act of telling or informing or announcing to another one's deduction or reasoning, and not as an act of deducing or reasoning as such.

Close reading suggests that Austin usually does presume hearers of illocutionary acts, although he does not focus on them. Austin's descriptions of four of the five general classifications of illocutionary forces of utterances imply hearers: verdictives consist in "delivering . . ." presumably to another; exercitives in "giving of a decision" (not just deciding); expositives are "used in acts of exposition" and "of course, have reference to the communicational situation" (Lecture XII). Behabitives that "adopt attitudes" (XII) and are "concerned roughly with reactions to behaviour and with behaviour towards others" are also "designed to exhibit attitudes and feelings" (VII). Only Austin's general description of commissives, of which "promises" are a prime example, appears not to presume a hearer insofar as commissives simply "commit the speaker to a course of action" (XII). But Austin's account elsewhere of promising "normally" requires others. He writes (II, p. 22):

> It is obviously necessary that to have promised I must normally
>   (A) have been *heard* by someone, perhaps the promisee;
>   (B) have been understood by him as promising.[6]

Despite the implicit "other" or "you" in Austin's analysis, his text privileges speaking. Privileging speaking is Austin's way of turning philosophical thinking about language away from static propositions toward what language does and what we do with it. By focusing on speaking, Austin turns both logicians' propositions and other sentences into active doings. He acknowledges, and indeed argues, that understanding what we do with words requires considering speaking within its "total speech situation" but does not emphasize, as does Reinach, the mutuality of speaking and hearing. Even though speech situations "normally" include being heard by another for Austin then, the active or dynamic character of speech appears to stem for Austin from the source, or speaker, of utterances.

As Chapter One pointed out though, law often emphasizes hearing. Claiming requires speaking and hearing. In aiming to persuade, claims are passionate utterances in Stanley Cavell's terms. Cavell, recall, contrasts the focus on the "I" of the performative speech act to the focus on the "you" of what he dubs "passionate utterance," a category that includes insults, reassurance, seduction, and persuasion. Like claims, insults are sensible utterances that are neither constative nor performative. On the one hand, they are not propositions that can be assessed simply in terms of accuracy. On the other hand, they are unlike promises and bets, in that they cannot be performed by saying, "I insult you." Rather, insulting, reassuring, seducing, and persuading, do what they do in being heard a particular way by "you," argues Cavell. One ("I") indeed insults (reassures, seduces, or persuades) another ("you") through words, but saying what one is doing in these cases—as one may do in the case of promising or inviting—will not do. Speech is not magic (170). As sensible utterances that indicate essentially perlocutionary designs, successful passionate utterances require a particular response from you.

Reinach's account of social acts allows one to recognize that illocution, insofar as it makes the "I" its focus, and perlocution, in the manner of passionate utterances that focus on the "you," need not refer to different acts or even to the division of a single utterance into force and effect. Rather illocution and perlocution are two aspects or dimensions of a single jointly enacted or performed "social act." Hearing, Reinach argues, is a receptive act; it is not passive. Social acts involve both speaking and hearing, so they require at least two participants who are both actors or subjects, not mere objects acted on. (Recall from the first sections of Chapter One and Chapter Two, that our English language attributes "intention" to persons who act but not to objects such as scales that fall.) The "performative" utterances or illocutionary acts of informing, promising, and warning, then, no less than the "passionate" ones of persuading, insulting, and seducing, are social acts that must be heard. Reinach's social act emphasizes the presence of "you" both in the Austinian illocutionary act *and* in the passionate and performative utterances that Cavell would distinguish.

The explicit conditions that law places on its own social acts show how legal acts depend on "you." They happen *as much* in apprehension or reception or hearing as in speaking and voice. Although, for Reinach, social acts need to be apprehended or heard, they do not require oral utterance: A nod of the head may be "heard" as agreement or threat.[7] Today, apprehension among human beings largely requires verbal expression, whether oral or written, as the current emphasis on "having a voice" suggests and as both Reinach and Austin agree. Legal acts are no exception. They often require guarantees of delivery or receipt. Some acts, such as marriages and wills, require witnesses. Verdicts, rulings, and regulations both follow and require hearing. Acts of delivery, notification, witness, and hearing in turn have their own conventions, many articulated in law, which of course require the presence of someone other than the speaker(s). There are often more than two participants in social acts, as the ambiguity of an officiant "marrying" parties even as parties "marry" one another, or the very common depiction of a court as triad, indicate. The concern that law shows for these others and for the integrity of its processes of hearing (Chapter One, Section Two) confirms the essential significance of hearing to law. The conditions or conventions required for a legal act such as marriage to be successful refer not only to felicity conditions associated with the act of utterance but also to comparable conditions associated with the act of hearing.

As Chapter One showed, Austin makes clear that a marriage is problematic when the wedding ceremony is interrupted, when the words are not correctly or completely uttered, when an officiant has no authority, or when one of the parties is already married. The act is also problematic, this section has argued, when it is improperly heard: when there are no witnesses,[8] when a license is not filed or recorded, when a form lacks validation or when, as in the case of a marriage made abroad, for instance, a record cannot be translated or otherwise authenticated. Austin's Γ2 condition, with its reference to "subsequent conduct," does not quite capture the ways in which hearing or apprehension, although subsequent to expression, does not simply follow a social act. Rather, apprehension is essential to the way in which the social act of which it is part transforms what Reinach calls "states of affairs," discussed further in the next section.

Two. Marriage Acts and States of Affairs

What are the implications of understanding legal acts not so much as Austinian speech acts but as Reinachian social acts? The union of two actors participating in a single social act complicates simple chronological or causal accounts of the transformation wrought in a social act (of informing, complaining, promising, persuading, marrying . . .). Transformation of a state of affairs is not caused by either the speaking or the hearing of the social act.[9] It occurs only upon joint speaking-and-hearing. The joint social act that transforms and initiates states of affairs is conceptually distinct from a linear sequence of expression, then hearing, then effect.

Consider marrying, an ostensibly mundane speech act that appears even before promising in *How to Do Things with Words*. In Lecture I, Austin offers the following example of a performative utterance: "'I do (sc. take this woman to be my lawful wedded wife)'—as uttered in the course of the marriage ceremony."

Austin's editor, J. O. Urmson, notes that "Austin realized that the expression 'I do' is not used in the marriage ceremony too late to correct his mistake. We have let it remain in the text as it is philosophically unimportant that it is a mistake" (Note 2, p. 5). Actually, "I do" *is* used in some marriage ceremonies. Austin and Urmson were apparently referring to traditional wedding ceremonies in which bride and groom vow to "take" one another as husband and wife. Although "philosophically unimportant," Austin's ostensible confusion as to precisely which expression marries attests to a real proliferation of possible moments of marrying.

As Chapter Two pointed out, legal acts involving verbal utterances occur over or take time. Pinpointing a singular moment of occurrence may sometimes be unnecessary. It is also difficult. In some wedding ceremonies, marriage arguably occurs after the vows when the groom places the ring on the bride's finger while declaring, "With this ring, I thee wed." In other ceremonies, vows are "sealed" with a kiss. In the past, marriages were said to "begin" with betrothal. In all fifty American states, a couple, whatever their vows, is not formally wed until the filing of a marriage license with an officiant's signature attesting to the ceremony. Despite a range of possible religious and civil marriage vows and pronouncements, many officiants "now" declare couples to be husband and wife. The precise moment of marrying thus appears elastic.

Such elasticity as to the moment in which legal acts can be said to occur points, as in Chapter Two, to the different temporal registers in which they happen. First, a marriage act or ceremony, like the reading or writing of an opinion for instance, takes minutes or more. Marriage proceedings occur or take place over a period of time during which speakers-hearers participate. Second, legal acts are nevertheless taken to occur at a particular "moment" or in a singular "present" that may precede the completion of the ceremony. At or on *this* hour or day or year, the act of marriage or announcement of a judgment *hereby* transforms these parties' marital status or their legal liability. Third, the new status that begins at the ostensible moment of the act endures for some time. Legal judgments may endure until they are remanded, overturned, superseded, or reversed; their conditions fulfilled or revoked; and so forth. A couple's marriage lasts until another act, such as annulment or divorce, transforms it or until an event, such as death, acknowledged explicitly in marriage vows as the end of the state of marriage, do the parties part. (That there are different names for "divorcee" and "widow" again reveals the importance, as in Chapter Two, Sections One and Two, that language accords to the distinction between act and event. That "divorcée," unlike "spinster," "wife," and "widow," for many years had no male-gendered analog is also telling, but another story). Annulment differs from both act of divorce and event of death in that, as an act, it retrospectively denies that the original act of now so-called marriage transformed the state of affairs.

Modern law often specifies not only the conditions of a social act's expression and hearing but also, as we have just seen, the moment of a social act and the duration of the state of affairs that ensues from it. That an officiant "now" pronounces a couple husband and wife, for instance, identifies a precise deictic moment at which the social and legal condition of marriage begins. This is the "present" in the "present indicative active" of Austin's explicit performative formula. In U.S. and U.K. contract law, the traditional mailbox rule specifies that the social-legal act of acceptance of an offer occurs at the moment of its posting in a mailbox. The "shrink-wrap" and "click-wrap" agreements of a digital age occur with notice that on opening (often software) packaging or clicking a button online, one accepts or assents to terms, including terms of installation, within. Contracts often contain clauses specifying when the making of an agreement has in effect been completed or when its terms become operative and the new state of affairs being agreed to begins. The California Penal Code "takes effect at twelve o'clock, noon, on the first day of January, eighteen hundred and seventy-three" (2). Legal writings are especially prone to "herebys" and "heretofores" that purport to fix moments of occurrence.

That the "now" or the present of the social act may occur during the period of its utterance and before the actual completion of the utterance or ceremony, even as it marks the initiation of a state of affairs that depends on such completion, highlights the peculiar "future perfect" temporality ascribed to speech acts by Derrida in Chapter Two.[10] While they are being spoken and heard, in their own present, social acts—like speech acts—are ongoing or incomplete or grammatically imperfect. The chronological disjunct of the expression of an utterance from its hearing reinforces this sense of incompleteness or imperfection and contrasts with the unity of the ostensibly singular, present "moment" attributed to the social act.

The point here is not only that the Austinian speech act fails to do justice to the complexity of temporality (as well as to the bodily character of the social act, addressed further in Chapter Four). In the Austinian account of the uptake of a speech act, hearing *follows* expression chronologically, even if at the speed of sound. The point is that the unification of speaking and hearing in the "moment" of the specifically *social* act means that a *social* act is not a linear sequence or "sum" of speaking plus hearing.[11]

In arguing that the obligation that arises in promising is a matter of convention (and not of intention as some have mistakenly read him to say), Austin can be taken to suggest that obligation follows as a consequence of the speech act and conventions of promising and invites fulfillment. Fulfillment, as Austin puts it, "requires a second act by the speaker or another person; and it is a commonplace of consequence-language that this cannot be included under the initial stretch of action" (117). Reinach recognizes with Austin that fulfillment of a promise may not occur and that, if it does, it constitutes a further act. Reinach points out, however, that *in* the very act of promising, or at the expansive yet singular nonchronological moment of "I do" that marks joint speaking and apprehension, or the unity of expression and hearing in a social act, a state of affairs is transformed: A claim and an obligation come into being. The existence of a claim differs from the possible later social act of claiming, just as the promise as obligation differs from the possible later act of fulfillment of it. The state of affairs of one subject having an obligation to another who has a claim does not follow, strictly speaking, as an effect caused by the speaking or by the hearing or by uptake of the promise or even from some combination. Rather, it happens on the occurrence of or in the promise.[12]

So far, we have seen that social acts require not only speaking but also hearing. They *transform* and *initiate* "states of affairs" in the moment of their performance before one who apprehends them. They may also invite responses, as Austin points out of speech acts, but they necessitate no particular response. Some social acts, such as adjournment, arguably close or complete a particular sequence of social acts. Others, such as requests or promises or commands, call in the usual course of things for or "invite" particular acts or performances. Invitations generally are accepted or are declined with regret, but an invitee may equally well forget to respond, take offense and refuse to reply, decline gleefully, or do any number of other things. The invitation may nevertheless have been appropriately uttered and heard; in so doing it will have changed a state of affairs, such that an invitation will have been issued, a state that may or may not remain open. Questions likewise are also usually answered or addressed, but they may also be countered with further questions, parodied, or ignored and may remain open.

In their transformation of states of affairs, legal acts often invite responses that themselves invite response in more or less formal dances of claims and counter-claims. Legal exchanges often involve verbal chains: offer and acceptance, acceptance and agreement; objection and ruling, ruling and exception, exception and appeal; complaint and demurrer, demurrer and summary judgment; and so forth. Warrants or summonses whose service guarantees that hearing has occurred also call for response or action: the appearance of the hearer or recipient at a particular place and time. Such appearance, interestingly, is in turn often a precondition for further legal acts or proceedings in which the party who must appear will be heard (or in the case of juror notice to appear, will hear others).

The shifting states of affairs that accompany the accomplishment of social and legal acts mean that new contexts continually emerge. The best sociolegal scholarship recognizes that particular legal or social acts in any number of venues transform states of affairs and invite without determining responses. Robert P. Burns, for instance, describes criminal trials as sophisticated "linguistic practices and performances" that culminate in verdicts, which are themselves skilled performances that cannot be adequately captured by rules.[13] Paying close attention to trial transcripts, Justin Richland shows how Hopi tradition and Anglo-American-style law interact in new ways when invoked in Hopi trial courts.[14] John L. and Jean Comaroff write about the "unexpected incarnations" of ethnic identity that manifest themselves in today's consumer economy through the legal incorporation of identity and the commodification of culture.[15] Like the postcolonial appropriation of "rights" in South Africa that the Comaroffs discuss elsewhere, these uses of law suggest that language does not have the "power" to determine responses nor does it simply produce conventionally expected states of affairs.

In different contexts, even the most stale or conventional utterances may unexpectedly take on new meaning or raise new issues. Citing dicta or working with precedent in fresh cases, for instance, may reconfigure states of affairs in previously unthought and certainly underdetermined ways. Recall the history of the famous *Carolene Products* footnote.[16] The case before the 1938 Supreme Court concerned the transportation of filled or mixed milk products across state lines. In footnote four, Justice Stone wrote:

> It is unnecessary to consider now whether legislation which restricts those political processes which can ordinarily be expected to bring about repeal of undesirable

legislation, is to be subjected to more exacting judicial scrutiny under the general pro-
hibitions of the Fourteenth Amendment than are most other types of legislation.

Nor need we inquire whether similar considerations enter into the review of statutes directed at particular religious . . . or national . . . or racial minorities . . . : whether
prejudice against discrete and insular minorities may be a special condition, which
tends seriously to curtail the operation of those political processes ordinarily to be
relied upon to protect minorities, and which may call for a correspondingly more
searching judicial inquiry.[17]

By the 1970s, Stone's tangential suggestion, in dicta of a 1938 case, of an alternative approach both to that of the former hands-off *Lochner* era and to that
actually used in *Carolene Products*, had become "equal protection" orthodoxy.
As Jack Balkin explains, by the 1970s "government action either received no [ju-
dicial] review at all or a virtually irrebuttable presumption of unconstitution-
ality. The only issue in most cases was which level of scrutiny applied, which
in turn reduced to the question whether a suspect class or a fundamental right
was affected." Although Stone's successors and later cases have offered their own
variations on the theme of a two-tiered level of scrutiny, writes Balkin, they have
allowed Stone's suggestions "to ossify into an unthinking paradigm of judicial
practice."[18] The story of the *Carolene Products* note suggests that new meanings
may themselves become conventions or orthodoxies, even as reiteration of the
"same" writing or speech takes on new force or meaning in different contexts, as
Derrida has repeatedly and variously demonstrated.

Austin's description of the conventional game of football as having been initiated by "the man who first picked up the ball and ran" likewise acknowledges
that conventions (or procedures) may come about where no convention may have
existed before:

> What could be meant by the suggestion that sometimes a procedure may not even ex-
> ist—as distinct from the question whether it is accepted, and by this or that group, or
> not? . . . We have . . . the case of procedures in which someone is initiating. Sometimes
> he may "get away with it" like, in football, the man who first picked up the ball and
> ran. Getting away with things is essential, despite the suspicious terminology. (30)

Actions (or instances) initiate and establish paradoxically "new" conventions.
Even conventional legal acts happen at least in part as responses to states of affairs among persons whose particular interactions with one another are not
fully determined by preexisting conventions or rules.[19] Those social acts and the

transformations that issue from them manifest precisely the initiative or free-dom that Austin suggests. As in Austin's example, to initiate is not the same as to cause an effect; to begin is not the same as to produce a result.

Social acts, in other words, involve a particularly human capacity to insti-gate a future perfect act that will be done. Hannah Arendt calls this capacity for beginning or for transforming and in this way initiating new states of affairs "natality."[20] The capacity to initiate, she argues, involves a particular sort of free-dom that belongs to specifically human speech and action, although it is never in the complete control of the one who speaks or acts. It must—unsurprisingly now—be exercised with others or, as Section One of this chapter emphasized, be-fore those who hear (or hear of) it. In the jointly held capacity to initiate that ac-companies social acts, participants in ostensibly conventional acts nevertheless possess unpredictable transformative potential. They take up possibilities from out of routine, habitual, undifferentiated ways of living and transform them into acts. *While they were living there* [in the imperfect], *he said* [a past act], *"I bet it will rain tomorrow,"* [using a first-person present active indicative grammatical form], *as a way of tempting her* [through passionate utterance] *to go on a walk* [how did she respond? Did she go?]. One can never completely determine how a social act, or the state of affairs it initiates, will be taken up—or for how long it will endure. For Arendt, the new emerges from human beings' acting and speak-ing with one another in what Reinach calls "social acts." The meaning and sig-nificance to history of words and deeds must be heard or seen by others and then passed on through their telling to yet others, according to Arendt. So too, legal acts must occur as social acts that are heard by others. In being heard, they initi-ate new states of affairs. The significance of those acts and the states of affairs they initiate emerge, against speakers' and hearers' shared background knowl-edge of speaking and living, over time—and, as Section Three shows, through dialogue.

Three. Speech as Dialogue: "You" and "I"

In a simple dialogue, a speaker and a hearer, who begin as "I" and as "you," change places. The first person's utterance addresses the second and initiates a new state of affairs. The "you" first addressed by "I" then has an opportunity to talk back or to respond in any number of ways, as *another* first-person "I," establishing yet another state of affairs to which the new "you" may then respond in any number of ways. Consider the following exchanges:

> A: I'd like pizza tonight. How would you like to go to that Italian
>   place by the bay?
> B: I guess I could have salad if you really want to go.
> A:

Or:

> C: You have the right to remain silent . . .
> D: I want a lawyer.
> C:

Or:

> E: XXX
> F: Objection, Your Honor.
> G: Overruled.
> F: Exception!

The first and second persons constituting the "I" and the "you" of dialogue need not use first- and second-person pronouns directly. Nor need they be alone. In law, only the most schematic examples, such as stereotypical lawsuits involving Buyer and Seller, or brief circumscribed exchanges, such as those between cross-examiner and witness, involve two participants. Ostensibly simple dialogues and even what we take to be monologues—such as the California Penal Code—are fragments of more complex interactions of language that always involve more than two persons.[21] The law student to whom a lawsuit appears as two-sided has already engaged with legal authority, as Mertz explains.[22] The bilateral contracts that emerge from corporate law firms always involve multiple actors.[23] Testimony occurs in settings that depend on the social acts of many others: parties, lawyers, judges, witnesses, clerks, and so forth. And a penal code presumes "knowers" of its language.

The relations of even two subjects in dialogue are complex. Nineteenth-century legal positivism viewed subjects of law as objects of commands issued by the sovereign-subject, but the addressees of legal acts and legal claims today seldom appear this way. Modern legal subjects nevertheless resemble the addressees of *grammatical* imperatives. In grammar, the imperative is not restricted to commands but may be used for requesting, prohibiting, permitting, and so forth. The imperative is not strictly in the second person. Eugen Rosenstock-Huessy writes,

> As the six persons in search of an author in the play of Pirandello, the imperative is in search of a subject. It is said "to whom it may concern." "Go" does not contain the second person "you" or "thou"; what it does is to create this person. It is pure verb without an ending. He who does just this, becomes the second person by answering the first person. The listener, who says "I will do it," becomes the person to whom "go" was addressed.[24]

In doing what an imperative says to do or shall be done, that is, an actor retrospectively constitutes him- or herself as the implicit addressee of an imperative.[25] In responding "I will do it," the actor constitutes him- or herself not only as hearer and addressee of an imperative but also as actor and speaker.[26] Through speech or sometimes simply through action, that is, a hearer constitutes him- or herself retrospectively vis-à-vis the imperative and its speaker. Again recalling the temporality of the future perfect, the hearer who responds to an imperative *will* turn out, in the future in relation to the present of the utterance, to *have been* its addressee.

One who responds affirmatively to the imperatives, such as they are, of modern law also retrospectively becomes law's implicit addressee. In responding to the ostensible imperative of a legal enactment, for instance, one becomes the "whom" concerned and, in some sense, not only a "you" but also an "I" who does what "it" says. Insofar as this "I" unites with other subjects, a collective of "I"s becomes possible. A collective of "I"s is a "we" of sorts. On its own, this collective "I" is not the "we" whose "word is bond," however. "We" is ambiguous: It may be "I and I" or "I and you." Two "I"s speaking at once without any "you" make neither dialogue nor law. At best, they resemble, when speaking as one, a choral or royal "We."[27]

For the *we* of "our word" or "our bond" to emerge, *I* must become *you*, and *you*, *I* to one another.[28] I say "hello" to you: *I* have greeted *you*, a social act. You say "hello" back to me: Now *we* have greeted one another. In dialogic exchanges and chains of social acts, you and I join together as "we" over our shared concerns. Our relations are not those of an equality or identity of "I"s (even when our word, "Hello," is the same, and even when, having once established ourselves, only one of us says it). Far from it. Rather *we* speak, in the turn-taking differences of the dialogue of "you" and "I," then "I" and "you," not as one, but as two. We speak, for instance, as teacher and student, as child and parents, as partners or friends or neighbors, even as law and its addressee, with one another. In such dialogues, words show themselves to be "our" bond, and "we" emerge from our use of language with one another over common concerns.

The third-person grammar of *he, she, it* supplements *I, you*, and *we*, showing further the complexity of dialogue. Let us begin with *it*. Insofar as speaking says something, the "something" or *what is said* is an "it." (Speaking is also say*ing* or do*ing* something, as we have seen, but let us bracket for the moment the activity of speaking and stick to a perfected or completed utterance or thing said.) When speakers say things, the "things said"—the *what* that the speaker says—may be thought of either as words *or* as what words say. What words say may further be grasped as things said ("I'd like pizza tonight") or as things in the world (persons, desires, pizzas, dining suggestions). The formulation "what words say" (where *words* say "*what*") shows how "words" swivel between being grammatical objects that a speaker speaks and a hearer hears and being grammatical subjects that themselves predicate or say something. A written text or spoken utterance that says something may be third-person subject or object: Like words, speech, and dialogue, *it* says something, and what is said is also *it*.

This first-person speaking, second-person hearing, and third-person saying of an utterance or text complicates the ostensible equivalences of I speak; you speak; and she, he, or it speaks, presumed in the grammatical conjugations through which one learns foreign languages (and middle-school English). The I-who-speak corresponds less to you-who-speak and to an objectified he-who-speaks and it-that-speaks, than to you-who-hear (what I say) and it-that-says (what I utter) or, even, it-that-is-said (in my speaking). Grasping the relations between the I-speak, you-hear, and it-says is as important to speaking and writing as are the rules of proper usage (I speak, you speak, he/she/it speaks).[29]

The centrality of such relations is evident in composition—and legal writing—classes. The written text of a student's paper or brief (a *what* or an objective "it") enables a teacher to bring to the fore the disjuncts between the (first-person) student's "what I meant" and "what it says" through the teacher's "what I read." The (first-person) teacher's "what I read" conveys to a (second-person) student *what you wrote*. A student who listens (who not only hears but is at peace with a teacher) learns how "what it says," now associated with "what you, the [second-person] teacher, heard," falls short of the student's (now first-person) "what I meant." A student comes to realize and work on minimizing the disjunction among *what-I-mean*, *what-you-hear*, and *what-it-says*.

In learning, student and teacher respond to one another, alternating as first- and second-person participants in dialogue. They may adjust what they intend to say, what they understand to have been said, and what they say. What they have already said ("it") remains what has been said, however. The words of Obama's first oath stand as what was said before the second oath. Words that have been spoken or written constitute the text of a particular moment. True, student and teacher can say new words and add to their conversation. You and I may revise and discard soon-to-be-forgotten drafts. Legislation can be amended. Obama can swear a new oath. But once spoken or written, a given iteration or set of words—"it"—remains constant and continues to say (although, again as Derrida points out, not necessarily to mean or to do) the same thing.

Plato's teacher Socrates says as much to Phaedrus (although not directly to Plato) in the *Phaedrus*:

> SOCRATES: Writing, Phaedrus, has this very strange quality, and is
> very like painting; for the creatures of painting stand like living beings,
> but if one asks them a question, they preserve a solemn silence. And so
> it is with written words; you might think they spoke as if they had intel-
> ligence, but if you question them, wishing to know about their sayings,
> they always say only one and the same thing. And every word, when once
> it is written is bandied about, alike among those who understand and
> those who have no interest in it, and it knows not to whom to speak or
> not to speak; when ill-treated or unjustly reviled, it always needs its fa-
> ther to help it; for it has no power to protect or help itself. (259d–e)[30]

What Socrates means and what Phaedrus hears are arguable; what Plato meant is highly contested; what the reader understands may yet change. But the words of the text at 259d–e (in Greek or in a given translation) remain the same, a third-party constraint—although as we shall see, not the only constraint—on what a second-person (whether that be Phaedrus or the reader) hears of the speech of a first (whether that be Socrates as character or Plato as author). Although the text will admittedly do different things in different contexts, its words remain the same. That they remain the same but are uttered in a different time and place nevertheless makes them different.[31] When we quote those words, however, the words—as text or as third-person *it*—still constrain what the second person hears.

As was previously noted of legal acts, spoken exchanges and written dialogues may explicitly include and always gesture toward more than two interlocutors. They may involve a silent third party. In standing by, this third party is *he* or *she*—not simply *it*. He or she serves as a reminder that the understandings of first- and second-person characters do not exhaust the possibilities of response to any given utterance. He or she may say nothing during the course of the exchange. But the silence of the third-person bystander at any given moment is not the same as the continuous and repetitive present imperfect saying of the third-person text. *He* or *she* is a subject who is presumed to have a capacity to hear and to act or to predicate in a particular way. He or she could be thinking—or doing—anything. Like the second person, he or she can hear what is said. But insofar as he or she is not the addressee of the utterance (or a direct participant in the social act), he or she may say or do anything, initiatory or conventional, as response or nonresponse to what he or she hears. He or she, for instance, may overhear the wedding ceremony yet continue indifferently to sweep up in the back of the church. But he or she may also make a ruckus or later testify as to the marriage.

The range of possibilities of such a third party's actions challenge another seeming grammatical equivalence: that of *he* and *she* with *it*. The possibilities of third-party response contrast to third-person textual repetition and serve to remind us—and may, through interruption for instance, remind the two persons in dialogue also—that neither separately nor together do first- and second-person participants or even the third-person text control the way of the dialogue.

In other words, the third-person party, in some sense like the words of a text, draws attention to the limits of the power or control of a first-person speaker over an utterance. (Even as *I* say, "I am speaking" or "Go!" or "The wind blew the church door shut," my utterance exceeds what *I* mean to say and do.) The text, as a third-person *it*, draws attention to these limits by falling short of the first person's intentions (as the teacher points out) and constraining what the second person can hear. The third-party presence of *he* or *she* shows further that speech and writing occur in a world that is greater even than a dialogue comprised of the first two characters and their words. On the one hand, the third-person text reiterates the words of first persons; on the other, the presence of a third-person party, a *he* or *she* that is not yet an *I* nor a *you* nor quite an *it*, reveals a world that includes more than *I* and *you* and the *it* of their words.

This greater world grants to all hearers, second-person addressees and third parties alike, their possibilities of response, including nonresponse. It grants to all potential speakers their possibilities of speech and action. These possibilities are not the same for all, as sociolegal studies, such as that of Galanter discussed in Chapter One, point out of legal actors. Nor are possibilities of speech and act unlimited. Words must fit the world to which they belong. In so doing, they bring a particular world—the world in which and of which we speak—near.[32] We are bound—responsive and responsible—to a given world through the words it offers us. Responses suit their own time and place, which is why written dialogues from Plato to Heidegger take such care to establish when and where they occur. Plato's Phaedrus cannot reply to Socrates using Twitter as his example.

That responses are both offered by and must suit their circumstances again suggests, as in Chapter One, that responses can be assessed along various dimensions, as more or less appropriate, skilled, responsive, and so forth. As social or speech acts, responses are neither static texts nor propositions that either do or do not correspond to the world, but dynamic interactions. That responses do not always suit their situations suggests that some acts and some words will not work at all and that some manners of action or speech work better than others. Without learning the right words, one does not have the means to respond well to particular utterances; one does not know the conventions of particular social acts. When one knows these conventions, by contrast, one shares with those with whom one speaks a common knowledge of how to use, or rather how we who speak with one another use, words in the world. We—nonlawyers and lawyers alike—are thus bound in our use of language not only to the actual world but to the proper use of speech. One who is ignorant of conventions is in effect a foreigner or a stranger in our world, having to confront issues not only of haves and have-nots but also of translation, initiation, and access, before being able to fully participate.[33] Contemporary concerns about bilingual education, the translation of voting materials, and the right to public education of the undocumented resident children of illegal aliens are just a few examples that show how issues of membership, language, and knowledge are bound.

Knowing how to speak and act with one another can be said to constitute a practical knowledge of how to name and judge states of affairs in the world.

Knowing what to say requires the ability to judge. In their classic article on "The Emergence and Transformation of Disputes: Naming, Blaming, and Claiming," sociolegal scholars Felstiner, Abel, and Sarat show how knowledge of language is key to legal claims and relations.[34] They argue that "disputes" emerge through three transformations: first, the transformation of an experience into something perceived as an injury; second, the transformation of that perception into a grievance about a wrong; and third, the rejection of a claim for a remedy. Interestingly, "claiming"—the speech act par excellence of law—is, in this three-moment account, elided. For Felstiner and his colleagues, the first moment involves recognition on my part that "I" have been injured, the second that "you" are to blame. The third transformation then moves directly to rejection of a claim. Despite its title, the article appears to leave out the making of the claim or my grieving against you in the name of how "we" judge. Before a claim can be rejected, though, naming and blaming must be turned into claiming!

Claiming, a social act, indeed involves relations between "you" and "I" and, in particular, an assertion as to my injury and a demand that "I" be made whole by "you," as Felstiner and his coauthors argue. Before a dispute emerges, however, naming and blaming, as assertion and demand, must be articulated in a claim that appeals, through dialogue or exchange, to *our* ways of judging. Claims that appeal to our ways of judging involve more than one person's knowledge of naming and blaming; they invoke a common—if imperfect, as the possibility of its rejection shows—sense of responsibility. The next section offers a brief example to illustrate the relation of this common knowledge to dialogic social acts or speech events; the subsequent section returns to claiming and to what it is to claim in the name of our law.

Four. Knowledge and Event: The Temporalities of Law and Language

English-language speakers practice their knowledge of how to conduct themselves in dialogue with one another in many different kinds of social acts: when they answer questions, acknowledge thanks, fulfill requests, decline invitations, accept advice, rebut objections, and so forth. In claims and counterclaims of law, made in broken and unbroken chains of dialogue, they participate in social acts and judge and respond to states of affairs that issue from them. A question has *now* been posed, an answer has *now* been given, an objection has *now* been raised, a promise has *now* been made. At the moment of each new social act, the state of affairs and the issue changes: how now to respond? what next to do? Knowing what to do in these instances suggests shared practical knowledge, not of a Kantian moral law as such, but rather of language.[35] On the basis of their certainly incomplete, various, and variable knowledges of a "common" tongue, speakers and hearers take turns acting and responding to one another.

Exchanges around the *Miranda* warning illustrate how turn-taking social acts occur in law, producing new occasions for claims and at least provisionally terminating other opportunities of response. In warning an accused that any statement may be used against him or her, as Chapter One pointed out, police acknowledge the potential limitations of representatives of law to grasp the accused's speech, inculpatory and exculpatory. In offering to the accused an opportunity to accept the law's acknowledgment that the terms of in-custody police interrogation may not do justice to his or her speech, officials presume common knowledge of speech. They presume that the accused is already engaged enough in the language in which their exchange is taking place to be able to understand the warning and that they themselves will understand enough of an accused's response to act accordingly.

Prosecutors', defendants', and courts' responses to the warning since *Miranda* have troubled the terms of these presumptions. A veritable welter of case law and commentary raise issues about warnings and waivers that before *Miranda* would have been irrelevant. Understanding *Miranda* warnings, waivers, and rulings as social and dialogic acts allows one to situate discussions that since 1966 have addressed, in the piecemeal fashion that is case law, the expression, hearing, and conditions of, and states that ensue from, warning and waiver. Questions have arisen in particular cases, for instance, as to: when warnings are warranted (courts have carved out public safety exceptions to the requirement that the warning must precede questioning); whether warnings are understandable to foreign-language-speaking parties; what sorts of utterances count as invocations, requests for counsel, and waivers (Austin's B1 and B2 felicity conditions); what responses must follow (Γ2); and how long the state of affairs pursuant to invocation of a particular aspect of the right endures. How long, for instance, does an assertion of the right to counsel, or a demand for counsel, endure before a second round of questioning may begin? Courts have ruled that an accused must "understand" the warning and that waivers must be "knowing, intelligent, and voluntary."

The invocation of the right is nevertheless problematic. While early *Miranda* practices allowed the right to remain silent to be claimed or invoked through silence, recent decisions now require explicit "assertion" of the right as well as of the right to counsel.[36] Requiring explicit spoken assertion of one's right to silence following an official's warning about speech both undermines official utterances and reveals a lack of understanding of how legal speech acts. First, the requirement of a particular assertion undermines the integrity of the speech of those who issue the warning. It rejects what the official has just said, as Janet Ainsworth points out, in effect taking back the offer or invitation to silence (or the recognition of silence as appropriate) that law enforcement officials have just made. (Recall in this context the "if the individual indicates *in any manner*" language of the *Miranda* opinion cited in Chapter One.) As Ainsworth explains, in cases where an accused responds to the warning by hedging or using indirect language, such as asking for a phone to call a lawyer rather than baldly and directly saying "I want a lawyer," police are unlikely to stop questioning, and courts have upheld the practice (2008, p. 11). These cases, as Ainsworth writes, appear to "exemplify the very concern that led the Supreme Court in *Miranda* to interpose a right to counsel in the police interrogation context" (10), the inability of legal officials to grasp the speech of the accused. Likewise courts have considered "I don't wanna talk no more" and similar utterances, as well as "stony silence," to be too ambiguous to constitute invocation of the right to remain silent (9–10). The court's "hyperliteral readings" of invocation have deemed the accused's replies to be "infelicitous legal speech acts because they took the form of questions, or were framed in the subjunctive mood, or preceded the request with softening expressions of emotion or desire" (11). In conjunction with the court's conversely expansive understanding of waiver, its "stingy" understanding of invocation eviscerates not only *Miranda*, as Ainsworth argues, but the very integrity of the social act of warning.

Second, the requirement that an accused must assert the right in a particular way implies that activation of the right to remain silent must occur through what appears to be taken as a discrete and acontextual statement. The requirement of a particular assertion completely ignores that the invocation of the right occurs as a claim or as a social act in an exchange or dialogue in which common knowledge of speech is already presumed and one party has just acknowledged its potential inability to properly hear or apprehend the words of the other. Any utterance, claims the official, "will" be used against the accused; if utterance is required for invoking the right to silence, then the accused confronts the horns of a dilemma.

Exchanges that happen around the *Miranda* warning allow one to distinguish between the legal and social acts that occur in the dialogue between official and accused (warnings, waivers, invocations, questions, replies) and the shared, yet imperfect, knowledge of language that must already be present for the very dialogue to occur. Both are associated with "law." The former "law" consists of social acts that occur in a present (indicative or imperative) mood and that may be said to initiate new states of affairs. In the future, such social acts can be considered or treated and recounted as completed or perfected past acts or events. After the act of warning, one can describe what has happened as an event or set of events: "The official warned the accused of the danger of speaking. The accused then asked for a lawyer." Or: "The official read the accused his rights. The accused waived the right to remain silent." Or, perhaps: "The accused asserted the right." Again, particular *social acts* occurring on the basis of the shared practical knowledge of the official and the accused can be relegated to a past. (Chapter Four will consider in part what may be made of "The accused remained silent.")

In contrast to particular social acts, the *shared knowledge or practice of language* that is presumed by those acts, as well as by those who later interpret them, corresponds to the continuous or imperfect aspect of the law of the situation: "The official and the accused *were speaking* in a common tongue, when the official issued the warning," or "While the accused was being *Mirandized*, sirens wailed." That courts and officials do not always apprehend or understand the speech or the silence of an accused also reveals the incompleteness or imperfection of our speech and the incapacities and limitations of its speakers and hearers. The English language is neither universal nor seamless in its use, and it is also susceptible to misuse (again, a matter to which Chapter Four turns).

The dual aspect of law, as social acts and as shared knowledge of language, means that law cannot be fully grasped as a set of events in a linear chronology of cause and effect. (Nor indeed can language, properly understood.) As they are issuing, utterances in some sense await their hearing to complete themselves as social acts in an elastic "present" moment. Insofar as social acts transform states of affairs, their temporal structure appears to be that of the future perfect, as we saw in Chapter Two. Insofar as social acts also depend on shared albeit imperfect and incompletely articulable practical knowledge, however, they also reveal ways of speaking and living together that correspond to the continuous and habitual, ongoing and yet interruptible, law of a "community"—or of "we" who speak with and hear one another.

Not only explicit legal dialogues such as those surrounding the *Miranda* warning presume interlocutors who can hear and know. Even grammatically third-person legal enactments addressed "to whom it may concern" do so. They presume practical knowledge of language that not only constitutes speaker and hearer as "you" and "I" in dialogue, as we have seen, but also as "we" who make claims of one another, as the next section shows, in the name of law.

Five. Speaking Imperfectly

Modern law is explicit in recognizing, as in *Miranda*, that although we may speak a common language and apprehend one another's speech, we do not always understand one another, much less agree, in language or in law. Modern U.S. law not only articulates conditions for many of its own acts but also allows for their contestation.[37] Contestations often seem in large part a matter of conventional legal practices or of performative utterances or illocutionary acts: complaints, lawsuits, objections, proposed amendments, and other claims. Legal claims often appear articulable in the conventional first-person present indicative active form of the explicit performative that Austin pointed out: "I claim xyz," "I object to abc," "I propose 123," "I authorize . . . ," "I dissent . . . ," "I waive . . ." But legal claims, as Chapter One also pointed out, are explicitly designed to persuade or "make demands upon you," in Cavell's description of passionate utterance, "in a way that an illocutionary force (if all goes well) forgoes" (173). Even conventional social acts of law, in claiming to be law, to be in accordance with law, or even to be better law, do not simply make demands on you that you may or may not fulfill (much less do they simply name and blame). They also appeal to you, this section shows, to recall who "we" are and what "we" know. This invocation exceeds both the "I" of Austin's performative formula and the focus on "you" of Cavell's passionate utterance.

Social acts or claims of law of both officials and nonofficials, that is, are designed to single *you* out, to recall to *you*, their addressee, how *we* name or judge or act *otherwise* than would *you* alone. Recall that while performative utterance stakes itself on the conventions followed by the speaking "I," passionate utterance according to Cavell draws the "'you' . . . essentially into the picture" (180). In law, when *I* enact or amend laws, or for that matter, initiate or pursue legal grievances, accuse others and defend myself (or vice versa), propose compromises and protest them, or make any other claims, *I* address *you*. While addressing you, I make my claims in the name of what *we*, rather than I or you, take law to be. My appeal to law seeks to move you beyond your—possibly indifferent, possibly contested—relation with me, to remind you of *us* or of who *we* are. That in making claims of you, I may do so through a third party or in the third person ("May it please the Court . . .") reinforces the point that my appeal is not a simple appeal to a second person alone and that speech, though dialogic, is not binary.

The crux is that when *I* seek to move or persuade *you*, "desire" undergirds my claims. As already noted, legal claims are rhetorical: They are simultaneously passionate in their appeals and performative in their doing. Recall (from Chapter One) Cavell's contrast between the performative utterance that offers "participation in the order of law" and the passionate utterance that "is an invitation in the disorder of desire" (185). As acts designed precisely to persuade others of one's assertions and demands, legal claims trouble not only Felstiner's ostensible tripartite sequencing of a dispute (discussed above), but also what Cavell apparently perceives as the conventionality of the "order of law." That legal claims often require thought, tact, and imagination, qualities that Cavell associates with passionate utterances, implies that any strong distinction between a conventional "order of law" and a passionate "disorder of desire" does not do justice to the appeal of legal speech or, ultimately, of any speech. (Might Cavell himself see this?[38])

Legal claims are utterances made in the name of the law. Speaking in the name of another is to speak as a proxy for or representative of that third-party other. Legal officials speak in the name of an ostensibly impersonal law when they make official claims, as did Cardozo in *Palsgraf*. Yet as Chapter Two also discussed, so too did Andrews dissent in the name of the law. Acts done in the name of the law, no less than acts done in the name of any third party, are vulnerable to not being as the represented party would have it. In being represented or invoked in name, law is the third party in whose name both official and nonofficial claimants speak.[39] It is a third party of a peculiar sort, in that it also functions as the first-person plural or "we" to which claimants, in their desire to persuade, would recall their hearers. In the name of the law, that is, officials engage retrospectively identifiable, concerned, addressee-hearers through seemingly conventional practices, although "citizens" and other hearers may equally well contest such official articulations in the name of law. As persuasive utterances, the legal speech acts of representatives of official law as well as the claims of their critics are performative and passionate, designed to evoke in their respective hearers a shared sense of obligation that is not only conventionally performed but also a matter of desire.

As social acts that address *you* in the name of "our" third-party law, even formal enactments or mandates can only *ask*—to draw on the Latin meaning of the term *mandare*—for their recognition as a claim of law from you. The assertions of a particular claim may be false and its demands unmet and even challenged, but recognition that a particular act is a claim shows that, as an act of claiming, of asserting and demanding, it belongs to desire and initiates a state of affairs in which particular sorts of responses are more appropriate than others. Contestations of its mandates are also claims, no less than the official announcements and enactments of positive law, all of which appeal in the name of law to who "we" are and how we judge what is to be done.

The *fulfillment* of claims as of other social acts, such as requests and invitations, that is, can be distinguished from their *accomplishment*. Claims are contestable social acts, subject to infelicities and other mishaps and failures of speech and action. They take place incompletely against a background of imperfect—incomplete, habitual, overlapping, often routine, yet interruptible—ways of speaking or of knowing our language and the world. Such imperfection refers not only to the open-endedness of a future perfect temporal structure but also to the relations of speakers and hearers. Imperfection belongs not only to assertion and to the fit of words to their so-called objects or world but also to speaking and hearing subjects who misspeak and misunderstand. Recall the discussion of the relation of the adverb "faithfully" to subject and object in Obama's oath: We imperfectly claim imperfectly.

Even within so-called community, claimants and knowers of a given law or language do not constitute a completely harmonious or cohesive whole. *You* may not accept my characterization not only of the world but also of who *we* are. That we at times neglect or ignore or even at times deceive one another indeed attests to the incomplete, sometimes interrupted, nevertheless ongoing character of our dialogic dance. Its "imperfect" aspect, grammatically speaking, corresponds to our speech and our bond. Imperfect, incompletely articulated shared knowledge of how we are speaking and living together is a precondition for the particular social acts that we know as legal acts to take place in a present, even as they will only be perfected or completed if ever in the future.

In sum, in the unfulfilled expectant present of a social act, the words and language we know, even unspoken, bind speaker-hearers to one another. Insofar as you understand my claim and accept my invitation to consider the question of who we are or, rather, the question of how we name our current concerns and differences, you engage with my desire and matters of "our" law. You deal with the issue. You in effect acknowledge my claim as being in a language you know, even if you do not yet, or ever, consider it right. Indeed you answer me (*I* answer *you*) with an objection, with denial, with protest, with excuse, with your (my) own passionate utterance. In lawsuits as elsewhere, we are joined in dialogue through our shared practices or common knowledges of speaking over the very issue, the naming and name of our law, that simultaneously divides us into plaintiff and defendant, official and accused.

. . .

This chapter has argued in part that imperfection or incompleteness in the sense of open-endedness, continuity, variability, and interruptibility are characteristics of human speech and action, as Austin and Arendt and many others point out. The chapter has also argued that speech and action cannot be disentangled from human community. Community, as the ragged commonality of knowledge of speakers and hearers, does not follow from acts of agreement but rather makes agreement, like other social acts, possible. The social character of legal acts suggests that "we" who are bound to one another in law do not follow from our promises, but are already—or will already have been—sharing, imperfectly, language and speech. That legal acts take place in the context of language and speech does not diminish the force of positive law. "So *saying*," Virgil's *Aeneid* concludes, "Aeneas buried his sword into his [opponent's] chest"—thereby founding Rome.[40]

When social contract theorists, in incarnations from Hobbes and Locke to Rawls and Habermas, seek to ground society in promises or in intersubjective agreement, they attribute to acts of speech *too* powerful a role. For, if promises or agreements are needed to transform a state of nature into a state of society, then we shall never get there. Either promises and agreements are impossible in a state of nature, or, if they are possible, they are possible only on the basis of a shared (practical) knowledge of language such that a society (in which social acts occur) already exists. In other words, social contract theories assert that language and promise *precede* and *produce* society or law. But to make promises, as well as to deceive, we must *already* be in society, capable both of negotiating conventional speech acts and of claiming and hearing the appeals that are made in the passionate utterances we address to one another in the name of "our" law. Even as we call on promises to be kept, our appeals take place in a world that need not meet our demands, as the next chapter discusses. It turns from the admittedly imperfect bond of language within communities of speaker-hearers to the situatedness of law and language in a larger world.

CHAPTER FOUR

When Words Go Wrong

The Master said, "If names are not correct, language is not in accordance with the truth of things. If language is not in accordance with the truth of things, affairs cannot be carried on to success."

—*Confucian Analects*, trans. James Legge, 1970[1]

In *The Scandal of the Speaking Body*, Shoshana Felman argues that the story of the philandering Don Juan and his unkept promises conveys a joint impossibility: that of keeping the promise of meaning and that of not promising and believing in promises.[2] In other words, she writes, literature shows the impossibility of choosing between giving the lie to one's words and not promising. Mortals will continue both to promise and to breach their promises. This chapter considers literature's insight that truth is the fallible promise of language in the context of law. It argues that if the promise of language is to reveal the world, then the claim of law is that promises—including those of language—must be kept. Law, one might say, insists imperfectly on keeping the impossible promises of language. Contract law and criminal law address through their words, however incompletely, the injustice that corresponds with the unhappiness of speech or the inadequacy of words to truth.

The chapter focuses on Euripides' *Hippolytus*,[3] the Greek play cited by J. L. Austin in the first lecture of *How to Do Things with Words*, to explore promising, the ur-example of speech act theory and the ostensible ground of law, before turning to modern contract law. In his first lecture, Austin contrasts his view of promising, as a conventional and performative act, with a mistaken view of a promise that he identifies with Hippolytus's utterance. A promise is neither a true-or-false description of a speaker's intention or state of mind nor an internal act, Austin argues, but depends on convention. Section One shows how Austin misreads Hippolytus's utterance, "my tongue swore, but my mind did not" even as he claims that "accuracy and morality alike are on the side of the plain saying that *our word is our bond*" (10). For those unfamiliar with *Hippolytus*:

> The play opens with Aphrodite, the goddess of love, marriage and procreation, declaring that she will punish Hippolytus, the son of Theseus, for not paying proper respect to her. She announces that she has made Phaedra, Theseus's wife and Hippolytus's stepmother, fall in love with him. Aphrodite will cause this to become known to Theseus, who will, through the curses that the god Poseidon has granted him, kill his son. Aphrodite declares that she "shall now show you the truth of these words" (9). Upon Hippolytus's return from the hunt, he indeed pays homage to the virgin goddess of the chase, Artemis, but disdainfully refuses, despite his old servant's urging, to honor Aphrodite with the appropriate salutations. The play then unfolds as Aphrodite has predicted. At a key moment, Phaedra, who has confided her secret to her Nurse, overhears Hippolytus proclaiming to the Nurse what vile things he has just heard. The Nurse shushes him and begs him to keep his oath, presumably to remain silent. He replies, "My tongue swore, my mind did not" (612). At the midpoint of the play, believing that her secret is out, Phaedra hangs herself backstage.

Despite what Austin and Phaedra think, Hippolytus does keep his word:

> Theseus returns as the frenzied Nurse and Chorus announce Phaedra's death. He finds in his dead wife's hands a written tablet that "cries out insufferable things" (877). Echoing and inverting what in part Phaedra had overheard Hippolytus saying to the Nurse (589–90), Theseus learns that Hippolytus "dared to touch my marriage bed by force" (885–6). Over the appeals of the Chorus, he calls on Poseidon, god of the sea, to use the first of the three curses that he has promised to Theseus, on Hippolytus. Hippolytus reappears, oblivious to what has just happened. He denies Theseus's angry accusation and protests his virtue without revealing his conversation with the Nurse. He swears an oath to Zeus, the god of oaths, to no apparent avail. Theseus proclaims that Hippolytus be exiled: if Poseidon does not kill him, he will be forced to wander foreign soil. After Hippolytus leaves, a messenger enters and informs Theseus that Hippolytus's life hangs "by a slender thread." As Hippolytus sets out along the beach, the messenger reports, Hippolytus's horses, spooked by a sound like thunder as a wild bull roared out of the sea, entangled him in their reins. Hippolytus is brought back to the palace where, as he lies dying, Artemis urges his forgiveness of Theseus and swears that Hippolytus will not be forgotten.

Accuracy and morality have more complicated relations to the bond of words than Austin implies, the chapter goes on to argue. Were Hippolytus to have broken his promise, he might have—accurately—refuted Phaedra's lies to Theseus about himself and—morally—defended himself against false accusations. That

Hippolytus dies for his oath of course also forcefully reveals the greatness of Austin's insight that words are serious bonds. They implicate mortals as much in the disorder of desire, as Cavell puts it, as in the order of law.

Section Two draws on Hippolytus's and Phaedra's passionate utterances to show how words bind mortals, not simply to one another, but in a world that exceeds conventional moral demands and challenges assertions of accuracy. Section Three transfers this insight to a modern context, showing how contract law and criminal law, as well as the laws encountered in earlier chapters, like Hippolytus's unfortunate utterance, acknowledge the fallibility of human speech and action, even as they seek to counter it. In short, promises and claims are both imperfect. Nevertheless, the chapter concludes, just as language promises truth, or to show the world as it is, so too law claims justice or to hold us to our words through its own jointly passionate and performative utterances.

Note that "truth" here refers not to the mere accuracy of propositions nor to the correspondence of propositional statements to external realities. Neither does it refer to the coherence of language use among subjects speaking the same tongue. Rather, at issue in the truth of language is the showing or revealing of a world that is not completely of human making, through a human capacity to speak that is not completely within human control.[4] At issue in law, likewise, is the perpetual danger that speech may go awry, whether through human fallibility or deceit or through the recalcitrance of a world that need not show itself to be as humans, with their imperfect and incomplete conventional moralities and articulations, would have it.

One. "My Tongue Swore . . .": Passionate Utterance

Austin turns to Hippolytus's promise to highlight his own view that the felicity or success of (what he at first calls) a performative utterance is a matter of fulfilling appropriate conventions. That Austin misreads or misremembers *Hippolytus* is not crucial to his own argument. He argues that there is more to a promise than intention. (Searle conversely emphasizes that some inner life is needed to promise. Derrida reads Austin as if Austin were Searle; Cavell attempts to mediate.[5]) Settling whether intentions or conventions are more important to promises is not the point here. Rather, the infelicity, or at least incompleteness, of Austin's reading of Hippolytus's utterance enables two insights: first, into the limitations of taking promises and other utterances to be purely conventional social acts that can be grasped in terms of accuracy and morality; and, second, into the ways that passion may call forth conventional performance or into the ways that what Cavell calls "invitation into the disorders of desire" may be congruent with appeals to "the order of law."

A promise, recall Austin argues, is not "true" or "false" in terms of its propositional content; like an oath, it may be complete or incomplete, valid or void, sincere or insincere, depending on circumstance. The mistaken view, against which Austin argues, would maintain that any utterance that makes sense reflects what is going on in someone's mind. The mistaken view would make of a promise, for instance, "(merely) the outward and visible sign, for convenience or other record or for information, of an inward and spiritual act" (9). From here, Austin claims,

> It is but a short step to go on to believe or to assume without realizing that for many purposes the outward utterance is a description, true or false, of the inward performance. The classic expression of this idea is to be found in the *Hippolytus* (l. 612), where Hippolytus says . . . i.e. "my tongue swore to, but my heart (or mind or other backstage artiste) did not." (9)

Countering a view that would equate acting, and hence responsibility, with what someone wills or intends, Austin writes, "One who says 'promising is . . . an inward and spiritual act!' is apt to appear as a solid moralist . . . Yet he provides Hippolytus with a let-out, the bigamist with an excuse for his 'I do' and the welsher with a defence for his 'I bet'" (10). In other words, he fails to recognize, Austin continues, that "accuracy and morality alike are on the side of the plain saying that *our word is our bond*" (10).

It is appropriate for a promisor to have a certain intention, Austin acknowledges. But lack of intention to keep one's word—such as Austin attributes to Hippolytus, based on line 612—makes a promise "misleading," "deceitful," or "wrong," he argues. (In Reinach's terms, it is "shadowy" or "inauthentic.") It does not make the utterance a false statement or a misstatement or a lie. It is, rather, a promise "given in bad faith" (which we may also call a "'false' promise"). If it turns out to be beyond the speaker's power, it is "not implemented" or not able to be implemented (11). A promise, however insincere or deceitful, has been made, one says accurately, according to Austin, when the utterance fulfills certain external or conventional requirements. And morality, according to Austin again, calls for that promise to be kept.

When Hippolytus says, "My tongue swore, but my mind did not," then, Austin takes him to mean to say that he has not actually promised, although admitting that he uttered the words. Hippolytus appears to Austin to follow the mistaken view that equates a promise with an act of intention. Austin refuses to provide Hippolytus with such a let-out. Hippolytus's earlier words, however insincere, he insists, constitute a promise. (Interestingly, those words are never heard onstage; the "backstage artiste" is Hippolytus's tongue, not his mind—or perhaps Austin's mind, not his ears!) They involve acting in a particular way that corresponds with conventions of promising. In acknowledging the insincerity of his words, Hippolytus now in effect seeks—immorally, Austin suggests—to repudiate his earlier promise or action. Hippolytus's utterance at line 612 or the illocutionary act in which Hippolytus now engages, to use the terminology of Austin's later lectures, amounts to disavowal or repudiation of an earlier illocutionary, if infelicitous, act of promising.

Repudiation or disavowal is indeed how Hippolytus's stepmother Phaedra, overhearing at least part of Hippolytus's conversation with her Nurse and reporting what she hears to the Chorus, seems to understand Hippolytus's words. Recall that, for Austin, an illocutionary act need not take any particular grammatical form (103), although as a performative utterance, it can be made explicit by the first-person present indicative active formula: *I repudiate my words*, for instance, or *I hereby declare that I shall not keep my promise*. Phaedra hears Hippolytus berating the Nurse for what the Nurse has apparently divulged to him of his stepmother's desire for him. Phaedra takes Hippolytus's words to be, in the context of his refusal to be quiet, if not direct repudiation of a promise, at least an indication that her secret is out. She kills herself on the basis of this premature understanding, leaving the written tablet with its false accusation. Phaedra acts out of an (honorable) shame about her (dishonorable) passion so as to preclude its revelation.

Hippolytus, however, does keep his word, not as a promise to the Nurse, as Austin seems to have it, but as an oath to the gods. The Nurse has no power to relieve him of his commitment. Oaths and promises, as social acts, both involve giving one's word to another. A promise creates in a promisee a claim against the promisor to an obligation that the promisee (not to be confused with a possible third-party beneficiary) has the power to revoke.[6] By contrast, the power to release someone from an oath appears to be in the power of the one *in whose name* it is sworn. (Recall Obama's oath, uttered before Chief Justice Roberts and made in the name of God, although presumably given to the American people.[7])

That Austin does not simply take Hippolytus to be breaking his word but also equates his oath with a promise, testifies to the twentieth-century absence of the gods! So too does Scalia's twenty-first century dismissal of the relevance of the oath to testimony (in Chapter One). In English common law, oaths used to function through appeal to God. In the "old days," writes Maitland, oaths (along with ordeals) used to be common modes of proof in actions of debt. "It is adjudged," Maitland writes,

> in an action for debt that the defendant do prove his assertion that he owes nothing by his own oath and the oaths of a certain number of compurgators, or oath-helpers. The defendant must then solemnly swear that he owes nothing, and his oath-helpers must swear that his oath is clean and unperjured. If they safely get through this ceremony, punctually repeating the right formula, there is an end of the case; the plaintiff, if he is hardy enough to go on, can only do so by bringing a new charge, a criminal charge of perjury against them. They have not come there to convince the court, they have not come there to be examined and cross-examined like modern witnesses, they have come there to bring upon themselves the wrath of God if what they say be not true.[8]

This process, Maitland continues, "is known in England as 'making one's law'; a litigant who is adjudged to prove his case in this way is said to 'wage his law' (*vadiare legem*) when he finds security that on a future day he will bring compurgators and perform this solemnity" (15–16). Contrast the "solemnity" here with the solemnity that Scalia attributes to unsworn testimony.

Hippolytus recognizes the bindingness of his oath. He even tells the Nurse, in the context of his rant against women shortly after line 612, that he will keep his oath:

> My piety saves you:
> if I hadn't been caught off guard by taking oaths to the gods,
> I would never have kept from declaring this to my father.
> But, as things are, I will go away from the house so long as Theseus
> is out of the country, and I will keep my mouth silent. (656–660)

That Hippolytus keeps his word and stays silent suggests that there is a way of understanding line 612 that neither returns to a mistaken view of the line as a true-false or constative utterance, nor accepts Phaedra's interpretation of it as performing an illocutionary act of repudiation. This alternative, as we shall see, shows how the binding of words involves more than either a dynamic conventional act of promising or an again conventional human morality that calls for the keeping of promises. That Hippolytus keeps his word suggests that his outburst is a *passionate* utterance. And it occurs, as Section Two will show, against the backdrop of a world of imperfect mortal speech.

Recall from earlier chapters Cavell's description of a passionate utterance as an utterance that "makes demands upon" another "in a way that an illocutionary force (if all goes well) forgoes" (173). The illocutionary act is conventional and reparable, he points out. A performative utterance can be undone, he suggests; passionate utterance, in being defined through its perlocutionary effects on another, cannot. In principle, promises can be repudiated. But repudiation of Hippolytus's oath is not so simple; the utterance through which he ostensibly tries to do so is, in Cavell's terms, a passionate one.

As Cavell indicates, the passionate utterance that is designed to have an effect on you requires more than a speaker's knowledge of conventions. It requires the skillful singling out of a second person. "Failure to have singled you out appropriately in passionate utterance," Cavell explains, "characteristically puts the future of our relationship, as part of my sense of my identity, or of my existence, more radically at stake. One can say: the 'you' singled out comes into play in relation to the declaration of the 'I' who thereby takes upon itself a definition of itself, in, as it may prove, a casual or fateful form" (184–185). Insofar as the "I" defines itself in terms of its moving (persuading, seducing, disappointing) you, the passionate utterance "appears as deeply characteristic and revelatory of both the utterer and his or her addressee" (180).

Insofar as legal claims aim to persuade, Chapters One and Three argued, they are not only performative but also passionate. So too Hippolytus's utterance. Hippolytus's remark follows the previously mentioned scene in which the horrified Phaedra, with whom Hippolytus never speaks directly in the play, overhears part of his conversation with the Nurse. Phaedra has called for the Chorus to be silent and describes to the Chorus leader what she hears. Hippolytus, she cries, "clearly declares [the Nurse] 'matchmaker of evils,' 'betrayer of your master's bed'" (589–590). Immediately afterwards, Hippolytus appears on stage, exclaiming over the "unspeakable words I heard uttered" (602). In several sentence-long turn-taking exchanges (stichomythia) with the Nurse, Hippolytus goes on about what he has just heard, while the Nurse begs him to be quiet and to honor his oath. Hippolytus finally answers with the famous, "My tongue is sworn, my mind unsworn" (612).

The dialogue between Hippolytus and the Nurse shows Hippolytus's growing aggravation with the Nurse as she continues to shush him, following what he takes to be her shameful disclosure of Phaedra's dishonorable lust for him. Several lines express his indignation and repugnance over what the Nurse has revealed. (Or perhaps what she has proposed. Like Hippolytus's earlier oath of silence, the Nurse's earlier words to him are neither heard by the spectators nor conveyed by Phaedra's description of what she overhears.) Hippolytus's words at line 612 show his profound dismay at the way in which his earlier words have bound him to something that is not virtuous at all: Keeping his oath, as virtue demands, binds him to concealing his repugnance at the Nurse's revelations. His earlier words, he passionately protests to the Nurse, have bound him to a world in which all is not right; they have committed him to injustice. His exclamation expresses anger, at himself perhaps as much as at the Nurse, as he realizes that he has committed himself—or his tongue has sworn him—through the earlier words of his backstage oath, to silence about something the shameful nature of which he—or his mind—has only now come to know. His words appear designed to upset and shame the Nurse as she has upset and shamed him.

Hippolytus's words engage and confront the Nurse precisely over matters of convention and law, in an unconventional way. He does not quite repudiate his promise or oath, nor quite ask to be released from it. Instead, his words "make demands upon" the Nurse for recognition of the injustice of the position in which he claims they now find themselves. His words involve a claim on his part as to the injustice of a world that would require oaths such as his to be kept and an invitation to the Nurse to share in his passionate desire for something else. Again neither quite repudiation nor request, Hippolytus's utterance entangles him in the messiness of happenings in the world, even more deeply than the Nurse had done in revealing Phaedra's passion and presumably inviting him into the disorder of desire.

On its face, then, Hippolytus's "my tongue swore, my mind did not" may be read, as Austin seems to have done, as a classic expression of a mistaken view that equates promising with a mental act or intention. It can also be read, though, as a proposition toward which Austin might indeed have been sympathetic: There is something unsatisfactory about a promise in which one commits oneself without quite knowing to what. The utterance may even be read as the illocutionary act of proclaiming the infelicitousness of the earlier oath or promise. It can be read as Phaedra and the Nurse seem to hear it: as a conventional repudiation of an earlier promise, as an ultimately ineffective yet felicitous speech act of protest against the promise, as an unmet demand for recognition of the unfairness of being bound to the oath, as a rejection of the Nurse's invitation, and so forth.

More to the point, as a passionate utterance that fails to persuade the Nurse, line 612 reveals, in fateful form, who and what Hippolytus is: a self-righteous and chaste prince, dedicated to the virgin goddess Artemis, whose pious commitment to virtue has led him, in his angry response to the Nurse's revelations of Phaedra's shameful desires, precisely to "improvisation in the disorders of desire," as he threatens not to keep an earlier oath that he has made to the gods. Furthermore, the Nurse's subsequent protest against his words—a self-interested appeal that he not harm his "friends" by speaking—in turn challenges who and what he has revealed himself in his passionate utterance to be: no friend to her or to her impure mistress. Passionately appealing to Hippolytus to stick to the conventions of his earlier performative act, the Nurse's utterance, like that of Hippolytus at line 612, again reveals a role for passion and desire in calling for the performance of conventional acts.

That, despite his passionate outburst, the virtuous, chaste and pious Hippolytus ultimately and yet fatally keeps his oath suggests that the binding of words involves both passion and performance. *Our word is our bond* is not quite as "plain" a "saying" as Austin suggests, although the bonds of words are indeed great. Accuracy and morality alike are not necessarily on the side of keeping promises: Hippolytus's keeping of his word sustains inaccuracy and leads to the condemnation of an innocent man. Silences and utterances entangle Hippolytus, like other mortals, as we shall see, in both the order of law and the disorder of desire.

Two. Binding Words: Hippolytus and Phaedra

The unfolding of the events of the tragedy of *Hippolytus* reveal much about how human speech and action go wrong. The play is chock-full of dynamic utterances or social acts, divine and human: oaths, promises, declarations, predictions, accusations, supplications, wishes, curses, rebuttals, proclamations, repudiations, acknowledgments, and so on. The speech acts of the gods are effective (or "magic"); those of humans continually go awry. Not only Aphrodite's predictions, but those of Artemis, and the curses of Poseidon, come true. Artemis calls on Hippolytus to forgive Theseus ("I urge you not to hate your father" [1435]) and promises to establish a cult for Hippolytus. Hippolytus forgives Theseus before dying ("I dissolve the strife with my father, since you wish it" [1442]), and such a cult indeed existed, as contemporary audiences would have known. Artemis also takes care of Hippolytus's own oath to Zeus, that if he be an evil man he perish with no name, by swearing that unmarried maidens will not only offer locks of their hair but also sing songs to him so that Phaedra's love will not "fall away nameless and be kept silent" (1424–1430). Even the secondhand curse of Poseidon, promised by Poseidon to Theseus and invoked by Theseus against Hippolytus, is effective. In destroying Hippolytus (by sending a wild bull from out of the sea), Poseidon "gave [to Theseus] only what he had to, since he had agreed," explains Artemis (1319).

In contrast to divine speech, human speech in *Hippolytus* is susceptible to all manner of difficulties. Words are not false as such, other than those in Phaedra's tablet, which, significantly, is written. Words are spoken "rashly" (119), go "too far" (924), and "go astray" (934). They are spoken in excess, in haste (Theseus), in anger (Hippolytus), in pride (Hippolytus), and in weakness (Phaedra). They both hide and reveal. "Fine words" hide what is not fine (988), destroying "well-governed cities" (486–487), while others reveal shameful things that should stay hidden (363). There is no assurance that speech reveals truth nor that any truth that speech reveals is a happy one. Words "foretell woe" (881); they show the "unendurable" (354, 875), the "insufferable" (877), even the "unspeakable" (602, 875).

Moreover, words are concealed by many, including Hippolytus and the Chorus of married women. They are not said by those who should speak them (Hippolytus to Aphrodite); they are spoken by those who claim to prefer silence (Phaedra to Nurse); they are told to those who should not hear them by those who should not speak (Nurse to Hippolytus); they are heard by those for whom they are not intended (Phaedra). They are misheard or misunderstood (Phaedra of Hippolytus; Theseus and Hippolytus of one another). Human utterances are unhappy as acts, unsuccessful as speech, and infelicitous as performances. They "misfire" and are "abused," to use Austin's terminology.[9]

Human words are tied to morality, as Austin suggests, as well as to mortality and the body. Phaedra's words are linked as much to honor and shame (*aidos*, meaning not only shame but also the modesty or respect or reverence that is the opposite of dishonor) as Hippolytus's are linked to *sophrosyne* or temperance and moderation. In his pious devotion to chastity and the purity of the virgin goddess Artemis and his rejection of the virtues of Aphrodite, Hippolytus appears almost pathological. Phaedra by contrast is sick with shame. Early in the play, responding to the Nurse, the delirious Phaedra reluctantly confesses her feelings for Hippolytus with a locution that foreshadows and inverts that of Hippolytus: "My hands are pure, my mind polluted" (317). Phaedra's utterance not only parallels Hippolytus's passionate utterance at line 612, but is also "deeply characteristic and revelatory" of who she is (Cavell 180). She can admit her shame only because of her relation to her Nurse. Out of concern for her honor, she asks the Nurse not to tell anyone of her love for Hippolytus, whose name she cannot even bear to utter (another crucial silence). Her concern for honor or reputation, also a matter of words, is such that when she overhears part of the Nurse's conversation with Hippolytus, she immediately expresses her fear that, through her disgrace, her children too will lose their own good name.[10]

In choosing whether to speak, Phaedra and Hippolytus appear to follow human moralities or laws. (Phaedra does not share the [slightly later] Socratic view that "no one errs knowingly." She tells the Chorus, "We know what's good and we recognize it, but we don't toil to accomplish it, some through laziness, others because they have given priority to some pleasure other than the good." [377–381]) Phaedra submits to social conventions (*nomoi*) of honor and shame (*aidos*) that accord good reputation or good name to moderation and disgrace to passion. Hippolytus devotes himself to piety even as his very mortal commitment to virtue or chastity (*sôphron*)[11] leads him to favor one goddess over another and binds him to his oath to be silent. Further, in his exchange with and condemnation of Hippolytus, Theseus also judges on the basis of human laws or conventions. He judges as husband, father, ruler. He draws inferences from his wife's written text that he uses as a basis for "persuasive" argument. He refuses to be swayed by Hippolytus's oaths of chastity or to turn to divination or prophets or other kinds of trials (1053). Many of Theseus's accusations and Hippolytus's rebuttals, like line 612, can be characterized as conventional performative utterances or illocutionary speech acts; commentators sometimes refer to Theseus's and Hippolytus's agonistic exchange as a scene of hearing or trial. But the utterances of the two, spoken at cross-purposes, are also social acts or passionate utterances that anger, astonish, disgrace, outrage, and humiliate the other and indeed are designed to do so (1038–1101).

In death, Hippolytus and Phaedra are literally bound up with words. Before hanging herself and leaving the lying tied-up tablet, Phaedra asks herself how she can "loosen the knot of words" that ties her (670–671). The messenger tells

Theseus that the injured Hippolytus's life hangs "by a slender thread" (Kovacs, 1162–1163)[12]; Hippolytus's horses entangled him in their reins. Bound by the words of one of his earlier oaths to the gods, he has been "thrown in the air" above the beach and dragged by his horses in a zigzag course (1200–1230) such that in keeping with those earlier words he is received by "neither land nor sea" (1030).

Finally, for all Hippolytus's disdain of the body and of the passion that Aphrodite represents and his chaste adoration of the virgin goddess Artemis, his fate is bound to his body. He is condemned by his own "tongue" in having sworn as well as by Phaedra's "pure hand." Phaedra's fate too comes from overhearing Hippolytus's words and by her own hand. Although Phaedra and Hippolytus neither speak to nor touch one another, their mortal words bind them in bodily ways. Given the role of bodies and desires in the unhappiness of the speech and action of human beings, it is perhaps not coincidental that the gods do not manifest themselves to mortals in bodily form. Artemis is invisible, a scent for Hippolytus and a sound; Aphrodite is a statue at the threshold of the palace. Poseidon and Zeus do not appear in the play except in successful, if ultimately tragic, invocations of curses and oaths.

Words and silence represent the horns of an impossible dilemma for Hippolytus and Phaedra. If Hippolytus speaks the words he has heard, he breaks the word he has given; if he stays silent, he is true to his word but allows the false world of Phaedra's written words to stand. When he speaks he is misunderstood; when he is silent he shows disrespect. He tells Theseus, "It is not right for me to say more" (1033); "I will not . . . violate the oaths which I swore" (1063); and "I know these things but I don't know how to reveal them" (1091).

It is not only Hippolytus's own reticence that seals his doom, however. His silence itself comes from his earlier oath, the words and performance of which spectators must infer. The Chorus, too, keeps its promise to Phaedra (709–714) to stay silent. The Chorus can only appeal to Theseus: "By the gods, take this back and undo this prayer; for you will recognize later that you erred" (891–892) in an apparent mirroring of the Nurse's passionate appeal to Hippolytus to keep his promise. Just as Hippolytus fails to take back his words and so keeps his promise, so too Theseus fails to take back his words, responding, "Impossible." He does not follow through on the "reparability" to which his prayer to Poseidon, as an ostensibly conventional utterance, would be subject in Cavell's account. In yet another silence, Theseus also fails to investigate the words he finds when he unties Phaedra's tablet, as the Chorus and Hippolytus urge him to do.

For her part, if Phaedra stays silent, she conceals the truth of the passion from which she suffers. When she speaks, as she does to her Nurse, she reveals her shame and risks her reputation and that of her children, a matter so serious, she would rather die! And her writings, however persuasive, lie. So too does argument: Theseus's argument is "persuasive," Hippolytus concedes, but not "in fact." The words of the tablet that Theseus unties and cannot hold within the gates of his mouth (883) entrap him into confronting and condemning Hippolytus without properly waiting for proofs and prophets. Phaedra's dying words "cry aloud," and despite his suspiciousness about the live Hippolytus's words, Theseus considers Phaedra's written ones "witness most reliable" (970).[13] As in Plato's *Phaedrus*, so too in Euripides' *Hippolytus*, writings always say one and the same thing: "If one asks them a question, they preserve a solemn silence"; they need their authors if they are to say more (*Phaedrus* 259 d–e). Or, as Artemis later says to Theseus, "Your wife in dying did away with the refutation of her words, so that she persuaded your mind" (1335–1337).

Mortals are bound then to conventional human moralities and laws, as well as to their unruly bodies, desires, and words. But that is not all to which they are subject. In the words of the Chorus:

> Greatly does the gods' concern, when it comes to mind,
> relieve my distress; and although one conceals his understanding in hope,
> he falls short of it when looking among the fortunes and deeds of mortals.
> For things come and go from here and there, and the life of men changes,
> always wandering. (1104–1110)

Men and women are subject to "fortune" (*tuxê*) (268, 679, 673, 818, 827, 832), to "fate" (679, *moira*) (1434), to "destiny and necessity" (*moira tou xreôn t'*) (1256), and to the desires and judgments of the gods. Gods do follow some conventions or law. (Indeed the "all too human" character of the Greek gods is frequently remarked.) The law (*nomos*) that hates pride in mortals (90–95), for instance, is shared by the gods. It justifies proud Aphrodite's anger at the pride manifest in Hippolytus's disdain for the conventional act of respectful prayer to her and in his rash words about her (102–113). Artemis follows conventions of moral and criminal responsibility that are compatible with those of today (discussed in Chapter Two, Section One). She considers, for instance, the extent to which Theseus acted "knowingly." She first accuses Theseus of killing Hippolytus, then extends the excuse of his ignorance to him. Theseus killed Hippolytus who,

Artemis claims, did not "retract the pledge of his oath when he was abused by you, since he is pious by birth" (1308–1309). "Your not knowing," though, "frees your error from wickedness," Artemis says later (1334); and again, "In ignorance you killed him" (1433).

The laws of the gods are not identical to human law. The "custom" (*nomos*) that holds among gods prevents Artemis, for instance, from directly opposing the expressed desire of Aphrodite (1328–1329). Instead, she initiates, as Aphrodite has done earlier, her own vengeful actions. After the messenger tells Theseus of Hippolytus's accident with the horses, Artemis swears to take vengeance herself on "whatever mortal is [Aphrodite's] very dearest" (1422), while giving Hippolytus "the greatest honors in the city" (1424).

In contrast to the many ways in which human speech acts go wrong, divinities magically effectuate "I avenge myself on you!" among themselves in simultaneously happy and felicitous, performative and passionate, social acts. Emerging out of passion and designed precisely to affect others, yet ruled by conventions of speech and judgment, the speech acts of the gods unerringly do what they say and cannot be directly contravened. Their words provoke responses. And, in a world of other gods, those responses too take effect. The gods' speech acts thus bind them into endless improvisational chains of intention and act, act and effect, response and revenge.

As happenings that cannot always be taken back or undone and in accord with a "law" that trumps the conventions of human beings then, speech acts bind both gods and mortals *and* bind gods and mortals together through curses and oaths. The speech produced by the tongues and hands and apprehended by the ears and eyes of mortals shows human speech acts to be convoluted happenings that bind human beings to one another unhappily even beyond their lifetimes. The conventions or laws of custom (*nomos*), honor (*aidos*), moderation (*sophrosune*), and virtue (*sophrôn*) that ostensibly govern mortals and their acts cannot rule what lies beyond human control: not only their own desires and those of others, but fate or fortune and the wills and passions of gods.

Human attempts to abide by conventional standards of morality and law, including those of social honor (Phaedra) and piety (Hippolytus), are subject to interference from powers and desires beyond their control and beyond their speech. Although Hippolytus is bound by various oaths, including that to silence, and Phaedra is, arguably in another sense, bound by Aphrodite to speak her secret passion, the choice offered to mortals between silence and speech is not symmetrical. For Hippolytus and Phaedra, as for other mortals in the play, *speech comes out of silence* and, once out, even ostensibly conventional performative utterances go wrong and are not easily taken back. Like the Nurse in her indiscretion and Theseus in his proclamations, and as is presumed in the formulation of the contemporary right to *remain* silent, Hippolytus's and Phaedra's choice is to *stay* silent or to speak; their choice is not to stay speaking or to be silent. As in *Miranda*, the choice to remain silent or to speak occurs against a backdrop of common and imperfect knowledge of speaking and of the world. Conventional moral commitments (to honor and to piety, in Hippolytus's and Phaedra's case) inform but do not determine their choices.

Human speech is in such a state that even truth and justice, at least in their conventional guises of accuracy and morality, appear to side against the innocent Hippolytus's keeping his promise not to speak of what he hears from the Nurse. His oaths lead him to an unjust fate. His fate, like that of Phaedra, shows how words and deeds, and words as deeds, performative and passionate, bind mortals to one another in a world in which there is no guarantee of justice, despite passionate human calls for it. The wayward speech of unhappy mortals in *Hippolytus* binds them to unruly fates in a dramatic world that is no more subject to the conventional standards of human laws and moralities than is the modern world—to which the final section now turns.

Three. Contracts and the Promises of Law and Language

Euripides' *Hippolytus* depicts a range of difficulties with human words and promises. Despite these kinds of difficulties, human affairs rely on the words with which we speak and judge. Speaking and judging must rely on the promise that words suit the world or that speech reveals truth, although often they do not. Speaking and judging rely too on assurances that promises will be kept and agreements will be met, although often they will not. Recognition that the promise of language is impossible to guarantee appears not only in literature, as in *Hippolytus*, but also in law, this section shows. Indeed, law addresses just such impossibility. Contract law, for instance, responds to the passionate calls for justice made in the face of the surprises and injustices that beset humans and their speech acts of agreement. It cannot do so seamlessly, however. Even as utterances and acts of contract law epitomize in many ways the conventionality of promises and the illocutionary aspect of speech that Austin draws attention to, the interventions of contract law themselves are, like Hippolytus's utterance at line 612, simultaneously passionate and performative, all-too-human claims.

Contract law enforces promissory agreements. A growing literature proposes the irrelevance of theories of promise to contract,[14] but the still-dominant view follows the Restatements' link of the two. Restatements are treatises, prepared by the now-4,000-member American Law Institute (ALI)[15] of lawyers, judges, and teachers, to combat the complexity and uncertainty of the common law and to systematize common law principles. Begun in 1923, the Restatements appeared in a second series in the 1950s and in a third in the late 1980s. Despite their status as secondary authority, ALI publications are extremely influential. In addition to developing Restatements and Model Codes, the ALI worked with the National Conference of Commissioners on Uniform State Laws to design the Uniform Commercial Code (UCC), which has been adopted, with regional variations, in forty-nine states.

The systematization of common law principles in the Restatements and the format of the ALI's Model Codes lend themselves to being read as statements of rules and may reinforce a sense of law as a system of rules. As earlier chapters have shown, though, law involves more than statements of rules, and ostensible statements of rules are more than they appear. The agreements of contract law, no less than the subject matters of other areas of law, involve much more than formal doctrines.[16] Further, no system of rules is completely discrete.

Contract law then, as a body of law that appears recognizably even if incompletely in texts often taken to be offering rules, protects promissory agreements and modulates unfairness related to them. It does so in the name of what have, tellingly, come to be called parties' "expectation" interests. Expectation interests are threatened precisely by the unexpected or surprising events that happen in a world, as in *Hippolytus*, that human beings do not completely control.

Protecting agreements and modulating unfairness may pull in different directions. To protect agreements, contract law tries to ensure that particular accepted conventions—of social acts of offer and acceptance, for instance—are followed. To assess unfairness, it looks more broadly to the entirety of circumstances in which an agreement was made (Austin's "total speech situation"). A valid agreement may be unfair; a technically improper agreement may be fair. Either may be upheld or rejected. When an agreement is upheld, the remedy for its breach is often not the performance of the promise by the breaching party, but some form of compensation.

Contract law, like Austin, does not take the outward utterance of the social acts of either offer or acceptance that constitute agreement to be a "description, true or false, of . . . inward performance." Nor does it consider promising to be an "inward and spiritual act" (9). Agreement is neither a matter of correspondence with, nor a representation of the coincidence of, two parties' mental states or inward acts. Rather, contracts or the agreements that constitute them are matters of accepted conventions and ritualized procedures, which nevertheless change over time.[17] In today's contract law, an agreement is a matter of successfully executed or felicitous offer and acceptance.

Writers on contracts indeed illustrate Austin's (passionate) utterance that "you will appreciate that in this way and that writers on jurisprudence have constantly shown themselves aware of the varieties of infelicity and even at times of the peculiarities of the performative utterance" (19). Contract law addresses precisely the issues, discussed in Chapter One, that Austin identifies as relevant to the success of a performative utterance: Does an existing law govern this type of agreement? And, if so, which one? Do these promises constitute an agreement? Are these parties entitled to offer and accept the terms that they have? Have the terms of the agreement been articulated correctly and completely? How is one to deal with a misunderstanding between the parties? What is to be done when the world changes such that the terms of the agreement become impossible to carry out?

The history of contract law testifies to legal recognition of agreement as a conventional social act. The shift in contract law from a "meeting of the minds" to an ostensible "reasonable person" standard for determining that an agreement has been made, disputes and tensions as to the "subjective intent" versus "objective meaning" of contractual terms, and the demise of the nineteenth-century "will theory" of promise in favor of the modern "bargain test" for identifying the "consideration" necessary for agreement, epitomize the sorts of issues that surround speech acts. They accord with the dialogic quality of agreement.

That contract law recognizes agreement as a conventional speech act or, rather, a set of social acts does not mean that contracts completely coincide with, or have ever completely coincided with, promises. The Restatements' bargain test for determining the existence of an enforceable agreement is said to have supplanted an earlier "will theory" in which "a promise was enforceable because the promisor had 'willed' to be bound by the promise."[18] Even this earlier "willing" had required conventional and external communication, however, of the sort

Austin maintains of the promise. The modern requirement of "consideration," understood as a benefit to a promisor and a detriment to the promisee, followed from requirements for proof in the common law action of assumpsit (an action to recover damages for a breach of implied or express promise).[19] The Restatements redefined *consideration* in terms of "bargain," such that something is bargained for "if it is sought by the promisor in exchange for his promise and is given to the promisor in exchange for that promise."[20]

The contemporary legal requirement that there must be a bargain or exchange for an agreement to be enforceable makes some promises unenforceable that might formerly have been enforceable, such as those made outside of the marketplace in a family setting. In 1891, for instance, the New York Court of Appeals upheld an uncle's promise to pay his teenage nephew $5,000 on his twenty-first birthday if the nephew did not smoke, drink, or gamble before then.[21] The (unanimous) Court maintained in *Hamer v. Sidway* that, although the uncle was not benefited by the nephew's abstinence, the nephew's forbearance of a legal right constituted "consideration" for the promise, so that the agreement was binding. (See Baird's wonderful account filling out the "facts" of the case and offering alternative bases for possible rulings.[22])

As analysis of benefits and detriments has largely given way to requirements that contracts occur through bargaining or the mutual exchange of something of value, the act of acceptance has become key. In the context of a unilateral contract or of a contract where a promise is given in exchange for an act, as in *Hamer v. Sidway*, rather than in exchange for another promise, looking for an explicit speech act or utterance of "acceptance" becomes inappropriate.[23] A famous law school hypothetical illustrates the difficulties that the lack of a speech act of acceptance raises for a contract law that would enforce the bilateral exchange of spoken promises. A promises B $100 to climb to the top of a flagpole. Without speaking, B starts climbing. When B is one foot from the top of the flagpole, A revokes his promise. B sues. Attempts to resolve the case, as does U.S. law, on the basis of B's performing in "reliance" on A's promise, ground themselves in an expectation of detriment or harm to B that would not have occurred *but for* the promise. Such a utilitarian justification for a judgment in favor of B ignores that a promise, as a social act, creates not only an obligation on the part of a promisor but also a claim on the part of the promissee, in this case B, who would be the one entitled to grant the promisor any right of revocation.[24]

In addition to discounting some promises and making some previously enforceable agreements unenforceable, the bargain test of contract law also conversely makes some promises enforceable that might otherwise have been unenforceable. Before the Restatements' identification of contract with bargain, "unconscionability" or unfairness made some arbitration agreements (which provide for bypassing legal mechanisms in cases of dispute) and contracts of adhesion (which sell necessary goods) unenforceable. Under the new approach, unconscionability must be reconfigured in terms of bargaining power. In such reconfiguration, courts strain to reconcile "the ends of justice" with the procedural requirements of bargain.[25]

Over time, in other words, the edifices constructed by contract law around such doctrines as "unconscionability" and around such formalities as the "consideration" that ostensibly seals a bargain and makes of it an enforceable social act of agreement fail to coincide completely with any particular principle of morality, including the precept that promises must be kept. Just as conventional human standards of morality conflict in *Hippolytus* (keeping promises and not punishing an innocent man), so too in contract law. Articulations of human positive law conflict not only with its own prior articulations but also with the conventional morality of keeping promises. The world fails to conform once and for all to human standards, in contract law as in *Hippolytus*.

Contract remedies highlight the divergence of law from conventional morality, insofar as the latter is taken to require the keeping of promises.[26] Even in cases of breaches of clearly enforceable bilateral agreements, that is, law seldom requires fulfillment or actual or "specific performance" of a promise. Contract law most often remedies the breach of a promise (made in the context of an enforceable agreement) through the imposition of (monetary) damages. (Here contract law diverges from *Hippolytus*. Imagine the Nurse offering to pay Hippolytus for keeping quiet or Hippolytus paying off the Nurse, or Phaedra's children, for breaking his oath to remain silent![27])

That the broken promises of breached enforceable contracts sometimes come before the court as having become impossible to fulfill—because of bad harvests or earthquakes or volcanoes, for instance—confirms that human speech happens in a world that does not inherently conform to human demands and expectations, however conventional and moral those demands and expectations. Like Rawls's influential theory of justice, the assertions and demands of contract law in effect seek to neutralize "morally arbitrary" natural attributes.[28] Legal claims manifest an all-too-human protest against a world that is not in one's control. Things go wrong, and then they cannot be fixed. So too, words and claims.

In law as elsewhere, then, it is not so clear that promises must be kept, as conventional morality would have it. Nor, despite Austin, is the binding of words always a matter of accuracy and morality, as *Hippolytus* also revealed. Even the contract law that enforces "our word is our bond" through the recognition of agreements has not always and does not universally require the keeping of promises. Contract law and *Hippolytus* suggest that human law does not and cannot seamlessly rectify speech acts gone awry. Promises, the epitome of conventional performative speech acts, go wrong in ways, contra Cavell, that are often not reparable or correctable through proper procedures. Neither conventional procedures nor the morality that calls for the keeping of promises make the world just. Like *Hippolytus*, contract law occurs in and reveals a world that exceeds the human capacity to speak and to name, to judge and to control.

Like literature, that is, the law of contract treats of conventional speech acts, questions of obligation and debt, issues of misunderstanding, and revocations of promises. It responds to assertions of injustice and demands for justice with its own claims of and calls for justice. So too does criminal law. Again like *Hippolytus*, criminal law treats of accusations and confessions of guilt, excuses for action, and shameful deceptions of all sorts. Both contract law and criminal law respond to assertions of injustice and demands for justice with their own claims, asserting facts (as per Chapter Two) and making demands in their own right. Human beings today, along with Hippolytus, Phaedra, Theseus, and the Nurse, respond to the disorder of living in a world that is only imperfectly within their control with passionate recriminations, convictions of guilt, illicit proposals, and protestations of virtue. Or, despite their powerlessness, human beings, like the more primitive goddesses Artemis and Aphrodite, may demand revenge or compensation.[29]

Contract law acknowledges the imperfection of speech and of promises. It responds to and engages in its own social acts or passionate utterances, calling for some words to be kept and others be broken. It engages in legal fictions to get around what has indeed been said.[30] The fictions of law are no stranger than fantasies of literature. Powerful transformations and mysterious vanishing acts occur in law as in fairy tales. Declarations as of *this* moment turn you into someone or something else: a homeowner, a wife, a convict, a stone—a president. Strange disappearances accompany the nonlinear time of such linguistic events as annulments of marriage or nullifications of grants made in perpetuity. Recognizing the impossibility of demanding or ensuring the "specific" performance of promises, contract law simultaneously affirms the conventionality of acts of promise and agreement and addresses their breach in judgments and formulations that change over time.

Criminal law likewise heeds human calls for justice that comes from all directions in what appears to be an indifferent world. It allocates guilt. When it comes to judging deeds gone wrong, though, criminal law, too, modulates its judgments of responsibility. It requires intention and offers gradations of it. As the *Morissette* court puts it (recall Chapters One and Two), conviction requires "concurrence of an evil-meaning mind with an evil-doing hand." Language offers us adverbs, which modern criminal law takes up as excuses. Law inscribes grammatically inflected dualities of bodies and minds, of acts and intents, of nouns and verbs, of *mens rea* and *actus reus*, into its judgments, as Chapter Two showed. In the judgments made through its own passionate and performative utterances, law maintains that, at least by human standards, neither pure hand and polluted mind (Phaedra) nor pure mind and polluted tongue (Hippolytus) alone deserve the grief and punishment that they tragically incur.

Neither does tort law, in addressing what unintentionally befalls us, hold persons responsible for all of the unintended consequences of their actions, despite Andrews's claims in *Palsgraf* as to what the law "is and should be." Law grapples continuously with the fallibility of human speech and conventions, as earlier chapters have shown. It hears selectively, as in evidence law; it takes back utterances through revocations, amendments, and pardons; it even pretends they have never happened, as in depublications, annulments, and expungements.

Positive law never completely masters language, however. Linda Meyer cites

> the story of the Roman emperor, who was reproved by a distinguished grammarian for the use of an incorrect term, but justified by one Capito, on the ground that the unlimited power and will of the sovereign itself made the term correct. "Capito is a liar, Caesar," was the reply, "you can make a Roman citizen, but you cannot make a Latin word."[31]

Despite the attempts of constitutional law to fix the meanings of texts and utterances, of statutory interpretation to define words and classify statements, and of laws of evidence and of procedure to establish rules for speaking and hearing and then to establish rules for exceptions to those rules, law fails to control speech. Positive law cannot completely master language because language is neither a matter of falsehoods to be corrected nor of purely conventional human acts, whatever that could now mean, to be undone. The "imperfect" quality of speaking—its continuous, incomplete, habitual, routine, and interruptible aspect—attaches not only to the efforts of speakers, the receptivity of hearers, and the knowledge and conventions of speech of the so-called communities of language to which speakers and hearers belong, but also to words themselves vis-à-vis the world.

Language and word as phenomena belong to a world that has no need to conform to human will, that is. When we understand that as *zoon echon logon* (living beings having language),[32] we are necessitated and related to language, and that language, though necessarily humanly related, need not be human-centric, we open our ears to the ways that language allows things to show themselves to us as *they* are and not simply as we would have them. Things reveal themselves to us in a doing that is not completely of our will, nor of our hands and tongues.

In other words, human beings as speaking beings, both law and literature show, are bound to one another and to the world through language. Truth is possible only on the basis of our capacity to speak and of the promise of words to reveal the world. Not only truth, though, but also concealment and untruth, accidental and deliberate, of the sorts revealed in *Hippolytus* and addressed by contract and criminal law, tort law and evidence law, accompany the possibilities of speech.[33] We speak and hear imperfectly in and of a world that is greater than we are.

In addressing and making the claims that it does, modern law, especially positive or official law, largely appears to be a matter of conventional speech and performative utterances. But modern human law also acknowledges and domesticates, recognizes and incorporates, elaborates and improvises on, passionate utterances whose claims of injustice are not exhausted by appeal to convention. The utterances of law of officials and nonofficials alike or, rather, of claimants, their representatives, and representatives of their law, make passionate demands on those whom they would persuade of the truth of their words. They do so in the name of shared law or knowledge of their way of life. These claims often fail.

If truth is the often-failed promise of words to reveal the world, then justice accords with an imperfectly spoken insistence and passionate claim made in the name of the law that, despite our imperfections and the incompleteness of our speech and morality, the world nevertheless show itself as our desires and words—including but not limited to those of convention—would have it. Justice is the paradoxical claim by which we live or, in the case of Hippolytus, tragically die, and of which, in speaking, we persuade ourselves. As law, claims of justice assert and demand that the ever-imperfect promise of language be kept. As speech, claims of justice struggle to emerge from the silences in which truths lie. As passionate utterances, claims of law are claims of justice, protesting—however imperfectly—against the world and against the silences in which we would otherwise remain and to which the conventionality of our words would otherwise bind us.

·   ·   ·

In sum, in claims of contract and criminal law, as in literature, human beings call out—or rail or argue—against the imperfection of a world that does not conform to their expectations, utterances, and desires. The standards against which they judge the world and the demands that follow from their judgments are not inherent in the world however, but come from human beings themselves and from their language, as Nietzsche showed (Chapter Two). Human beings speak continually in ways that persuade them, as does much professional legal education (Chapter Two), that the world can indeed be grasped in the articulations and conventions of human language and law. The tragedies and broken promises of literature and law alike, however, show the necessary imperfection or incompleteness of human speech and human standards. They can never do complete justice in or to the world.

The Name of the Law

Ereignis[1] is the plainest and most gentle of all laws . . . *Ereignis*, though, is
not a law in the sense of a norm which hangs over our heads somewhere, it
is not an ordinance which orders and regulates a course of events: *Ereignis*
is *the* law because it gathers mortals into the appropriateness of their nature and there holds them.

—Martin Heidegger, On the Way to Language, pp. 128–129

At the most basic level, *Our Word Is Our Bond* argues, in plain or ordinary English, that modern U.S. law is a matter of language. U.S. law does the things it
does largely through speech. U.S. law recognizes that speech acts (Chapter
One). Professional law schools convey the importance of language by emphasizing reading and writing in legal education. Reading and writing law cannot be
captured by rules, though (Chapter Two). Law, like language, is interactive or
transactional or social in the sense that it requires another to hear it. Its temporality is such that it is not simply causal (Chapters Two and Three); neither
is it completely conventional (Chapters One, Three, and Four). Legal acts occur
through words (Chapter One), addressed as claims of speakers (Chapter Two) to
hearers that transform states of affairs (Chapter Three) and implicitly appeal to
justice (Chapter Four), in the name of the law. Acts of law, like the use of words,
are sometimes unpredictable and susceptible to going wrong in various ways.
An ongoing or continuous background of practical knowledge allows particular
legal acts to be done and to be known as the acts and events that they turn out
to be, even as this background knowledge, like knowledge of a given language, is
imperfect, incompletely articulable, and interruptible.

This basic argument will by now seem familiar. Its threefold target, recall
from the Introduction, is the contemporary professional legal education that acknowledges the primacy of reading and writing, while suggesting wrongly that
law is a system of rules; the sociolegal research that makes a strong distinction
between law-in-action and law-on-the-books and does not properly recognize

how legal speech acts; and the dominant philosophical view of law as a positivist or state system of human law in which there is no necessary connection between law and justice. Thinking about law as language, as does this book, or attending to how law is said and unsaid, heard and unheard, in claims and counterclaims made by persons who participate in law (including but not limited to practitioners, the legal professoriate, and other scholars) reorients various misunderstandings of law. No longer are legal texts to be grasped as static or atemporal statements or applications of rules. No longer are legal acts to be assessed solely in terms of their impact. Authority is not conflated with the power to coerce or to command. Finally, law need not be considered primarily as a regulatory science or a problem-solving technique with no necessary connection to justice. Instead, one enters a world in which law is an idiom of justice and in which words matter.

In this world, law is not reducible to words understood as the propositions and articulations of language; indeed, law cannot be *reduced* to anything. Speech is admittedly not the whole of law, nor for that matter of language, but it is as good as, if not better than, rules or empirical impact or violence or problem solving, for drawing attention to the way modern law acts or claims and hears. Attending to language shows how law relates us to justice and injustice, and to crucial issues of intention and action, cause and responsibility, community and obligation.

The turn to language in this book offers a fresh understanding of law that allows us to think about the ways that justice may be—and indeed sometimes is—done in our world. Our law talks about and claims justice. Some of our inherited thoughtways obscure this, however. The philosophical and theological commitments of a natural law that would intrinsically connect law and justice are increasingly unavailable to us. The empiricism of the social sciences precludes understanding justice as anything other than values to be measured or political commitments to reform. Legal deconstructionists tend to view justice as an inaccessible horizon of possibility. In being said, justice and truth are not only aspirations, though. Although justice may be partial and incomplete, it may be done, just as truths may be uncovered. That law and language are susceptible to manipulation does not mean that they do not sometimes work! They occasionally do what they say and say what is needed, eloquently addressing their hearers and circumstances. That they do so is bound up with how legal speech acts.

The relation between law and language presented here grows from the work of many thinkers. J. L. Austin, Adolf Reinach, Stanley Cavell, and Friedrich Nietzsche have all been important in developing the argument. The book began with a common understanding of Austinian speech acts as purely conventional performances, but the social acts of law that the book goes on to describe refuse, as does Reinach, the "normative reduction" that conventionality usually implies.[2] Rather than grounding what social acts do in a priori law, though, as does the natural lawyer Reinach, the argument here grounds legal acts in language. Language and legal utterances are always simultaneously performative and, in Cavell's terms, passionate, or "everywhere revealing desire," even if Cavell himself seems to withhold this attribute from utterances that he considers within a conventional "order of law." The argument also relies on Nietzsche's insights into the metaphysics of conventional language, but it suggests that Nietzsche also passes too quickly over the ways in which speech and writings, including his own, can break with rules and conventions.

The book associates law with the language of those to whom a language belongs, but it does not set out to identify an "ideal speech situation" or even "discourse ethics" à la Habermas.[3] It draws attention, rather, to the inarticulability of any given "community's" law. In thinking about how words bind us, it turns, contra Agamben, not to philosophy but to language for "a critique of the oath"; or, in Agamben's words, to "question the primacy of names" or "the sacramental bond that links the human being to language."[4] Readers will be in a better position than the author to gauge the extent to which the book's claims accord with those of Wittgenstein on "lifeform," of Bakhtin on "dialogue" and "heteroglossia," or of Levinas and Heidegger on ontology and ethics.

. . .

Our Word Is Our Bond basically argues, then, that although we are often told that our public discourse is in bad shape, words and claims matter, in law and elsewhere. As social acts, claims assert truths and demand recognition from others. Making legal claims, like using language more broadly, is an imperfect rhetorical art. It involves acting to persuade hearers of one's assertions and demands in singular contexts. The skilled performance of an act of claiming must generally conform to conventions, even as its success depends also on the attunement of speakers and hearers not only to one another, but also to their situation. Assessment of a claim, as of other acts of speech, may include consideration of its accuracy, but what a claim is and does is exhausted neither by its accuracy, its conformity with convention, nor its empirical impact or effect. Like other utterances, a claim is a more or less happy or eloquent and skilled act or performance that takes place simultaneously in a present moment *and* over time. It draws on a past that it interrupts and initiates a future that it awaits.

The many temporalities of claims of law challenge empirical or causal accounts of sociolegal positivism. That the meanings of legal rules are only retrospectively grasped, according to H. L. A. Hart, or that legal acts have the temporal character of the future perfect, according to Jacques Derrida, suggests the inadequacy of trying to predetermine or to permanently fix the meanings of statements or acts of law. One participates in or tells of an act or an event in the "present moment" of its happening without yet being able to foretell its meaning or significance. Recall the Million Man March, the writing of the *Carolene Products* footnote, or Austin's "first" picking up of the football and running. The significance of what happens emerges from a tradition of speaking and acting and interpreting in particular ways. This background tradition, into which a particular "legal" happening or deed may or may not assimilate and against which it may or may not stand out as an act or an event of history, is also called "law."

Within tradition yet potentially breaking with it, legal acts involve more than speakers' conventional utterances. Law acts through persuading hearers. The active engagements of speakers and hearers in dialogue transform states of affairs in their world. In responding to "I" who speak in the name of the law, hearers retrospectively become "you" whom an utterance or text concerns, who share with those who speak a common language and the law by which they live. Fluid and practical knowledge manifests itself in the turn-taking dialogues of speakers and hearers who talk with one another and recognize the same world, despite their differences.

In speaking, a speaker appeals not only to a hearing "you" who may disagree but also to the *we* that "I" hope that "you" take "us-in-our-speaking" to be. In social acts that depend on already-existing imperfect ways of speaking and also interrupt them, persons and groups appeal not only to official state law but also to their own conceptions of law. Think here not only of the law of other cultures but of the *mis*conceptions with which beginning students approach formal law and doctrine. Claims of injustice or of justice made in the name of law recall hearers to what a speaker takes, perhaps mistakenly, to be the common practices and judgments of the two or, rather, of the "community" to which they both belong. Itself only ever incompletely articulable, the practical reason or law of those who share a common language is shaped by, yet precedes, articulated conventions, norms, and rules.

Even the positive law of the state is bound to prior language or law. Its ostensibly impersonal enactments are mandates or imperatives that must *ask* for recognition of their claims, as assertions of truth and as demands of right, from hearers. The *Miranda* warning and the California Penal Code, for instance, depend on and occur against a backdrop of practical knowledge of language and law. As social acts done by "I"s and "you"s in the "name" of the third-party "law," they are not only conventional performances but also passionate utterances of speakers who would persuade hearers of their claims, in a world that need not conform to those conventions or claims.

Even as words fail to deliver on their promise of truth, law enables particular conditions of speech and negotiates failures of language. From the laws of evidence and procedure that structure ways of hearing, to the laws of tort and crime that name and judge causes of accidents and the responsibilities of persons for their acts, from the constitutional law that would keep speech free to the contract law that permits affairs to go on, law concerns itself with language, at the same time as it is itself a matter of language. Like literature, it both offers and mediates dramatic transformations and upheavals. Like the English language, its grammar of subject-predicate-object carries with it particular habits of judging and understanding.

Those habits of course can change. The emergence of "new" phrases, such as "click-wrap" and "*Daubert* standards" and even "suspect classifications," like changes in old phrases, such as "due process" or "free speech," point to the social and historical fluidity of language and of law. Law's unfamiliar ways of doing things may interrupt and challenge habitual or routine ways of hearing and judging, as anyone who has sat in on a law school class or attended a hearing can attest. Conversely, ordinary acts and ways of living can provoke controversy and disrupt ostensibly routine or established law. Think of gay marriage.

Although this book has highlighted issues of language and law at what may appear to be the expense of power and politics, it nevertheless leads to deeply political questions. Much work in anthropology, history, and religion already points to the inadequacy of taking the state and its law as a universal model of law. Thinking about law as language contributes further to understanding the limitations of state-centered sociolegal positivism. In a world of law as language, that is, the authority and so-called sovereignty of the state is as much a matter of "juris-diction" as of power and violence. Many other legal and linguistic nonstate communities exist, however, as conflicts law attests. The care that law accords to language highlights the significance of often underemphasized issues that actually underlie our civic culture and public sphere: literacy and access to educational and legal institutions; bilingualism and interpretation in class-rooms, courtrooms and elsewhere; the manner, availability and quality of politi-cal and legal representation; the character of discursive engagements in a variety of state and nonstate venues by intersecting public and private associations; and the transformation of knowledges and communities of speakers of vernacular tongues through the spread of uniform or dominant legal languages.[5] If words and deeds are matters of politics and law constitutes the walls of the polis, as Arendt puts it, then language is the ground that undergirds those walls and of-fers pathways through the city.

Today, the language of law is the language of policy. Over the centuries, juris-prudence, legal history, and other humanistic disciplines have offered a range of responses to perennial questions of what to do or how best to live, how we know, and who we are. In modern law, policy makers threaten to answer at least the first of these questions in ways that rely on economic and statistical methods and frameworks and that tacitly foreclose particular sorts of answers.

Policy depends on language. The vocabulary of administration testifies to a proliferation of procedures of accountability and transparency that rival any public articulations of a "people" or an aspiring democracy. If, as Michel Foucault notes in *Discipline and Punish*, the "carceral archipelago" has become a "carceral continuum," so too the jargon of bureaucracy has overflowed any institutional borders and become ubiquitous.[6] "Policy" controls not only within states and internationally but also in private entities and community groups. The develop-ment of policy generally involves the articulation of a problem and data gather-ing about it; consideration and analysis of options for addressing the problem; selection of a strategy or set of strategies; implementation of that strategy and of mechanisms for its assessment. Although policy in this sense sounds incredibly broad, its language is limited. Policies are developed and implemented as efficient and effective means to particular ends. Policy transforms otherwise incommen-surate material goods and immaterial "values" into fungible units that can be exchanged or analyzed in terms of costs and benefits. When law becomes policy, legal knowledge threatens to turn into a combination of empirical research and rational decision making that appears to produce solutions to problems.

The richness of the English tongue allows one to say one thing and do another, in multisyllabic Latinate vocabulary and in short Anglo-Saxon words! Touted as solutions, the general policy statements adopted by all manner of organizations promote regulatory expansion at the same time as their details trace elaborate inclusions and exclusions. The language of spokespersons from schools to hospitals to prisons diffuses responsibility at the same time as control over "problem populations" grows.[7] Passive constructions and nominalizations, which make nouns (such as "construction" and "nominalization") from verbs or other parts of speech, suit an institutional ethos that seeks to acknowledge that mistakes may have been made without necessarily holding anyone responsible.

When policy institutions come to "depend heavily on useful numbers and calculations," as Reid Hastie puts it, it indeed becomes useful to produce numerical scales for assessing the numerical judgments of legal decision-makers.[8] One must be alert to the inadequacy of numerical scales for assessing nonnumerical judgments and other speech acts, however.[9] Legal claims are neither calculable in the way that numbers are, nor propositional, as this book has emphasized, in the manner of symbolic logic.

To think law as language is to recognize the contemporary grip of policy talk on law, not simply to come up with better policies as such but to keep open to us ways of thinking and speaking that policy discourses appear to preclude or to disfavor, as useless, irrational, unnecessary, or inapplicable means to ends. It is not only to challenge philosophical accounts that define law as a system of rules or as sovereign power or force then, but also to counter discourses that make law into a set of optimal solutions or strategies and that consider the imperfect aspect of law to be its ineffectiveness and inefficiency. If one must be wary of gap studies that appear to take legal rules for granted when they point to the ways that law-in-action does not live up to law-on-the-books, then one must be equally wary of policy reports that say what they do in particular ways.

To think law as language then is to think beyond the jurisdiction of official state law. It is to encourage broader engagement with the imperfect aspects of international law, of traditions of law, and of the laws of other times and genres, by students, the legal professoriate, mainstream philosophers of law, and sociolegal scholars. It is to attend to the binding of law to language in a manner that is neither expressed by, nor of concern in, policy discourse.

Approaching law as language allows one to consider what law and policy say and do not say; to explore what law shows and does not show; to interpret what legal archives express, suppress, and repress; and to do so unconstrained by the demands of policy regulation. In speaking of the language of law, lawyers, philosophers, historians, social scientists, and others respond more freely to the assertions and demands of policy than can policy scientists and survey participants. We need not identify law as language with particular fields nor dub it "law and humanities." Rather, we are free to speak as who we are. With this freedom comes an indebtedness to language that is neither a policy problem nor a solution. In the indebtedness to language and the freedom to speak, all who speak—including policy makers—are bound, as if by law, to language.

·   ·   ·

Although for some the story can end here, for others the discussion so far barely touches on more profound matters. What is law? *Is* law language? Is *all* law a matter of language in the manner of the U.S. law depicted in Chapter One? Or is law *like* language, as Chapter Two suggests when it argues that neither law nor language are matters of rules, but sites of judgment and attributions of responsibility, which English-language speakers understand in the same terms as legal speech acts and events. Does language *accompany* law, as Chapter Three argues, insofar as law requires dialogue? Or if, as Chapter Three also claims, law is an imperfect practical knowledge or incompletely articulable way of speaking and living that is shared among community members, might language *be* law? In any case, if legal claims can go wrong in the many ways associated with human speech and action in Chapter Four, how do law or language implicate, not only politics, but justice?

When, as is often the case today, "law" is taken to refer to positive law, it sounds strange to say that legal speech draws attention to, much less implicates or relates us to, justice. Like other conventional laws and human moralities, like statements of rules and even like divine and natural law today, positive law is only possible on the basis of words or of language that, as we have seen, can go wrong. Claims of justice exceed positive law, as attested to by the law of colonial regimes and by the inability of U.S. law to speak coherently of justice in relation to Native Americans. As legal positivism itself proclaims, positive law is not necessarily just. The binding of positive law appears unjust and its otherwise garrulous texts seem to have nothing to say and little to do with justice. Justice, like injustice, however, may be done without being said. Indeed, elsewhere I have argued that justice today lies in the silences of positive law.[10]

When we begin to consider those silences and the struggle of speech to emerge from silences in which truth and justice lie, we get a more complex and encompassing sense of the bonds of law than what is offered by the causal and power-oriented accounts of sociolegal positivism or the sovereignty-centered interpretations of political philosophy. As Chapter One argues, U.S. law is bound or indebted to speech or language that exceeds it, as are legal rules and the statements of legal positivism. Although neither law nor language can be captured by rules, law's reliance on grammar, Chapter Two shows, binds or inscribes into it a particular metaphysics or commitment to responsibility and guilt, as Nietzsche claims of language.

Speech and writings are not simply conventional, however. As a matter of joint speaking and hearing, performing the social act of claiming obligates and entangles us, binds and commits us, albeit imperfectly, as Chapters Three and Four show, in a world that exceeds the assertions and demands of conventional morality and of positive law. Passionate calls for justice challenge conventional moralities and laws, but they also affirm them when established expectations are not met. Recall Hippolytus's outburst against the oath that unjustly binds him to a silence in which he nevertheless remains. Like the addressee of a *Miranda* warning, Hippolytus's choice is to speak or to *remain* silent. Speech comes out of silence.

What comes from silence into speech need not be just. Passionate calls for justice may be mistaken, misleading, deceptive, or wrong. They raise issues of justice, however, insofar as they are made in the name of the law. Law makes claims. In assertions and demands made in its name, law relates us implicitly—both closely and without always needing to say so directly—to the promise of words to truth. Our relation and that of our law to truth and to justice is not implicit in the sense of being absolute or unreserved. It is implicit, rather, in the sense of often being unspoken; unspoken and yet still there for the (imperfect) saying. Even when the words of our language are unspoken, that is, they relate us, commit us, and bind us, to each other and to a larger world.

In explicit events of speech, those bonds manifest themselves; they show up in the matters about which we speak. Just as the event of a lawsuit like *Palsgraf v. Long Island Railroad* gathers persons to speak in a common tongue of a matter that both joins and divides them over issues of fact and of law, that is, so too events of speech gather speakers and hearers together over matters of common concern. The concern of this book has been language and law. In the event of speaking or in language's "event-uality," language as "the plainest and most gentle of all laws" gathers and binds us, as speaking animals, to the world and to one another. Words alone cannot guarantee justice; even "plain English" has its instrumental uses. Strangely, words detach themselves from us. But without their speaking and hearing, we are not ourselves. We have no law without our language or without the potential it offers us to wend our ways through the world.

So: Is law language? Is law like language? Does language accompany law? Is language law? Yes, to all these questions. Law is a matter of language. Like language, it is a site of judgment and of ascriptions of responsibility. Law and language accompany one another. And language is our law, saying ever imperfectly who we are and what to do.

Epilogue

Old iconography sometimes represents justice as a chestnut tree. Today justice sometimes seems to be an old chestnut. Law is the garden of justice. Without ground, however, there are no gardens to nourish, no pathways to weed, nor walls to build, much less chestnuts, however shady or stale. Without language, there is neither law nor claim; nor is there politics, much less public discourse, empty, impoverished, or engaged.

Reference Matter

Transcript of Obama's First Oath

1. Roberts: I, Barack Hussein Obama [do solemnly swear]
2. Obama: [I, Barack]
3. Obama: I, Barack Hussein Obama, do solemnly swear.
4. Roberts: That I will . . . execute the office of President ~~of~~ **to** the United States faithfully.
5. Obama: That I will execute . . . (nods to Roberts)
6. Roberts: the off—faithfully the Pres—office of President [of the United States.]
7. Obama: [the office of President] of the United States faithfully.
8. Roberts: And will to the best of my ability.
9. Obama: I will to the best of my ability.
10. Roberts: Preserve, protect, and defend, the constitution of the United States.
11. Obama: Preserve, protect, and defend, the constitution of the United States.
12. Roberts: So help you God?
13. Obama: So help me God.
14. Roberts: Congratulations Mr. President.

*Brackets "[ ]" represent overlapping speech. Parenthesis represent paralinguistic cues. Periods "." represent pauses. Hyphens "—" represent truncated speech. Text in **bold** at line 4 represents a change made to the transcription (after the original post timestamp).*

Source: From the blog of the LGSA (Linguistics Graduate Student Association), "Constitution vs. Cooperation: The Case of Syntax and Oath of Office," January 20, 2009; retrieved on February 6, 2009, from http://fledgelings.blogspot.com/2009/01//constitution-vs-cooperation-case-of.html.

MORISSETTE v. UNITED STATES

Supreme Court of the United States
342 U.S. 246 (1952)

JUSTICE JACKSON delivered the opinion of the Court.

[Morissette, a junk dealer, openly entered an Air Force practice bombing range and took spent bomb casings that had been lying about for years exposed to the weather and rusting away. He flattened them out and sold them at a city junk market at a profit of $84. He was indicted and convicted of violating 18 U.S.C. §641, which made it a crime to "knowingly convert" government property.[a] The defendant admittedly knew that what he had taken were Air Force bomb casings, and there was therefore no question that the defendant had "knowingly convert[ed]" to his own use property that previously did not belong to him. His defense was that he honestly believed that the casings had been abandoned by the Air Force and that he was therefore violating no one's rights in taking them. The trial judge rejected Morissette's defense and instructed the jury that "[t]he question on intent is whether or not he intended to take the property." The court of appeals affirmed, ruling that the statute created several separate offenses, including stealing and knowing conversion. While the crime of stealing traditionally has required an intent to take another's property, in violation of the owner's rights, the court of appeals held that knowing conversion did not include an element of intent to violate the rights of another, because no such intent was expressly required by the statute. In other words, the court of appeals assumed that Congress meant the term "knowingly convert" to carry its conventional tort law meaning—simply an intentional exercise of dominion over property that is not one's own. The Supreme Court reversed, concluding that the defendant must be proven to have had knowledge of the facts that made the conversion wrongful, that is, that the property had not been abandoned by its owner.]

---

a. "Whoever embezzles, steals, purloins, or knowingly converts to his use or the use of another, or without authority, sells, conveys or disposes of any record, voucher, money, or thing of value of the United States . . . shall be fined not more than $10,000 or imprisoned not more than ten years, or both; but if the value of such property does not exceed the sum of $100, he shall be fined not more than $1,000 or imprisoned not more than one year, or both."—EDS.

Source: *Morissette v. United States*, 342 U.S. 246 (1952). Appendix B contains the excerpt reprinted in a student casebook, Sanford H. Kadish et al., *Criminal Law and Its Processes: Cases and Materials*, 9th ed. (New York: Aspen Publishers, 2012), pp. 284–288. The full version of the case can be found online at http://supreme.justia.com/cases/federal/us/342/246/case.html.

The contention that an injury can amount to a crime only when inflicted by intention is no provincial or transient notion. It is as universal and persistent in mature systems of law as belief in freedom of the human will and a consequent ability and duty of the normal individual to choose between good and evil. A relation between some mental element and punishment for a harmful act is almost as instinctive as the child's familiar exculpatory "But I didn't mean to," and has afforded the rational basis for a tardy and unfinished substitution of deterrence and reformation in place of retaliation and vengeance as the motivation for public prosecution. . . .

Crime, as a compound concept, generally constituted only from concurrence of an evil-meaning mind with an evil-doing hand, was congenial to an intense individualism and took deep and early root in American soil. As the states codified the common law of crimes, even if their enactments were silent on the subject, their courts assumed that the omission did not signify disapproval of the principle but merely recognized that intent was so inherent in the idea of the offense that it required no statutory affirmation. . . .

However, the *Balint* and *Behrman*[b] offenses belong to a category of another character, with very different antecedents and origins. The crimes there involved depend on no mental element but consist only of forbidden acts or omissions. This, while not expressed by the Court, is made clear from examination of a century-old but accelerating tendency, discernible both here and in England, to call into existence new duties and crimes which disregard any ingredient of intent. The industrial revolution multiplied the number of workmen exposed to injury from increasingly powerful and complex mechanisms, driven by freshly discovered sources of energy, requiring higher precautions by employers. Traffic of velocities, volumes and varieties unheard of, came to subject the wayfarer to intolerable casualty risks if owners and drivers were not to observe new cares and uniformities of conduct. Congestion of cities and crowding of quarters called for health and welfare regulations undreamed of in simpler times. Wide distribution of goods became an instrument of wide distribution of harm when those who dispersed food, drink, drugs, and even securities, did not comply with reasonable standards of quality, integrity, disclosure and care. Such dangers have engendered increasingly numerous and detailed regulations which heighten the duties of those in control of particular industries, trades, properties or activities that affect public health, safety or welfare.[20]

---

b. United States v. Behrman, 258 U.S. 280 (1922), a companion case to *Balint*, was another prosecution for a narcotics offense.—Eps.

20. Sayre, Public Welfare Offenses, 33 Col. L. Rev. 55, 73, 84 (1933), cites and classifies a large number of cases and concludes that they fall roughly into subdivisions of (1) illegal sales of intoxicating liquor, (2) sales of impure or adulterated food or drugs, (3) sales of misbranded articles, (4) violations of antinarcotic Acts, (5) criminal nuisances, (6) violations of traffic regulations, (7) violations of motor-vehicle laws, and (8) violations of general police regulations, passed for the safety, health or well-being of the community.

While many of these duties are sanctioned by a more strict civil liability, lawmakers, whether wisely or not, have sought to make such regulations more effective by invoking criminal sanctions to be applied by the familiar technique of criminal prosecutions and convictions. This has confronted the courts with a multitude of prosecutions, based on statutes or administrative regulations, for what have been aptly called "public welfare offenses." ... Many of these offenses ... are in the nature of neglect where the law requires care, or inaction where it imposes a duty. Many violations of such regulations result in no direct or immediate injury to person or property but merely create the danger or probability of it which the law seeks to minimize. [T]heir occurrence impairs the efficiency of controls deemed essential to the social order as presently constituted. In this respect, whatever the intent of the violator, the injury is the same, and the consequences are injurious or not according to fortuity. Hence, legislation applicable to such offenses, as a matter of policy, does not specify intent as a necessary element. The accused, if he does not will the violation, usually is in a position to prevent it with no more care than society might reasonably expect and no more exertion than it might reasonably exact from one who assumed his responsibilities. Also, penalties commonly are relatively small, and conviction does no grave damage to an offender's reputation. Under such considerations, courts have turned to construing statutes and regulations which make no mention of intent as dispensing with it and holding that the guilty act alone makes out the crime.[c] This has not, however, been without expressions of misgiving. ...

After the turn of the Century ... New York enacted numerous and novel regulations of tenement houses, sanctioned by money penalties. Landlords contended that a guilty intent was essential to establish a violation. Judge Cardozo wrote the answer:

> The defendant asks us to test the meaning of this statute by standards applicable to statutes that govern infamous crimes. The analogy, however, is deceptive. The element of conscious wrongdoing, the guilty mind accompanying the guilty act, is associated with a concept of crimes that are punished as infamous.

---

c. But see Henry M. Hart, The Aims of the Criminal Law, 23 Law & Contemp. Probs. 401, 431 n.70 (1958):

> "In relation to offenses of a traditional type, the Court's opinion seems to be saying, we must be much slower to dispense with a basis for genuine blameworthiness in criminal intent than in relation to modern regulatory offenses. But it is precisely in the area of traditional crimes that the nature of the act itself commonly gives some warning that there may be a problem about its propriety and so affords, without more, at least some slight basis of condemnation for doing it. Thus, Morissette knew perfectly well that he was taking property which, at least up to the moment of caption, did not belong to him.
>
> "In the area of regulatory crimes, on the other hand, the moral quality of the act is often neutral; and on occasion, the offense may consist not of any act at all, but simply of an intrinsically innocent omission, so that there is no basis for moral condemnation whatever."—EDS.

Even there, it is not an invariable element. But in the prosecution of minor offenses there is a wider range of practice and of power. Prosecutions for petty penalties have always constituted in our law a class by themselves. That is true, though the prosecution is criminal in form.

Tenement House Dept. v. McDevitt, 109 N.E. 88, 90, (1915). . . .

Thus, for diverse but reconcilable reasons, state courts converged on the same result, discontinuing inquiry into intent in a limited class of offenses against such statutory regulations. . . .

Before long, similar questions growing out of federal legislation reached this Court. Its judgments were in harmony with this consensus of state judicial opinion, the existence of which may have led the Court to overlook the need for full exposition of their rationale in the context of federal law. . . .

Neither this Court nor, so far as we are aware, any other has undertaken to delineate a precise line or set forth comprehensive criteria for distinguishing between crimes that require a mental element and crimes that do not. We attempt no closed definition, for the law on the subject is neither settled nor static. The conclusion reached in the *Balint* and *Behrman* Cases has our approval and adherence for the circumstances to which it was there applied. A quite different question here is whether we will expand the doctrine of crimes without intent to include those charged here.

Stealing, larceny, and its variants and equivalents, were among the earliest offenses known to the law that existed before legislation; they are invasions of rights of property which stir a sense of insecurity in the whole community and arouse public demand for retribution, the penalty is high and, when a sufficient amount is involved, the infamy is that of a felony, which, says Maitland, is ". . . as bad a word as you can give to man or thing." State courts of last resort, on whom fall the heaviest burden of interpreting criminal law in this country, have consistently retained the requirement of intent in larceny-type offenses. . . .

Congress, therefore, omitted any express prescription of criminal intent from the enactment before us in the light of an unbroken course of judicial decision in all constituent states of the Union holding intent inherent in this class of offense, even when not expressed in a statute. Congressional silence as to mental elements in an Act merely adopting into federal statutory law a concept of crime already so well defined in common law and statutory interpretation by the states may warrant quite contrary inferences than the same silence in creating an offense new to general law, for whose definition the courts have no guidance except the Act. Because the offenses before this Court in the *Balint* and *Behrman* Cases were of this latter class, we cannot accept them as authority for eliminating intent from offenses incorporated from the common law. . . .

The Government asks us by a feat of construction radically to change the weights and balances in the scales of justice. The purpose and obvious effect of doing away with the requirement of a guilty intent is to ease the prosecution's path to conviction, to strip the defendant of such benefit as he derived at common law from innocence of evil purpose, and to circumscribe the freedom heretofore allowed juries. Such a manifest impairment of the immunities of the individual should not be extended to common-law crimes on judicial initiative. . . .

We hold that the mere omission from §641 of any mention of intent will not be construed as eliminating that element from the crimes denounced. . . .

Of course, the jury, considering Morissette's awareness that these casings were on government property, his failure to seek any permission for their removal and his self-interest as a witness, might have disbelieved his profession of innocent intent and concluded that his assertion of a belief that the casings were abandoned was an after-thought. Had the jury convicted on proper instructions it would be the end of the matter. But juries are not bound by what seems inescapable logic to judges. They might have concluded that the heaps of spent casings left in the hinterland to rust away presented an appearance of unwanted and abandoned junk, and that lack of any conscious deprivation of property or intentional injury was indicated by Morissette's good character, the openness of the taking, crushing and transporting of the casings, and the candor with which it was all admitted. They might have refused to brand Morissette as a thief. Had they done so, that too would have been the end of the matter.

Reversed.

Helen Palsgraf, Respondent,

v

The Long Island Railroad Company, Appellant.

Court of Appeals of New York
Argued February 24, 1928
Decided May 29, 1928

248 NY 339
CITE TITLE AS: Palsgraf v Long Is. R.R. Co.

[*340] OPINION OF THE COURT

CARDOZO, Ch. J.

Plaintiff was standing on a platform of defendant's railroad after buying a ticket to go to Rockaway Beach. A train stopped at the station, bound for another place. Two men ran forward to catch it. One of the men reached the platform of the car without mishap, though the train was already moving. The other man, carrying a package, jumped aboard the car, but seemed unsteady as if about to fall. A guard on the car, who had held the door open, reached forward to help [*341] him in, and another guard on the platform pushed him from behind. In this act, the package was dislodged, and fell upon the rails. It was a package of small size, about fifteen inches long, and was covered by a newspaper. In fact it contained fireworks, but there was nothing in its appearance to give notice of its contents. The fireworks when they fell exploded. The shock of the explosion threw down some scales at the other end of the platform, many feet away. The scales struck the plaintiff, causing injuries for which she sues.

The conduct of the defendant's guard, if a wrong in its relation to the holder of the package, was not a wrong in its relation to the plaintiff, standing far away. Relatively to her it was not negligence at all. Nothing in the situation gave notice

Source: Retrieved from www.nycourts.gov/reporter/archives/palsgraf_lirr.htm.

that the falling package had in it the potency of peril to persons thus removed. Negligence is not actionable unless it involves the invasion of a legally protected interest, the violation of a right. "Proof of negligence in the air, so to speak, will not do" (Pollock, Torts [11th ed.], p. 455; *Martin v. Herzog*, 228 N. Y. 164, 170; cf. Salmond, Torts [6th ed.], p. 24). "Negligence is the absence of care, according to the circumstances" (WILLES, J., in *Vaughan v. Taff Vale Ry. Co.*, 5 H. & N. 679, 688; 1 Beven, Negligence [4th ed.], 7; *Paul v. Consol. Fireworks Co.*, 212 N. Y. 117; *Adams v. Bullock*, 227 N.Y. 208, 211; *Parrott v. Wells-Fargo Co.*, 15 Wall. [U. S.] 524). The plaintiff as she stood upon the platform of the station might claim to be protected against intentional invasion of her bodily security. Such invasion is not charged. She might claim to be protected against unintentional invasion by conduct involving in the thought of reasonable men an unreasonable hazard that such invasion would ensue. These, from the point of view of the law, were the bounds of her immunity, with perhaps some rare exceptions, survivals for the most part of ancient forms of liability, where conduct is held to be at the peril of the actor ([*342] *Sullivan v. Dunham*, 161 N.Y. 290). If no hazard was apparent to the eye of ordinary vigilance, an act innocent and harmless, at least to outward seeming, with reference to her, did not take to itself the quality of a tort because it happened to be a wrong, though apparently not one involving the risk of bodily insecurity, with reference to some one else. "In every instance, before negligence can be predicated of a given act, back of the act must be sought and found a duty to the individual complaining, the observance of which would have averted or avoided the injury" (McSHERRY, C. J., in *W. Va. Central R. Co. v. State*, 96 Md. 652, 666; cf. *Norfolk & Western Ry. Co. v. Wood*, 99 Va. 156, 158, 159; *Hughes v. Boston & Maine R. R. Co.*, 71 N. H. 279, 284; *U. S. Express Co. v. Everest*, 72 Kan. 517; *Emry v. Roanoke Nav. Co.*, 111 N. C. 94, 95; *Vaughan v. Transit Dev. Co.*, 222 N. Y. 79; *Losee v. Clute*, 51 N. Y. 494; *DiCaprio v. N. Y. C. R. R. Co.*, 231 N. Y. 94; 1 Shearman & Redfield on Negligence, § 8, and cases cited; Cooley on Torts [3d ed.], p. 1411; Jaggard on Torts, vol. 2, p. 826; Wharton, Negligence, § 24; Bohlen, Studies in the Law of Torts, p. 601). "The ideas of negligence and duty are strictly correlative" (BOWEN, L. J., in *Thomas v. Quartermaine*, 18 Q. B. D. 685, 694). The plaintiff sues in her own right for a wrong personal to her, and not as the vicarious beneficiary of a breach of duty to another.

A different conclusion will involve us, and swiftly too, in a maze of contradictions. A guard stumbles over a package which has been left upon a platform. It seems to be a bundle of newspapers. It turns out to be a can of dynamite. To the eye of ordinary vigilance, the bundle is abandoned waste, which may be kicked or trod on with impunity. Is a passenger at the other end of the platform protected by the law against the unsuspected hazard concealed beneath the waste? If not, is the result to be any different, so far as the distant passenger is concerned, when the guard stumbles over a valise [*343] which a truckman or a porter has left upon the walk? The passenger far away, if the victim of a wrong at all, has a cause of action, not derivative, but original and primary. His claim to be protected against invasion of his bodily security is neither greater nor less because the act resulting in the invasion is a wrong to another far removed. In this case, the rights that are said to have been violated, the interests said to have been invaded, are not even of the same order. The man was not injured in his person nor even put in danger. The purpose of the act, as well as its effect, was to make his person safe. If there was a wrong to him at all, which may very well be doubted, it was a wrong to a property interest only, the safety of his package. Out of this wrong to property, which threatened injury to nothing else, there has passed, we are told, to the plaintiff by derivation or succession a right of action for the invasion of an interest of another order, the right to bodily security. The diversity of interests emphasizes the futility of the effort to build the plaintiff's right upon the basis of a wrong to some one else. The gain is one of emphasis, for a like result would follow if the interests were the same. Even then, the orbit of the danger as disclosed to the eye of reasonable vigilance would be the orbit of the duty. One who jostles one's neighbor in a crowd does not invade the rights of others standing at the outer fringe when the unintended contact casts a bomb upon the ground. The wrongdoer as to them is the man who carries the bomb, not the one who explodes it without suspicion of the danger. Life will have to be made over, and human nature transformed, before prevision so extravagant can be accepted as the norm of conduct, the customary standard to which behavior must conform.

The argument for the plaintiff is built upon the shifting meanings of such words as "wrong" and "wrongful," and shares their instability. What the plaintiff must [*344] show is "a wrong" to herself, i. e., a violation of her own right, and not merely a wrong to some one else, nor conduct "wrongful" because unsocial, but not "a wrong" to any one. We are told that one who drives at reckless speed through a crowded city street is guilty of a negligent act and, therefore, of a wrongful one irrespective of the consequences. Negligent the act is, and wrongful in the sense that it is unsocial, but wrongful and unsocial in relation to other travelers, only because the eye of vigilance perceives the risk of damage. If the same act were to be committed on a speedway or a race course, it would lose its wrongful quality. The risk reasonably to be perceived defines the duty to be obeyed, and risk imports relation; it is risk to another or to others within the range of apprehension (Seavey, Negligence, Subjective or Objective, 41 H. L. Rv. 6; *Boronkay v. Robinson & Carpenter*, 247 N. Y. 365). This does not mean, of course, that one who launches a destructive force is always relieved of liability if the force, though known to be destructive, pursues an unexpected path. "It was not necessary that the defendant should have had notice of the particular method in which an accident would occur, if the possibility of an accident was clear to the ordinarily prudent eye" (*Munsey v. Webb*, 231 U. S. 150, 156; *Condran v. Park & Tilford*, 213 N. Y. 341, 345; *Robert v. U. S. E. F. Corp.*, 240 N. Y. 474, 477). Some acts, such as shooting, are so imminently dangerous to any one who may come within reach of the missile, however unexpectedly, as to impose a duty of prevision not far from that of an insurer. Even today, and much oftener in earlier stages of the law, one acts sometimes at one's peril (Jeremiah Smith, Tort and Absolute Liability, 30 H. L. Rv. 328; Street, Foundations of Legal Liability, vol. 1, pp. 77, 78). Under this head, it may be, fall certain cases of what is known as transferred intent, an act willfully dangerous to A resulting by misadventure in injury to B (*Talmage v. Smith*, 101 Mich. 370, 374) [*345] These cases aside, wrong is defined in terms of the natural or probable, at least when unintentional (*Parrot v. Wells-Fargo Co. [The Nitro-Glycerine Case]*, 15 Wall. [U. S.] 524). The range of reasonable apprehension is at times a question for the court, and at times, if varying inferences are possible, a question for the jury. Here, by concession, there was nothing in the situation to suggest to the most cautious mind that the parcel wrapped in newspaper would spread wreckage through the station. If the guard had thrown it down knowingly and willfully, he would not have threatened the plaintiff's safety, so far as appearances could warn him. His conduct would not have involved, even then, an unreasonable probability of invasion of her bodily security. Liability can be no greater where the act is inadvertent.

Negligence, like risk, is thus a term of relation. Negligence in the abstract, apart from things related, is surely not a tort, if indeed it is understandable at all

(BOWEN, L. J., in *Thomas v. Quartermaine*, 18 Q. B. D. 685, 694). Negligence is not a tort unless it results in the commission of a wrong, and the commission of a wrong imports the violation of a right, in this case, we are told, the right to be protected against interference with one's bodily security. But bodily security is protected, not against all forms of interference or aggression, but only against some. One who seeks redress at law does not make out a cause of action by showing without more that there has been damage to his person. If the harm was not willful, he must show that the act as to him had possibilities of danger so many and apparent as to entitle him to be protected against the doing of it though the harm was unintended. Affront to personality is still the keynote of the wrong. Confirmation of this view will be found in the history and development of the action on the case. Negligence as a basis of civil liability was unknown to mediaeval law (8 Holdsworth, History of English Law, p. 449; Street, Foundations of Legal Liability, vol. 1, pp. 189, 190). For damage to the person, the sole remedy was trespass, and trespass did not lie in the absence of aggression, and that direct and personal (Holdsworth, op. cit. p. 453; Street, op. cit. vol. 3, pp. 258, 260, vol. 1, pp. 71, 74.) Liability for other damage, as where a servant without orders from the master does or omits something to the damage of another, is a plant of later growth (Holdsworth, op. cit. 450, 457; Wigmore, Responsibility for Tortious Acts, vol. 3, Essays in Anglo-American Legal History, 520, 523, 526, 533). When it emerged out of the legal soil, it was thought of as a variant of trespass, an offshoot of the parent stock. This appears in the form of action, which was known as trespass on the case (Holdsworth, op. cit. p. 449; cf. *Scott v. Shepard*, 2 Wm. Black. 892; Green, Rationale of Proximate Cause, p. 19). The victim does not sue derivatively, or by right of subrogation, to vindicate an interest invaded in the person of another. Thus to view his cause of action is to ignore the fundamental difference between tort and crime (Holland, Jurisprudence [12th ed.], p. 328). He sues for breach of a duty owing to himself.

The law of causation, remote or proximate, is thus foreign to the case before us. The question of liability is always anterior to the question of the measure of the consequences that go with liability. If there is no tort to be redressed, there is no occasion to consider what damage might be recovered if there were a finding of a tort. We may assume, without deciding, that negligence, not at large or in the abstract, but in relation to the plaintiff, would entail liability for any and all consequences, however novel or extraordinary (*Bird v. St. Paul F. &*

M. Ins. Co., 224 N. Y. 47, 54; *Ehrgott v. Mayor*, etc., of N. Y., 96 N. Y. 264; *Smith v. London & S. W. Ry. Co.*, L. R. 6 C. P. 14; 1 Beven, Negligence, 106; Street, op. cit. vol. 1, p. 90; Green, Rationale of Proximate Cause, pp. 88, 118; cf. *Matter of Polemis*, L. R. 1921, 3 K. B. 560; 44 Law Quarterly Review, 142). There is room for [*347] argument that a distinction is to be drawn according to the diversity of interests invaded by the act, as where conduct negligent in that it threatens an insignificant invasion of an interest in property results in an unforseeable invasion of an interest of another order, as, e. g., one of bodily security. Perhaps other distinctions may be necessary. We do not go into the question now. The consequences to be followed must first be rooted in a wrong. The judgment of the Appellate Division and that of the Trial Term should be reversed, and the complaint dismissed, with costs in all courts.

ANDREWS, J. (dissenting).

Assisting a passenger to board a train, the defendant's servant negligently knocked a package from his arms. It fell between the platform and the cars. Of its contents the servant knew and could know nothing. A violent explosion followed. The concussion broke some scales standing a considerable distance away. In falling they injured the plaintiff, an intending passenger.

Upon these facts may she recover the damages she has suffered in an action brought against the master? The result we shall reach depends upon our theory as to the nature of negligence. Is it a relative concept the breach of some duty owing to a particular person or to particular persons? Or where there is an act which unreasonably threatens the safety of others, is the doer liable for all its proximate consequences, even where they result in injury to one who would generally be thought to be outside the radius of danger? This is not a mere dispute as to words. We might not believe that to the average mind the dropping of the bundle would seem to involve the probability of harm to the plaintiff standing many feet away whatever might be the case as to the owner or to one so near as to be likely to be struck by its fall. If, however, we adopt the second hypothesis we have to inquire only as to the relation between cause and effect. We deal in terms of proximate cause, not of negligence.

Negligence may be defined roughly as an act or omission which unreasonably does or may affect the rights of others, or which unreasonably fails to protect oneself from the dangers resulting from such acts. Here I confine myself to the first branch of the definition. Nor do I comment on the word "unreasonable." For present purposes it sufficiently describes that average of conduct that society requires of its members.

There must be both the act or the omission, and the right. It is the act itself, not the intent of the actor, that is important. (*Hover v. Barkhoof*, 44 N. Y. 113; *Mertz v. Connecticut Co.*, 217 N. Y. 475.) In criminal law both the intent and the result are to be considered. Intent again is material in tort actions, where punitive damages are sought, dependent on actual malice—not on merely reckless conduct. But here neither insanity nor infancy lessens responsibility. (*Williams v. Hays*, 143 N. Y. 442.)

As has been said, except in cases of contributory negligence, there must be rights which are or may be affected. Often though injury has occurred, no rights of him who suffers have been touched. A licensee or trespasser upon my land has no claim to affirmative care on my part that the land be made safe. (*Meiers v. Koch Brewery*, 229 N. Y. 10.) Where a railroad is required to fence its tracks against cattle, no man's rights are injured should he wander upon the road because such fence is absent. (*Di Caprio v. N. Y. C. R. R.*, 231 N. Y. 94.) An unborn child may not demand immunity from personal harm. (*Drobner v. Peters*, 232 N. Y. 220.)

But we are told that "there is no negligence unless there is in the particular case a legal duty to take care, and this duty must be one which is owed to the plaintiff [*349] himself and not merely to others." (Salmond Torts [6th ed.], 24.) This, I think too narrow a conception. Where there is the unreasonable act, and some right that may be affected there is negligence whether damage does or does not result. That is immaterial. Should we drive down Broadway at a reckless speed, we are negligent whether we strike an approaching car or miss it by an inch. The act itself is wrongful. It is a wrong not only to those who happen to be within the radius of danger but to all who might have been there—a wrong to the public at large. Such is the language of the street. Such the language of the courts when speaking of contributory negligence. Such again and again their language in speaking of the duty of some defendant and discussing proximate cause in cases where such a discussion is wholly irrelevant on any other theory. (*Perry v. Rochester Line Co.*, 219 N. Y. 60.) As was said by Mr. Justice HOLMES many years ago, "the measure of the defendant's duty in determining whether a wrong has been committed is one thing, the measure of liability when a wrong has been committed is another." (*Spade v. Lynn & Boston R. R. Co.*, 172 Mass. 488.) Due care is a duty imposed on each one of us to protect society from unnecessary danger, not to protect A, B or C alone.

It may well be that there is no such thing as negligence in the abstract. "Proof of negligence in the air, so to speak, will not do." In an empty world negligence would not exist. It does involve a relationship between man and his fellows. But not merely a relationship between man and those whom he might reasonably expect his act would injure. Rather, a relationship between him and those whom he does in fact injure. If his act has a tendency to harm some one, it harms him a mile away as surely as it does those on the scene. We now permit children to recover for the negligent killing of the father. It was never prevented on the theory that no duty was owing to them. A husband may be compensated for [*350] the loss of his wife's services. To say that the wrongdoer was negligent as to the husband as well as to the wife is merely an attempt to fit facts to theory. An insurance company paying a fire loss recovers its payment of the negligent incendiary. We speak of subrogation—of suing in the right of the insured. Behind the cloud of words is the fact they hide, that the act, wrongful as to the insured, has also injured the company. Even if it be true that the fault of father, wife or insured will prevent recovery, it is because we consider the original negligence not the proximate cause of the injury. (Pollock, Torts [12th ed.], 463.)

In the well-known *Polemis Case* (1921, 3 K. B. 560), SCRUTTON, L. J., said that the dropping of a plank was negligent for it might injure "workman or cargo or ship." Because of either possibility the owner of the vessel was to be made good for his loss. The act being wrongful the doer was liable for its proximate results. Criticized and explained as this statement may have been, I think it states the law as it should be and as it is. (*Smith v. London & Southwestern Ry. Co.*, [1870–71] 6 C. P. 14; *Anthony v. Slaid*, 52 Mass. 290; *Wood v. Penn. R. R. Co.*, 177 Penn. St. 306; *Trashansky v. Hershkovitz*, 239 N. Y. 452.)

The proposition is this. Every one owes to the world at large the duty of refraining from those acts that may unreasonably threaten the safety of others. Such an act occurs. Not only is he wronged to whom harm might reasonably be expected to result, but he also who is in fact injured, even if he be outside what would generally be thought the danger zone. There needs be duty due the one complaining but this is not a duty to a particular individual because as to him harm might be expected. Harm to some one being the natural result of the act, not only that one alone, but all those in fact injured may complain. We have never, I think, held otherwise. Indeed in the *Di Caprio* case we said that a breach of a general [*351] ordinance defining the degree of care to be exercised in one's calling is evidence of negligence as to every one. We did not limit this statement to those who might be expected to be exposed to danger. Unreasonable risk being taken, its consequences are not confined to those who might probably be hurt.

If this be so, we do not have a plaintiff suing by "derivation or succession." Her action is original and primary. Her claim is for a breach of duty to herself— not that she is subrogated to any right of action of the owner of the parcel or of a passenger standing at the scene of the explosion.

The right to recover damages rests on additional considerations. The plaintiff's rights must be injured, and this injury must be caused by the negligence. We build a dam, but are negligent as to its foundations. Breaking, it injures property down stream. We are not liable if all this happened because of some reason other than the insecure foundation. But when injuries do result from our unlawful act we are liable for the consequences. It does not matter that they are unusual, unexpected, unforeseen and unforseeable. But there is one limitation. The damages must be so connected with the negligence that the latter may be said to be the proximate cause of the former.

These two words have never been given an inclusive definition. What is a cause in a legal sense, still more what is a proximate cause, depend in each case upon many considerations, as does the existence of negligence itself. Any philosophical doctrine of causation does not help us. A boy throws a stone into a pond. The ripples spread. The water level rises. The history of that pond is altered to all eternity. It will be altered by other causes also. Yet it will be forever the resultant of all causes combined. Each one will have an influence. How great only omniscience can say. You may speak of a chain, or if you please, a net. An analogy is of little aid. [*352] Each cause brings about future events. Without each the future would not be the same. Each is proximate in the sense it is essential. But that is not what we mean by the word. Nor on the other hand do we mean sole cause. There is no such thing.

Should analogy be thought helpful, however, I prefer that of a stream. The spring, starting on its journey, is joined by tributary after tributary. The river, reaching the ocean, comes from a hundred sources. No man may say whence any drop of water is derived. Yet for a time distinction may be possible. Into the clear creek, brown swamp water flows from the left. Later, from the right comes water stained by its clay bed. The three may remain for a space, sharply divided. But at last, inevitably no trace of separation remains. They are so commingled that all distinction is lost.

As we have said, we cannot trace the effect of an act to the end, if end there is. Again, however, we may trace it part of the way. A murder at Serajevo may be the necessary antecedent to an assassination in London twenty years hence. An overturned lantern may burn all Chicago. We may follow the fire from the shed to the last building. We rightly say the fire started by the lantern caused its destruction.

A cause, but not the proximate cause. What we do mean by the word "proximate" is, that because of convenience, of public policy, of a rough sense of justice, the law arbitrarily declines to trace a series of events beyond a certain point. This is not logic. It is practical politics. Take our rule as to fires. Sparks from my burning haystack set on fire my house and my neighbor's. I may recover from a negligent railroad. He may not. Yet the wrongful act as directly harmed the one as the other. We may regret that the line was drawn just where it was, but drawn somewhere it had to be. We said the act of the railroad was not the proximate cause of our neighbor's fire. Cause it surely was. The words we used were [*353] simply indicative of our notions of public policy. Other courts think differently. But somewhere they reach the point where they cannot say the stream comes from any one source.

Take the illustration given in an unpublished manuscript by a distinguished and helpful writer on the law of torts. A chauffeur negligently collides with another car which is filled with dynamite, although he could not know it. An explosion follows. A, walking on the sidewalk nearby, is killed. B, sitting in a window of a building opposite, is cut by flying glass. C, likewise sitting in a window a block away, is similarly injured. And a further illustration. A nursemaid, ten blocks away, startled by the noise, involuntarily drops a baby from her arms to the walk. We are told that C may not recover while A may. As to B it is a question for court or jury. We will all agree that the baby might not.

Because, we are again told, the chauffeur had no reason to believe his conduct involved any risk of injuring either C or the baby. As to them he was not negligent.

But the chauffeur, being negligent in risking the collision, his belief that the scope of the harm he might do would be limited is immaterial. His act unreasonably jeopardized the safety of any one who might be affected by it. C's injury and that of the baby were directly traceable to the collision. Without that, the injury would not have happened. C had the right to sit in his office, secure from such dangers. The baby was entitled to use the sidewalk with reasonable safety.

The true theory is, it seems to me, that the injury to C, if in truth he is to be denied recovery, and the injury to the baby is that their several injuries were not the proximate result of the negligence. And here not what the chauffeur had reason to believe would be the result of his conduct, but what the prudent would foresee, may have a bearing. May have some bearing, for the problem of [*354] proximate cause is not to be solved by any one consideration.

It is all a question of expediency. There are no fixed rules to govern our judgment. There are simply matters of which we may take account. We have in a somewhat different connection spoken of "the stream of events." We have asked whether that stream was deflected—whether it was forced into new and unexpected channels. (*Donnelly v. Piercy Contracting Co.*, 222 N. Y. 210). This is rather rhetoric than law. There is in truth little to guide us other than common sense.

There are some hints that may help us. The proximate cause, involved as it may be with many other causes, must be, at the least, something without which the event would not happen. The court must ask itself whether there was a natural and continuous sequence between cause and effect. Was the one a substantial factor in producing the other? Was there a direct connection between them, without too many intervening causes? Is the effect of cause on result not too attentuated? Is the cause likely, in the usual judgment of mankind, to produce the result? Or by the exercise of prudent foresight could the result be foreseen? Is the result too remote from the cause, and here we consider remoteness in time and space. (*Bird v. St. Paul F. & M. Ins. Co.*, 224 N. Y. 47, where we passed upon the construction of a contract—but something was also said on this subject.) Clearly we must so consider, for the greater the distance either in time or space, the more surely do other causes intervene to affect the result. When a lantern is overturned the firing of a shed is a fairly direct consequence. Many things contribute to the spread of the conflagration— the force of the wind, the direction and width of streets, the character of intervening structures, other factors. We draw an uncertain and wavering line, but draw it we must as best we can.

Once again, it is all a question of fair judgment, always keeping [*355] in mind the fact that we endeavor to make a rule in each case that will be practical and in keeping with the general understanding of mankind.

Here another question must be answered. In the case supposed it is said, and said correctly, that the chauffeur is liable for the direct effect of the explosion although he had no reason to suppose it would follow a collision. "The fact that the injury occurred in a different manner than that which might have been expected does not prevent the chauffeur's negligence from being in law the cause of the injury." But the natural results of a negligent act the results which a prudent man would or should foresee do have a bearing upon the decision as to proximate cause. We have said so repeatedly. What should be foreseen? No human foresight would suggest that a collision itself might injure one a block away. On the contrary, given an explosion, such a possibility might be reasonably expected. I think the direct connection, the foresight of which the courts speak, assumes prevision of the explosion, for the immediate results of which, at least, the chauffeur is responsible.

It may be said this is unjust. Why? In fairness he should make good every injury flowing from his negligence. Not because of tenderness toward him we say he need not answer for all that follows his wrong. We look back to the catastrophe, the fire kindled by the spark, or the explosion. We trace the consequences—not indefinitely, but to a certain point. And to aid us in fixing that point we ask what might ordinarily be expected to follow the fire or the explosion.

This last suggestion is the factor which must determine the case before us. The act upon which defendant's liability rests is knocking an apparently harmless package onto the platform. The act was negligent. For its proximate consequences the defendant is liable. If its contents were broken, to the owner;

if it fell upon and crushed a passenger's foot, then to him. If it exploded [*356] and injured one in the immediate vicinity, to him also as to A in the illustration. Mrs. Palsgraf was standing some distance away. How far cannot be told from the record—apparently twenty-five or thirty feet. Perhaps less. Except for the explosion, she would not have been injured. We are told by the appellant in his brief "it cannot be denied that the explosion was the direct cause of the plaintiff's injuries." So it was a substantial factor in producing the result—there was here a natural and continuous sequence—direct connection. The only intervening cause was that instead of blowing her to the ground the concussion smashed the weighing machine which in turn fell upon her. There was no remoteness in time, little in space. And surely, given such an explosion as here it needed no great foresight to predict that the natural result would be to injure one on the platform at no greater distance from its scene than was the plaintiff. Just how no one might be able to predict. Whether by flying fragments, by broken glass, by wreckage of machines or structures no one could say. But injury in some form was most probable.

Under these circumstances I cannot say as a matter of law that the plaintiff's injuries were not the proximate result of the negligence. That is all we have before us. The court refused to so charge. No request was made to submit the matter to the jury as a question of fact, even would that have been proper upon the record before us.

The judgment appealed from should be affirmed, with costs.

POUND, LEHMAN and KELLOGG, JJ., concur with CARDOZO, Ch. J.; ANDREWS, J., dissents in opinion in which CRANE and O'BRIEN, JJ., concur.

Judgment reversed, etc.

Selections from California Penal Code

Title of the Act

Section 1. This Act shall be known as THE PENAL CODE OF CALIFOR-
NIA, and is divided into four parts, as follows:
I.—OF CRIMES AND PUNISHMENTS.
II.—OF CRIMINAL PROCEDURE.
III.—OF THE STATE PRISON AND COUNTY JAILS.
IV.—OF PREVENTION OF CRIMES AND APPREHENSION
OF CRIMINALS.

Section 2. This Code takes effect at twelve o'clock, noon, on the first day of
January, eighteen hundred and seventy-three.

Section 3. No part of it is retroactive, unless expressly so declared.

Section 4. The rule of the common law, that penal statutes are to be strictly
construed, has no application to this Code. All its provisions are
to be construed according to the fair import of their terms, with
a view to effect its objects and to promote justice.

Section 5. The provisions of this Code, so far as they are substantially the
same as existing statutes, must be construed as continuations
thereof, and not as new enactments.

Section 6. No act or omission, commenced after twelve o'clock noon of the
day on which this Code takes effect as a law, is criminal or pun-

Source: California Penal Code, http://www.leginfo.ca.gov/ (last accessed June 23, 2013).

ishable, except as prescribed or authorized by this Code, or by some of the statutes which it specifies as continuing in force and as not affected by its provisions, or by some ordinance, municipal, county, or township regulation, passed or adopted, under such statutes and in force when this Code takes effect. Any act or omission commenced prior to that time may be inquired of, prosecuted, and punished in the same manner as if this Code had not been passed.

Section 7. Words used in this code in the present tense include the future as well as the present; words used in the masculine gender include the feminine and neuter; the singular number includes the plural, and the plural the singular; the word "person" includes a corporation as well as a natural person; the word "county" includes "city and county"; writing includes printing and typewriting; oath includes affirmation or declaration; and every mode of oral statement, under oath or affirmation, is embraced by the term "testify," and every written one in the term "depose"; signature or subscription includes mark, when the person cannot write, his or her name being written near it, by a person who writes his or her own name as a witness; provided, that when a signature is made by mark it must, in order that the same may be acknowledged or serve as the signature to any sworn statement, be witnessed by two persons who must subscribe their own names as witnesses thereto. The following words have in this code the signification attached to them in this section, unless otherwise apparent from the context:

1. The word "willfully," when applied to the intent with which an act is done or omitted, implies simply a purpose or willingness to commit the act, or make the omission referred to. It does not require any intent to violate law, or to injure another, or to acquire any advantage.

2. The words "neglect," "negligence," "negligent," and "negligently" import a want of such attention to the nature or probable consequences of the act or omission as a prudent man ordinarily bestows in acting in his own concerns.

3. The word "corruptly" imports a wrongful design to acquire or cause some pecuniary or other advantage to the person guilty of the act or omission referred to, or to some other person.

4. The words "malice" and "maliciously" import a wish to vex, annoy, or injure another person, or an intent to do a wrongful act, established either by proof or presumption of law.

5. The word "knowingly" imports only a knowledge that the facts exist which bring the act or omission within the provisions of this code. It does not require any knowledge of the unlawfulness of such act or omission.

. . .

16. Words and phrases must be construed according to the context and the approved usage of the language; but technical words and phrases, and such others as may have acquired a peculiar and appropriate meaning in law, must be construed according to such peculiar and appropriate meaning.

. . .

18. When the seal of a court or public officer is required by law to be affixed to any paper, the word "seal" includes an impression of such seal upon the paper alone, or upon any substance attached to the paper capable of receiving a visible impression. The seal of a private person may be made in like manner, or by the scroll of a pen, or by writing the word "seal" against his or her name.

19. The word "state," when applied to the different parts of the United States, includes the District of Columbia and the territories, and the words "United States" may include the district and territories.

. . .

Section 8. Whenever, by any of the provisions of this Code, an intent to defraud is required in order to constitute any offense, it is sufficient if an intent appears to defraud any person, association, or body politic or corporate, whatever.

Section 9. The omission to specify or affirm in this Code any liability to damages, penalty, forfeiture, or other remedy imposed by law and allowed to be recovered or enforced in any civil action or proceeding, for any act or omission declared punishable herein, does not affect any right to recover or enforce the same.

. . .

Section 12. The several sections of this Code which declare certain crimes to be punishable as therein mentioned, devolve a duty upon the Court authorized to pass sentence, to determine and impose the punishment prescribed.

Section 13. Whenever in this Code the punishment for a crime is left undetermined between certain limits, the punishment to be inflicted in a particular case must be determined by the Court authorized to pass sentence, within such limits as may be prescribed by this Code.

Section 14. The various sections of this Code which declare that evidence obtained upon the examination of a person as a witness cannot be received against him in any criminal proceeding, do not forbid such evidence being proved against such person upon any proceedings founded upon a charge of perjury committed in such examination.

Section 15. A crime or public offense is an act committed or omitted in violation of a law forbidding or commanding it, and to which is annexed, upon conviction, either of the following punishments:

1. Death;
2. Imprisonment;
3. Fine;
4. Removal from office; or,
5. Disqualification to hold and enjoy any office of honor, trust, or profit in this State.

Section 16. Crimes and public offenses include:

1. Felonies;
2. Misdemeanors; and
3. Infractions.

Section 17. (a) A felony is a crime that is punishable with death, by imprisonment in the state prison, or notwithstanding any other provision of law, by imprisonment in a county jail under the provisions of subdivision (h) of Section 1170. Every other crime or public offense is a misdemeanor except those offenses that are classified as infractions.

. . .

(c) When a defendant is committed to the Division of Juvenile Justice for a crime punishable, in the discretion of the court, either by imprisonment in the state prison or imprisonment in a county jail under the provisions of subdivision (h) of Section 1170, or by fine or imprisonment in the county jail not exceeding one year, the offense shall, upon the discharge of the defendant from the Division of Juvenile Justice, thereafter be deemed a misdemeanor for all purposes.

Notes

Introduction

1. Lawrence M. Friedman, "The Law and Society Movement," *Stanford Law Review* Vol. 38, no. 3 (1986); and . Robert Cover, "Violence and the Word," *Yale Law Journal* Vol. 95, no. 8 (1986).

2. Ward Farnsworth, *The Legal Analyst : A Toolkit for Thinking about the Law* (Chicago: University of Chicago Press, 2007), p. 164.

3. A nice transcript is available at the Blog of the LGSA (Linguistics Graduate Student Association) Fledgelings, "Constitution vs. Cooperation." See Appendix A.

4. Art. II, section I, of the U.S. Constitution states: "Before he [the President] enter on the Execution of his Office, he shall take the following Oath or Affirmation: 'I do solemnly swear (or affirm) that I will faithfully execute the Office of President of the United States, and will to the best of my Ability, preserve, protect and defend the Constitution of the United States.'"

5. "I Really Do Swear, Faithfully: Obama and Roberts Try Again," *The New York Times*, January 21, 2009. Available at www.nytimes.com/2009/01/22/us/politics/22oath.html?_r=0.

6. Justin Richland, "Jurisdiction: Grounding Law in Language," *Annual Review of Anthropology* Vol. 42 (2013): 209–226, at 211.

7. Jack Sammons, "Origin of the Opinion as a Work of Art," paper presented at Association for the Study of Law, Culture and the Humanities, Annual Meeting, March 2012, p. 2, citing Lydia Goehr, *The Imaginary Museum of Musical Works: An Essay in the Philosophy of Music* (Oxford, UK: Oxford University Press, 2007).

8. James Boyd White, *Justice as Translation: An Essay in Cultural and Legal Criticism* (Chicago: University of Chicago Press), pp. 46–86.

9. Jeffrey Toobin, *The Oath: The Obama White House and the Supreme Court* (New York: Doubleday, 2012), opens with a discussion of the decision to retake the oath.

10. J. L. Austin, "A Plea for Excuses," in *Philosophical Papers*, 3rd ed. (Oxford, UK: Oxford University Press, 1979), pp. 175–204, at 198–99.

11. Robert F. Blomquist, "The Presidential Oath, the American National Interest and a Call for Presiprudence," *UMKC Law Review* Vol. 73 (2004): pp. 1–52.

12. J. L. Austin, *How to Do Things with Words* (Cambridge, MA: Harvard University Press, 1962), p. 144. The book is divided into twelve lectures. Page numbers or lecture numbers appear within the body of the text.

13. "Sociolegal positivism" identifies a cluster of characteristics around which sociology and legal positivism converge. It relegates any connections between law and justice to empirically contingent social realities. It presumes that law is humanly articulable as the declarations of officials or in scholars' descriptions of human social systems. It posits the completeness of positive or human-made law as law and views law as exclusively social. It thus tends toward exhaustive and ahistorical accounts of powerful and controlling law that functions as instrument or strategy in a field of social power. Elsewhere I have referred to this as "sociolegal positivism"; see Marianne Constable, *Just Silences*, p. 10, and chapter 2. See also Christopher Tomlins, "Law and History," in *Oxford Handbook of Law and Politics*, print 2008 or online publication 2009, DOI 10.1093/oxfordhb/9780199208425.003.0042; and Christopher Tomlins, "'Law as . . .': Theory and Practice in Legal History," *UC Irvine Law Journal* Vol. 1, no. 3 (2011): 1039–1079.

14. Stanley Cavell, "Passionate and Performative Utterances," in *Philosophy the Day after Tomorrow* (Cambridge, MA: Harvard University Press, 2005), pp. 155–191. Page numbers henceforth appear within the body of the text.

15. Friedrich Nietzsche, *Twilight of the Idols*, trans. R. J. Hollingdale (London: Penguin, 1968).

16. *Palsgraf v. Long Island Railroad*, 248 N.Y. 339 (1928). See Appendix C.

17. Richard C. Wydick, *Plain English for Lawyers*, 5th ed. (Durham, NC: Carolina Academic Press, 2005), p. 5.

18. Jacques Derrida, "Declarations of Independence," *New Political Science*, Vol. 7, no. 1 (1986): 7–15.

19. Adolf Reinach, "The A Priori Foundations of Civil Law," *Aletheia* 3 (1983): 1–142.

20. The "imperfect" also refers doubly and adverbially to the manner of those who are speaking together. Recall Obama's oath. In imperfectly speaking and in speaking imperfectly, those who speak together here differ from the members of a Habermasian speech community who are ostensibly governed by norms.

21. Pierre Clastres, *Society against the State: Essays in Political Anthropology* (New York: Zone Books, 1987); Robert Cover, "Nomos and Narrative," *Harvard Law Review* Vol. 97, no. 4 (1983); Martin Krygier, "Law as Tradition," *Law and Philosophy* Vol. 5, no. 2 (1986).

22. Euripides, *Hippolytus*, trans. Michael R. Halleran (Newburyport, MA: Focus Classical Library, 2001); and Shoshana Felman, *The Scandal of the Speaking Body: Don*

Juan with J. L. Austin, or Seduction in Two Languages (Stanford, CA: Stanford University Press, 2003).

23. See also Christopher Tomlins, "Introduction: The Many Legalities of Colonization," in Christopher Tomlins and Bruce H. Mann, eds., *The Many Legalities of Early America* (Chapel Hill: University of North Carolina Press, 2001), pp. 1–20.

Chapter One

1. J. L. Austin, *How to Do Things with Words* (Cambridge, MA: Harvard University Press, 1962).

2. Stanley Cavell, "Passionate and Performative Utterances," in *Philosophy the Day after Tomorrow* (Cambridge, MA: Harvard University Press, 2005). See also "Introduction" and "Something Out of the Ordinary" in the same volume.

3. Ross Charnock, "Hart as Contextualist? Theories of Interpretation in Language and the Law," in Michael Freeman and Fiona Smith, eds., *Law and Language, Current Legal Issues*, Vol. 15 (2013), pp. 128–150, at p. 131.

4. H. L. A. Hart, *The Concept of Law* (Oxford, UK: Clarendon Press, 1961), pp. 124–125. Fuller and many others take up Hart's example, which Hart first presented in H. L. A. Hart, "Positivism and the Separation of Law and Morals," *Harvard Law Review* Vol. 71 (1958): 593–629. See also Lon L. Fuller, "Positivism and Fidelity to Law—A Reply to Professor Hart." *Harvard Law Review* Vol. 71 (1958): 630–672.

5. Charnock, p. 131.

6. Fuller, 661–669, ostensibly arguing against Hart, perhaps at cross-purposes, that one must understand the aim or purpose of a statute to be able to interpret its individual words.

7. *Leocal v. Ashcroft*, 543 U.S. 1 (2004).

8. *Flores-Figueroa v. United States*, 556 U.S. 646 (2009); cf. Adam Liptak and Julia Preston, "Justices Limit Use of Identity Theft Law in Immigration Cases," *The New York Times*, May 5, 2009.

9. Lawrence Solan, *The Language of Statutes: Laws and Their Interpretation* (Chicago and London: The University of Chicago Press, 2010).

10. *Smith v. U.S.*, 508 U.S. 223 at 228 (1993).

11. *Duncan v. Walker*, 533 U.S. 167 at 174 (2001).

12. The depublishing of court opinions offers a counterexample to the usual conventions. See Penelope Pether, "Inequitable Injunctions: The Scandal of Private Judging in the U.S. Courts," *Stanford Law Review* Vol. 56 (2004): 1435–1580.

13. The burgeoning literature on speech acts cuts across philosophy of language, philosophy of action, linguistics, and literary theory. My focus on Austin and on Cavell reflects the usefulness of their work for thinking about the utterances of law not only in conventional and institutional context, to which John Searle's work also contributes,

but as dialogic interactions that cannot be exhausted by rules. Searle replaces Austin's locutionary act with propositional acts of referring and predicating; he offers constitutive rules, which include speakers and hearers, for the various illocutionary acts whose content comes from propositions. John R. Searle, *Speech Acts: An Essay in the Philosophy of Language* (London: Cambridge University Press, 1969).

14. *Morissette v. United States*, 342 U.S. 246 (1952). Appendix B contains the excerpt reprinted in a student casebook, Sanford H. Kadish et al., *Criminal Law and Its Processes: Cases and Materials*, 9th ed. (New York: Aspen Publishers, 2012), pp. 284–288. The full version of the case can be found online at http://supreme.justia.com/cases/federal/us/342/246/case.html.

15. See discussion of case briefing in, for example, Linda H. Edwards, *Legal Writing and Analysis*, 2nd ed. (New York: Aspen Publishers, 2007), in Chapter 3; Richard K. Neumann, *Legal Reasoning and Legal Writing: Structure, Strategy, and Style*, 4th ed. (Gaithersburg, MD: Aspen Law & Business, 2001), now in its 6th ed. See also Elizabeth Mertz, *The Language of Law School: Learning to "Think Like a Lawyer"* (Oxford, UK, and New York: Oxford University Press, 2007), pp. 64–82. See Jane C. Ginsburg, *Introduction to Law and Legal Reasoning*, 3rd ed., for a casebook that invites students to ask whether "analysis leads to outcomes the student would have approved before starting an introductory law course" (New York: Foundation Press, 2003), p. v.

16. *Miranda v. Arizona*, 384 U.S. 436 (1966).

17. See Marianne Constable, *Just Silences: The Limits and Possibilities of Modern Law* (Princeton, NJ: Princeton University Press, 2005), chapter 7.

18. *Dickerson v. United States*, 530 U.S. 428 (2000).

19. George C. Thomas III and Richard Leo, "The Effects of *Miranda v. Arizona*: Embedded in Our National Culture?" *Crime and Justice* Vol. 29 (2002): 203–271.

20. Nicola Lacey, *A Life of H. L. A. Hart : The Nightmare and the Noble Dream* (Oxford. UK: Oxford University Press, 2004): "A number of jointly taught seminars over the years with philosopher colleagues echoed the electric sessions he had taught with Austin, in which Herbert provided legal examples to which Austin would apply his distinctive analytic techniques" (p. 168; cf. 142).

21. Lucy Salyer, "'You Never Loved Me': Allegiance and the Loss of Citizenship in Wartime America," paper presented at AHA, 2006.

22. Salyer, p. 35, citing *United States v. Wusterbarth*, district court of New Jersey, from archival material.

23. The locutionary act itself involves performing other acts: uttering noises, a phonetic act; uttering words, a phatic act; and uttering them with a certain meaning, a rhetic act. Austin, *How to Do Things with Words*, pp. 92–93.

24. Federal Rules of Evidence, Article VIII.

25. U.S. Constitution, First Amendment: "Congress shall make no law respecting an establishment of religion, or prohibiting the free exercise thereof; or abridging the free-

dom of speech, or of the press; or the right of the people peaceably to assemble, and to petition the Government for a redress of grievances."

26. *Crawford v. Washington*, 541 U.S. 36, (2004); and *Davis v. Washington*, 547 U.S. 813 (2006).

27. See Helen Silving, "The Oath: I," *The Yale Law Journal* Vol. 68, no. 7 (June 1959): 1329–1390, for a history of the oath as a self-curse that has never quite broken with its "primitive roots in the decisive magic rite" (1389). English legislation passed in 1697 to accommodate the Quakers' refusal to swear a religious oath officially allowed substitution of the affirmation for the oath, according to Sir Thomas Edlyne Tomlins, *The Law-dictionary, Explaining the Rise, Progress, and Present State of the British Law: Defining and Interpreting the Terms or Words of Art, and Comprising Also Copious Information on the Subjects of Trade and Government*, Volume 2, (under entry: "Quakers"). (London: J. and W. T. Clarke; Longman, Rees, Orme, Brown, Green and Longman, 1835). For a more contemporary account of the history of the oath that shows in part that credibility is a rhetorical matter, see Barbara Shapiro, "Oaths, Credibility and the Legal Process in Early Modern England," Part One, *Law and Humanities* Vol. 6, no. 2 (2012): 145–178; and Part Two, *Law and Humanities* Vol. 7, no. 1 (2013): 19–54. Martin A. Hewett, "Hearsay at Guantanamo: A 'Fundamental Value' Determination," *Georgetown Law Journal* Vol. 96 (2008): 1375–1409, implies that "reliability" too changes meaning in context.

28. Articles that ground themselves in speech acts and that focus on speaking in conventional context often turn to institutional analyses or to what Searle calls "institutional facts": Carlos L. Bernal, "A Speech Acts Analysis of Judicial Decisions," *European Journal of Legal Studies* Vol. 2, no. 1 (2007), available at www.ejls.eu/2/34UK.pdf ; Deborah Cao, "Illocutionary Acts of Chinese Legislative Language," *Journal of Pragmatics* Vol. 41, no. 7 (2009) 1329–1340; and H. L. Ho, "What Does a Verdict Do? A Speech Act Analysis of Giving a Verdict," *International Commentary on Evidence* Vol. 4, no. 2 (2002), available at www.bepress.com/ice/vol4/iss2/art1. Articles that recognize limitations of this way of understanding speech act and law include Ross Charnock, "Overruling as a Speech Act: Performativity and Normative Discourse," *Journal of Pragmatics* Vol. 41, no. 3 (2009): 401–426; and Sandra Laugier, "Performativité, normativité et droit," *Archives de Philosophie* Vol. 67, no. 4 (2004): 607–627, reading Austin as a criticism of conventional accounts of speech acts to help redefine the connection between language and law.

29. Bernard J. Hibbits, "Making Sense of Metaphors: Visuality, Aurality and the Reconfiguration of American Legal Discourse," *Cardozo Law Review* Vol. 16 (1994–1995): 229–356; Desmond Manderson, *Songs without Music: Aesthetic Dimensions of Law and Justice* (Berkeley: University of California Press, 2000); and James Parker, "The Soundscape of Justice," *Griffith Law Review* Vol. 20, no. 4 (2011): 962–993.

30. Austin is often read as deemphasizing the role of the hearer, although he need not be read this way. Chapter Three takes this up. See also Laugier (2004).

31. Sara Kendall, "Contested Jurisdictions: Legitimacy and Governance at the Special Court for Sierra Leone," PhD dissertation, Rhetoric, UC Berkeley, 2009; Marianne Constable, "Speaking the Language of Law: A Juris-dictional Primer," *English Language Notes* Vol. 48, no. 2 (Fall/Winter 2010); and Justin Richland, "Jurisdiction: Grounding Law in Language," *Annual Review of Anthropology* Vol. 42 (2013): 209–226.

32. Judith Resnik and Dennis E. Curtis, *Representing Justice: Invention, Controversy, and Rights in City-States and Democratic Courtrooms* (New Haven, CT: Yale University Press, 2011), pp. 289–292, citing, among others, John M. Kelly, "Audi Alteram Partem," *Natural Law Forum* Vol. 9, no. 103 (1964).

33. Cavell, "Passionate and Performative Utterances," cited in Introduction, note 14, is again especially relevant to the discussion that follows.

34. James Boyd White, *The Legal Imagination* (Chicago: University of Chicago Press, 1985); James Boyd White, *Heracles' Bow: Essays on the Rhetoric and Poetics of Law* (Madison: University of Wisconsin Press, 1985); James Boyd White, *Justice as Translation: An Essay in Cultural and Legal Criticism* (Chicago: University of Chicago Press, 1990); James Boyd White, *Living Speech Resisting the Empire of Force* (Princeton, NJ: Princeton University Press, 2006); and Peter Goodrich, *Oedipus Lex: Psychoanalysis, History, Law* (Berkeley: University of California Press, 1995).

35. William L. F. Felstiner, Richard L. Abel, and Austin Sarat, "The Emergence and Transformation of Disputes: Naming, Blaming, Claiming," *Law & Society Review* Vol. 15, no. 3/4 (1980): 631–654.

36. Lawrence M. Solan and Peter Meijes Tiersma, *Speaking of Crime: The Language of Criminal Justice* (Chicago: University of Chicago Press, 2005). Page numbers appear in the text. See also Roger W. Shuy, *Language Crimes: The Use and Abuse of Language Evidence in the Courtroom* (Cambridge, MA: Blackwell, 1993).

37. Jessica Fischweicher, "Perjury," *American Criminal Law Review* Vol. 45, no. 2 (Spring 2008): 799–824. The witness must have the "willful intent" to produce false testimony.

38. See P. R. Glazebrook, "Misprision of Felony; Shadow or Phantom?" *American Journal of Legal History* Vol. 8 (1964): 189–208 and 293–302.

39. Kim Scheppele, *Legal Secrets: Equality and Efficiency in the Common Law* (Chicago: University of Chicago Press, 1988).

40. Grace Soyon Lee, "Comment on Chapter 1: Our Word (or the Lack Thereof) Is Our Bond: The Regulation of Silence under Contract Law" in Austin Sarat, *Speech and Silence in American Law* (New York: Cambridge University Press, 2010), citing *Hill v. Jones* 725 P. 2d 1115 (1986).

41. Federal Rules of Evidence, 403.

42. *A Book Named "John Cleland's Memoirs of a Woman of Pleasure" v. Attorney General of Massachusetts*, 383 U.S. 413 (1966).

43. See Linda J. Demaine, "In Search of an Anti-Elephant: Confronting the Human Inability to Forget Inadmissible Evidence," *George Mason Law Review* Vol. 16 (Fall 2008): 99–140; and Saul M. Kassin and Samuel R. Sommers, "Inadmissible Testimony, Instructions to Disregard, and the Jury: Substantive Versus Procedural Considerations," *Personality and Social Psychology Bulletin* Vol. 23, no. 10 (1997): 1046–1054.

44. Jack M. Balkin, "The Footnote," *Faculty Scholarship Series* Paper 287 (1989); available at http://digitalcommons.law.yale.edu/fss_papers/287.

45. *Schenck v. United States*, 249 U.S. 47 (1919); "A Cry of Fire in a Crowded Theatre," *The New York Times* September 25, 1884, 4. See also Robert Tsai, "Fire, Metaphor, and Constitutional Myth-Making," *Georgetown Law Review* Vol. 93 (2004–2005): 181–240.

46. John M. Scheb, *An Introduction to the American Legal System*, New York: Aspen Publishers, 3d ed. (2012); Edgar Oakley, John B. Bodenheimer, and Jean C. Love, *Introduction to the Anglo-American Legal System*, 4th ed. (St. Paul, MN: West, 2004); and James V. Calvi and Susan Coleman, *American Law and Legal Systems*, 7th ed. (Boston: Longman, 2011); also see the bibliography attached to the Duke University Law website's "Introduction to U.S. Law" at http://law.duke.edu/lib/researchguides/usleg/, rev. 5/2013 JW/KA. Some texts distinguish among legal systems, identifying them through such adjectives as "formal," "governing," "the Western," and so forth. See Kitty Calavita, *Invitation to Law and Society: An Introduction to the Study of Real Law* (Chicago: University of Chicago Press, 2010).

47. Hart, *Concept*, p. 96; cf. 113.

48. See Law Commission of Canada, "Justice Within: Indigenous Legal Traditions," Discussion Paper (2006), available at http://www/lcc/gc.ca; John Borrows, *Recovering Canada: The Resurgence of Indigenous Law* (Toronto: University of Toronto Press, 2002) and other work; E. Adamson Hoebel and Karl L. Llewellyn, *The Cheyenne Way* (Norman, OK: University of Oklahoma Press, 1941); and Justin B. Richland, *Arguing with Tradition: The Language of Law in Hopi Tribal Court*, (Chicago: University of Chicago Press, 2008).

49. Katherine Lemons, "At the Margins of Law: Adjudicating Muslim Families in Contemporary Delhi." PhD dissertation, Anthropology, UC Berkeley (2010).

50. On colonial law, see Christopher L. Tomlins and Bruce H. Mann, eds., *The Many Legalities of Early America* (Chapel Hill and London: University of North Carolina Press for the Omohundro Institute of Early American History and Culture, 2001); and Samera Esmeir, *Juridical Humanity: A Colonial History* (Stanford, CA: Stanford University Press, 2012).

51. See Annelise Riles, "Cultural Conflicts," in *Law and Anthropology*, ed. Michael Freeman and David Napier (Oxford, UK: Oxford University Press, 2009); and Martti Koskenniemi, *The Politics of International Law* (Oxford, UK: Hart Publishing, 2011).

52. As to sovereignty, see canon of political theory. As to power, see canonical social theory. As to social control, criminology.

53. Hart, *Concept*, pp. 3–4 and chapter 10.

54. Elsewhere I argue that if state law no longer speaks of justice, then that may not be a reason to ignore or neglect justice but rather a reason to reconsider the claims of state law to exhaust the category of law. Marianne Constable, "The Silence of the Laws: Justice in Cover's 'Field of Pain and Death,'" in *Law, Violence, and the Possibility of Justice*, ed. Austin Sarat (Princeton, NJ: Princeton University Press, 2001). See also Peter Fitzpatrick, "Why the Law Is Also Nonviolent," in *Law, Violence, and the Possibility of Justice*, ed. Austin Sarat (Princeton, NJ: Princeton University Press, 2001), pp. 142–174. Many argue that the legal positivist claim that there is no necessary connection between law and justice is for Hart a way of preserving a space outside of the law for practical discussion of morality and justice, rather than neglecting or dismissing them. See Fuller's response, however, cited in note 4 above.

55. Patricia Ewick and Susan S. Silbey, *The Common Place of Law: Stories from Everyday Life* (Chicago: University of Chicago Press, 1998) and works by Mertz, Winter, and others, are indeed compatible with the claims of this book.

56. See Daniel J. Givelber, William J. Bowers, and Carolyn L. Blitch, "Tarasoff, Myth and Reality: An Empirical Study of Private Law in Action," originally published in *Wisconsin Law Review* Vol. 443 (1984) and reprinted in "Social Impact: The Importance of Communication Networks," in *Law & Society: Readings on the Social Study of Law*, eds. Stewart Macaulay, Lawrence M. Friedman, and John Stookey (New York: W. W. Norton and Company, 1995): 627–658. The article shows how a California appellate decision (*Tarasoff v. UC Regents*, 1976) that a therapist must exercise reasonable care to protect those threatened by the therapist's patient, becomes heard, translated, circulated, constructed, and understood as a rule of conduct.

57. CA Penal Code; see Appendix D.

58. Hart, *Concept*, chapters 5 and 6.

59. Jeremy Webber makes a similar point about Canadian indigenous orders and customary law more broadly in "The Grammar of Customary Law," *McGill Law Journal* Vol. 54 (2009): 579–626. See especially 606–611 and studies cited therein.

60. Martin Krygier, "Thinking Like a Lawyer," in *Ethical Dimensions of Legal Theory*, ed. Wojciech Sadurski (Amsterdam: Poznan Studies in the Philosophy of the Sciences and Humanities: B. R. Grüner Publishing Company, 1991), 67–90. See also Martin Krygier, "Law as Tradition," *Law and Philosophy* Vol. 5, no. 2 (August 1986): 237–262, arguing that written law is addressed to state actors rather than the general citizenry.

61. Ludwig Wittgenstein, *Philosophical Investigations*, 3d ed., section 241, trans. G. E. M. Anscombe (New York: Basil Blackwell and Mott, Limited, 1958).

62. Unlike the aspirational discourse ethics of a Habermasian speech community. See Danielle S. Allen, *Talking to Strangers: Anxieties of Citizenship since* Brown v. Board of Education (Chicago: The University of Chicago Press, 2004); and Martin Krygier's

understanding of "civil society" in "Public Values," in *Civil Passions: Selected Writings* (Melbourne: Black Inc., 2005).

63. See also Robert Gammon, "Guns and the Code of Silence," *East Bay Express*, August 17–23, 2011, p. 6.

64. Private international law or "conflicts law" traditionally addresses which law governs when parties disagree as to whose law should govern. Private international law distinguishes itself from public international law by its concern not with conflicts between states involving "public"—or criminal and constitutional—law, but with suits between "private" parties in such areas as torts, contracts, property, and family law. Today conflicts law is increasingly considered a law of private international transactions, although it is not limited to these. When private enterprises do not manage to take disputes out of the system, conflicts are largely addressed by state—or even interstate—institutions. Through conflicts law or private international law, members of overlapping and conflicting associations or communities may challenge a particular state's jurisdiction or assert standing as entities that have formerly not had it.

65. See essays in the volume on *Transdisciplinary Conflict of Laws*, Karen Knop, Ralf Michaels, Annelise Riles, eds., *Law and Contemporary Problems*, Vol. 71, No. 3 (2008).

66. Hence the scholarly emphasis on method and on locating oneself within the literature of a field. See Michel Foucault, "The Discourse on Language," Appendix to *The Archaeology of Knowledge* (New York: Pantheon Books, 1972).

67. Galanter, Marc, "Why the Haves Come Out Ahead: Speculations on the Limits of Legal Change," *Law & Society Review* Vol. 9, no. 1 (1974): 95–160. Page numbers appear in the body of the text.

68. See David Kazanijan, *The Colonizing Trick: National Culture and Imperial Citizenship in Early America* (Minneapolis: University of Minnesota Press, 2003), p. 16, on the "messy co-mingling of articulation's discursive and bodily meanings," citing Stuart Hall, "Race, Articulation and Society Structured in Dominance," p. 328.

69. There are several journals and a few collections, especially by linguists, that address law and language.

Chapter Two

1. Richard Wydick, *Plain English for Lawyers*, 5th ed. (Durham, NC: Carolina Academic Press, 2005), p. 5.

2. The text of *Palsgraf* appears in Appendix C. Wydick (p. 5) refers to the passage, which he cites, in the standard way, as "the statement of facts of the majority opinion."

3. Elizabeth Mertz, *The Language of Law School: Learning to "Think Like a Lawyer"* (Oxford, UK, and New York: Oxford University Press, 2007), available at http://site.ebrary.com/lib/berkeley/Doc?id=10171021. Page references appear in parentheses in the

text. For another version of how a particular sort of legal or juridical discourse transforms one's knowledge or experience of the world, see W. E. Conklin, *The Phenomenology of Modern Legal Discourse: The Juridical Production and the Disclosure of Suffering* (Aldershot/Brookfield: Dartmouth/Ashgate, 1998).

4. Friedrich Wilhelm Nietzsche, *Twilight of the Idols*, trans. R. J. Hollingdale (London: UK: Penguin, 1968). "Four Great Errors," section 8.

5. Nietzsche, *Twilight* "How the True World Became a Fable," pp. 40–41. I've elaborated on this in "Genealogy and Jurisprudence: Nietzsche, Nihilism, and the Social Scientification of Law," *Law & Social Inquiry* Vol. 19, no. 3 (1994): 551–590.

6. Friedrich Wilhelm Nietzsche, *Beyond Good and Evil: Prelude to a Philosophy of the Future*, trans. Walter A. Kaufmann (New York: Vintage Books, 1989), section 296.

7. Jonathan W. Cardi, "The Hidden Legacy of *Palsgraf*: Modern Duty Law in Microcosm," *Boston University Law Review, Forthcoming Wake Forest University Legal Studies Paper No. 1851316* (2011), available at SSRN: http://ssrn.com/abstract=1851316. See also G. Edward White, *Tort Law in America: An Intellectual History* (Oxford, UK: Oxford University Press, 2003), pp. 96–102, 124–127; and John Noonan, *Persons and Masks of the Law* (Berkeley: University of California Press), chapter 4 (1976). See also notes accompanying *Palsgraf* in William L. Prosser et al., *Cases and Materials on Torts*, 12th ed. (New York: Foundation Press, 2010).

8. See also Bryan A. Garner, *The Elements of Legal Style*, 2nd ed. (New York: Oxford University Press, 2002). Wydick's claims are compatible with what is known as the "plain English movement," which began in the 1970s and is associated with relatively recent requirements, in some states, that legal transactions and jury instructions be presented clearly and simply. According to Peter Tiersma, "The premise behind the plain English movement is that legal documents ought to be plainer—and more comprehensible—to the average person." See Peter Tiersma, *The Plain English Movement*, retrieved on May 30, 2013, from a sited hosted by Loyola Law School: www.languageandlaw.org/plainenglish.htm.

9. Wydick, p. 6, note 5. See also Garner, pp. 8–11, for criticisms by Jerome Frank and others of Cardozo's ornamental "Asiatic style," compared to Justice Holmes's swifter "Attic style."

10. Nietzsche, *Twilight*, "'Reason' in Philosophy," section 5.

11. Austin, "A Plea for Excuses," in *Philosophical Papers*, 3d ed. (Oxford, UK: Oxford University Press, 1979): 175–204, at p. 190.

12. See links provided by Matthew Salzwedel, "Scrubbing Adverbs from Legal Writing," September 5, 2012, available at http://lawyerist.com/scrubbing-adverbs-from-legal-writing/. On the "trouble case," see E. Adamson Hoebel, *The Law of Primitive Man* (Boston, MA: Atheneum, 1954) and Austin Sarat, Marianne Constable, David Engel, Valerie Hans, and Susan Lawrence, eds. *Everyday Practices and Trouble Cases, Fundamental Is-*

sues in Law and Society Research: Vol. 2 (Evanston, IL: Northwestern University Press, 1998).

13. Dorothy Lee, *Freedom and Culture* (Englewood Cliffs, NJ: Prentice-Hall, 1959), for instance, shows how Wintu refers to primary generic substance from which particulars emerge. "What to us is a class, a plurality of particulars, is to him a mass or a quality or an attribute"; there is no nominal plural form (124). In Greek, there exists a "middle voice" that corresponds to neither the active nor strictly passive voice in English. In German, subjects and objects are identified by suffix; its word order differs from English, however, such that a recommendation to juxtapose subject-verb-object (such as Wydick makes for English) would make little sense. None of this is to say that one is unable to perceive or to think in ways that appear ungrammatical. Compare "black English" to standard English; see June Jordan, "Nobody Mean More to Me Than You and the Future Life of Willie Jordan," *Harvard Educational Review* Vol. 58, no. 3 (1988): 363–375. It appears rather that habituation to grammar predisposes one to making particular sorts of judgments; see Guy Deutscher, *Through the Language Glass: Why the World Looks Different in Other Languages* (Croydon, UK: Arrow Books, Random House, 2010).

14. Nietzsche, *Twilight*, "Four Great Errors," section 7. In German, *schuld* is both guilt and debt. Christian theology teaches that we are indebted to God for the gift of free will. See Augustine, *On Free Choice of the Will*, trans. Thomas Williams (Indianapolis: Hackett Publishing Company, 1993).

15. But see the Australian case of Lindy Chamberlain, convicted of murdering her baby (1982). On appeal, she was exonerated (1988). The story received intense publicity following *Evil Angels*, a film starring Meryl Streep, also released as *A Cry in the Dark*, and Chamberlain's own book. At Chamberlain's insistence, a fourth coroner's inquest finally agreed in summer 2012 to change the cause of death from "unknown" to "dingo attack." Reference under s.433A of the Criminal Code by the Attorney General for the Northern Territory of Australia of Convictions of the Chamberlains, No. CA2 of 1988. "Baby Azaria's Mother Seeks Ruling That Dingo Killed Her," *BBC News Asia* (February 24, 2012); and "Dingo to Blame for Azaria's Death: Coroner," *The Age*, June 12, 2012. Available at www.theage.com.au/national/dingo-to-blame-for-azarias-death-coroner-20120612-206wo.html.

16. See Colin Dayan, *The Law Is a White Dog: How Legal Rituals Make and Unmake Persons* (Princeton, NJ: Princeton University Press, 2011), arguing in part that dog law is the rhetorical antecedent of slavery, in which slaves are criminally culpable but not otherwise legally capable.

17. See essays in Jeffrie G. Murphy, ed. *Punishment and Rehabilitation*, 3rd ed. (Belmont, CA: Wadsworth Publishing Company, 1994).

18. Jeffrey A. Meyer, "Authentically Innocent: Juries and Federal Regulatory Crimes," *59 Hastings Law Journal* Vol. 59, no. 137-194 (November, 2007). He argues that, in many

regulatory crimes, such as illegal firearms possession, illegal drug dealing, and illegal re-entry of deported aliens, juries convict regardless of whether a defendant actually knew he or she was doing wrong and instead on the basis of whether he or she knew the elements of the crime. Compare the discussion of cases in Chapter 1, Section One.

19. For a more sophisticated account of tort law and causation, see Nancy Weston, "The Metaphysics of Modern Tort Theory," *Valparaiso University Law Review* Vol. 28, no. 3 (1994): 919–1006. For ways in which what count as accidents change, see Michael Witmore, *Culture of Accidents: Unexpected Knowledges in Early Modern England* (Stanford, CA: Stanford University Press, 2001).

20. Austin. "A Plea for Excuses," in Philosophical Papers, 3d ed., (Oxford, UK: Oxford University Press, 1979): 175–204.

21. Nietzsche, *Twilight*, "Four Great Errors," sections 4 and 5.

22. See Bruno Latour, writing as Jim Johnson, "Mixing Humans and Nonhumans Together: The Sociology of a Door-Closer," *Social Problems* Vol. 35, no 3 (1988): 298–310.

23. Michel Foucault, *Discipline and Punish: The Birth of the Prison*, trans. Alan Sheridan (New York: Pantheon Books, 1977); Martin Heidegger, "The Origin of the Work of Art," in *Basic Writings: From Being and Time (1927) to the Task of Thinking (1964)*, ed. David Farrell Krell (New York: Harper & Row, 1977); and Martin Heidegger, "The Way to Language," in *On the Way to Languag*, trans. Peter D. Hertz (New York: Harper & Row, 1982).

24. *New Yorker* collection 1996, by Frank Cotham, in David Alan Sklansky, *Evidence: Cases, Commentary and Problems*, 2d ed. (Austin, TX: Aspen Casebooks; Wolters Kluwer, 2008), 1.

25. Compare yet another account of the *Palsgraf* facts from the headnote for 248 NY 339, retrieved on November 5, 2010, from www.nycourts.gov/history/cases/palsgraf_lirr.htm:

> A man carrying a package jumped aboard a car of a moving train and, seeming unsteady as if about to fall, a guard on the car reached forward to help him in and another guard on the platform pushed him from behind, during which the package was dislodged and falling upon the rails exploded, causing injuries to plaintiff, an intending passenger, who stood on the platform many feet away. There was nothing in the appearance of the package to give notice that it contained explosives. In an action by the intending passenger against the railroad company to recover for such injuries, . . .

26. H. L. A. Hart, "The Ascription of Responsibility and Rights," in *Logic and Language*, ed. Antony Flew (Garden City, NY: Anchor, Doubleday, 1965), pp. 151–174.

27. Austin, "Truth," in *Philosophical Papers*, 3d ed. (Oxford, UK: Oxford University Press, 1979), pp. 117–133, p. 130.

28. See works cited in note 7 above. White writes that the Palsgraf case "helped usher in a new approach to negligence issues" (125).

29. See Pintip Hompleum Dunn, "How Judges Overrule: Speech Act Theory and the Doctrine of Stare Decisis," *Yale Law Journal* Vol. 113, no. 2 (2003): 493–531, arguing that ruling is a performative act (while going on to argue that overruling involves lying). See also Keith Bybee, *All Judges Are Political—Except When They Are Not: Acceptable Hypocrisies and the Rule of Law* (Stanford, CA: Stanford University Press, 2010).

30. See Robert Kagan et al., "The Evolution of State Supreme Courts," *Michigan Law Review* Vol. 76 (1978): 961–1005, p. 999, cited in Post: A study of state supreme courts found that "between 1940 and 1970, the supreme courts with high discretion wrote fewer opinions than the other courts. Their opinions tended to be longer and to cite more cases. They also reversed lower court decisions more often. Their opinions contained more dissents and concurrences." Robert C. Post, "The Supreme Court Opinion as Institutional Practice: Dissent, Legal Scholarship, and Decisionmaking in the Taft Court," *Faculty Scholarship Series* Paper 186 (2001), in *Minnesota Law Review* Vol. 85 (2000–2001): 1267–1390.

31. Post, ibid., at 1274. See also Robert Post, "Defending the Lifeworld: Substantive Due Process in the Taft Court Era," *Faculty Scholarship Series* Paper 193 (1998): 489–546. *Boston University Law Review* Vol. 78: 1489–1586.

32. Adam Liptak, "Justices Are Long on Words but Short on Guidance," *The New York Times*, November 17, 2010, A1.

33. Ward Farnsworth, *The Legal Analyst: A Toolkit for Thinking about the Law* (Chicago: University of Chicago Press, 2007), p. 164.

34. For the ways that "rules" partake in both fact and value, see Stanley Cavell, *Must We Mean What We Say?* (Cambridge, UK: Cambridge University Press, 1976), 14–24. For a critique of the "received view" of the fact/law distinction at trial, see R. P. Burns, *A Theory of the Trial* (Princeton, NJ: Princeton University Press, 2001).

35. Hubert L. Dreyfus and Stuart E. Dreyfus, "From Socrates to Expert Systems: The Limits of Calculative Rationality," *Technology in Society* Vol. 6 (1984): 217–233; Stuart E. Dreyfus, "The Five-Stage Model of Adult Skill Acquisition," *Bulletin of Science, Technology & Society* Vol. 24, no. 3 (2004); and Hubert L. Dreyfus, "The Current Relevance of Merleau-Ponty's Phenomenology of Embodiment," *Electronic Journal of Philosophy*, no. 4 (1996).

36. Nietzsche, *Twilight*, "Maxims and Arrows," chapter 2, page 72.

37. W. Farnsworth, *Legal Analyst*. Compare Reinach, "A Priori Foundations," section 8, pp. 103–104, referring to the opening words of the German Civil Code:

> The proposition, "The ability of man to be a subject of rights begins with the completion of birth," has just as little a *hypothetical* character as does the proposition, "Man is mortal." . . . We do not have here a positing of being which, according as this being is really there or not, could be judged as true or false; we rather have an *enactment* (*Bestimmung*), which stands beyond the alternative of true or false. The only

reason why it was possible to be misled about this is that the very different kinds of proposition can be given the same linguistic expression.

Read in a textbook of law, Reinach argues, the same sentence

> is really a judgment which is made, [in which] it is asserted that in Germany today the ability of man to be a subject of rights begins at birth, and this assertion goes back as to its ground to the first paragraph of the Civil Code. But this paragraph does not contain another assertion—how could one ground one judgment through identically the same judgment—it rather contains an enactment. Because the Civic Code enacts that the ability to be a subject of rights begins at birth, the jurist can *assert* that *in virtue of this enactment* it really is so in Germany at the present. The proposition of the jurist can be true or false; quite different predications are appropriate for the enactment of the Civil Code.

38. A rulelike formulation may also describe an act of inference. Recall *Morissette.* The Court describes Congress as "borrow[ing] terms of art." It then argues: "Where Congress borrows terms of art in which are accumulated the legal traditional meaning of centuries of practice, it presumably knows and adopts the cluster of ideas that were attached to each borrowed word in the body of learning from which it was taken and the meaning its use will convey to the judicial mind unless otherwise instructed." Is the Court stating a rule or describing its inference?

39. Cavell, *Must We Mean What We Say?* p. 15, finds statements of rules in *Hoyle's Rules of Games and in Robert's Rules of Order* to be "statements in the indicative, not the imperative, mood."

40. Jacques Derrida, "Declarations of Independence," *New Political Science* Vol. 7, no. 1 (1986): 7–15. Cf. B. Honig, "Declarations of Independence: Arendt and Derrida on the Problem of Founding a Republic," *The American Political Science Review* Vol. 85, no. 1 (1991): 97-113.

41. Jed Rubenfeld, *Freedom and Time: A Theory of Constitutional Self-Government* (New Haven, CT: Yale University Press, 2001).

42. The late Professor Ronald Walters, then head of Howard University's political science department, quoted in Charles Bierbauer, "Its Goal More Widely Accepted than Its Leader," *CNN.com* (October 17, 1995).

43. Although White, *Tort Law*, largely refers to *Palsgraf* in the past tense, pp. 96–102 and 124–127, he writes that "both opinions *jettison* the physical model of 'proximate causation,'" and explains what cases of proximate cause "become" (note 7, p. xv, emphasis added).

44. Discussion as to whether judges make or discover and declare the law will no doubt continue. See Zechariah Chafee Jr., "Do Judges Make or Discover Law?" *Proceedings of the American Philosophical Society*, Vol. 91, no. 5 (Dec. 3, 1947): 405–420.

45. Robert Cover, "Nomos and Narrative," *Harvard Law Review* Vol. 97, no. 4 (1983): 4–68.

Chapter Three

1. Roscoe Pound coined the term *sociological jurisprudence* to refer to efforts to fit the law to social problems and is credited with distinguishing "law in books" from "law in action." See Roscoe Pound, "Law in Books and Law in Action," *American Law Review* Vol. 44 (1910): 12–36. The legal realists who followed aimed their critiques against judicial decision making in particular, invoking empirical social science to claim that "facts and legal rules are ambiguous and socially contingent," according to Malcolm Feeley, "Theoretical Issues and Authodological Problems: Three Voices of Socio-Legal Studies," *Israel Law Review* Vol. 35, no. 2 (2001): 175–204, at 180. See Laura Kalman, *Legal Realism at Yale, 1927–1960* (Chapel Hill: University of North Carolina Press, 1986). Despite critiques of the "gap" between what has come to be called "law-in-action" and "law-on-the-books," the distinction is alive and well in the scholarship, as well as in grant proposals. See Kitty Calavita, *Invitation to Law & Society: An Introduction to the Study of Real Law* (Chicago: University of Chicago Press, 2010) and analysis in Christopher Tomlins, "Memo Prepared as Background Reading for Panel on Social Science and Legal Scholarship," in *Berkeley-NSF Workshop, The Interplay between Social Science and Law Schools* (Berkeley: UC Berkeley School of Law, May 2012), and works cited therein. Although studies of legal consciousness may fill the "gap," such studies often share with "impact" studies an attachment to causal explanation. See references in Marianne Constable, "Reflections on Law as a Profession of Words," in *Justice and Power in Sociolegal Studies*, ed. Bryant G. Garth and Austin Sarat (Evanston, IL: Northwestern University Press, 1998); and Marianne Constable, "On Not Leaving Law to the Lawyers," in *Law in the Liberal Arts*, ed. Austin Sarat (Ithaca, NY: Cornell University Press, 2004). For examples of more forgiving readings and uses of the relation between legal realism and language, see Justin Richland, "Jurisdiction" (cited Introduction, note 6); Richard K. Sherwin, *Visualizing Law in the Age of the Digital Baroque: Arabesques and Entanglements* (London: Routledge, 2011); Susan Silbey, "J. Locke, op. cit.: Invocations of Law on Snowy Streets," *Journal of Comparative Law*, Vol. 5, no. 2 (2010); and Steven L. Winter, *A Clearing in the Forest: Law, Life, and Mind* (Chicago: University of Chicago Press, 2001).

2. Adolf Reinach, "Die apriorischen Grundlagen des bürgerlichen Rechtes," in *Jahrbuch für Philosophie und phänomenologische Forschung* (Halle: Max Niemeyer, 1913); translated as Adolf Reinach, "The A Priori Foundations of Civil Law," in *Aletheia*, Vol. 3: *Philosophy of Law* (Irving, TX: International Academy of Philosophy Press, 1983). In what follows, I draw from Reinach's ideas about social acts and states of affairs, without adopting his argument for an a priori ground of law. If anything, I understand the "ground" of law to be language. I am indebted to commentary about Reinach's work:

John Crosby, "Adolf Reinach: Reinach's Discovery of the Social Act," in *Aletheia, Vol. 3, Philosophy of Law* (Irving, TX: International Academy of Philosophy Press, 1983): 143–194; Josef Seifert, "Is Reinach's *Apriorische Rechtslehre* More Important for Positive Law Than Reinach Himself Thinks?" in *Aletheia: Philosophy of Law* (Irving, TX: International Academy of Philosophy Press, 1983): 197–230; Kevin Mulligan, ed., *Speech Act and Sachverhalt: Reinach and the Foundations of Realist Phenomenology* (Dordrecht, Boston, and Hingham, MA: M. Nijhoff, Kluwer Academic Publishers, 1987); James M. Dubois, *Judgement and Sachverhalt: An Introduction to Adolf Reinach's Phenomenological Realism* (Dordrecht: Kluwer Academic Publishers, 1995); Lucinda Ann Vandervort Brettler, "The Phenomenology of Adolph Reinach: Chapters in the Theory of Knowledge and Legal Philosophy" (Dissertation, McGill University, 1973). Sandra Laugier, "Actes de langage et états de choses: Austin et Reinach," *Les Études philosophiques*, no. 1 (2005): 73–97; and Barry Smith, "Towards a history of speech act theory," in *Speech Acts, Meaning, and Intentions: Critical Approaches to the Philosophy of John R. Searle*, ed. Armin Burkhardt (Berlin and New York: W. de Gruyter, 1990).

3. Judith Butler, *Gender Trouble: Feminism and the Subversion of Identity* (New York: Routledge, 1990).

4. Adolf Reinach, "The A Priori Foundations of the Civil Law," *Aletheia* 3 (1983): 19.

5. *Apprehend, recognize*, and *receive* are possible translations of *vernehmen*. "It is clear that neither German nor English has any natural and unambiguous word for expressing the highly meaningful concept of a receptive act which refers precisely to an act of another person addressed to the recipient," writes Crosby (translator's note 18, p. 49). I also use *hear* because of its legal connotations.

6. See also J. L. Austin, "Performatif-Constatif," in *Cahiers de Royaumont, Philosophie no. IV, La philosophie analytique* (Paris: Editions de Minuit, 1962): 271–304.

7. Reinachian social acts, like both Austinian illocutionary acts and Cavellian passionate utterances, are distinguishable from acts that only incidentally require speech and hearing, such as frightening someone by giving a person (or an animal) a shock. Reinach points out that we would not even need to express ourselves at all if we were the sorts of beings who could directly perceive each other's experiences. For him, even a silent prayer to a God who grasps our thoughts is a social act (20-1). The history of the language of the deaf shows too that gestures can be social acts. Austin also points out that conventional illocutionary acts—such as warnings and agreements—may occur through gesture (119).

8. Except in Connecticut, where no witnesses are required. See Christopher Roy, "Marriage in Connecticut: A Guide to Resources in the Law Library," in *Connecticut Judicial Branch Law Series* (New Britain: Judicial Branch, State of Connecticut, 2012). The license must still be signed by an authorized officiant and filed within sixty-five days for marriage to have taken place.

9. Again, I adapt Reinach's terminology, although I do not follow his distinctions among ontological "states of affairs" (*Sachverhalt*) that "exist" a priori without obtaining.

10. Jacques Derrida, "Declarations of Independence," *New Political Science*, Vol. 7, no. 1 (1986): 7–15, at 10.

11. To be fair, Austin does try to articulate this. He associates hearing with the "securing of uptake" and the "taking effect" of the successful illocutionary act, which he attempts—unsuccessfully, according to his critics—to distinguish from "the producing of effects which is characteristic of the perlocutionary act" (116–118). He also writes that "the sense in which saying something produces effects on other persons or *causes* things, is a fundamentally different sense of cause from that used in physical causation by pressure, &c." [In an apparent nod to persuasion, he also adds that "this is probably the original sense of cause." (113, n. 1)] He notes that this cause has to operate through conventional language. At the same time though, he writes that "it [the sense in which saying something produces effects] is a matter of influence exerted by one person on another." When he notes that "many illocutionary acts invite by convention a response or sequel," invitation follows utterance chronologically, then however "fundamentally different" the sense of cause. Although Austin distinguishes successful accomplishment of an invitation from its being fulfilled, he does not specify that the hearing needed to accomplish the inviting is part of a joint enterprise of inviting in which hearer and speaker mutually engage. He leaves the impression that hearing is an aspect of the chronologically subsequent "uptake" of the utterance and an "effect" of sorts. One might rather say here with Reinach that although "hearing" is necessarily subsequent to the utterance as a noun and to the speaker's uttering as a verb, hearing cannot be subsequent to—or caused by—the social act to which it essentially belongs.

12. Again, this may be what Austin tries to get at when he distinguishes "mere conventional consequences" from "the real production of real effects" (103) and when he considers "the securing of uptake" to be "a bringing about [of] the understanding of the meaning and of the force of the locution" (117). In Austin's chronological or "commonplace consequence-language," however, uptake necessarily appears "subsequent to" the (locutionary) act of uttering sounds in a grammar and vocabulary that have sense and reference; it does not happen in or upon the performance of the social act.

13. R. P. Burns, *A Theory of the Trial* (Princeton, NJ: Princeton University Press, 2001), p. 3.

14. Justin B. Richland, *Arguing with Tradition: The Language of Law in Hopi Tribal Court* (Chicago: University of Chicago Press, 2008).

15. John L. Comaroff and Jean Comaroff, *Ethnicity, Inc.* (Chicago: University of Chicago Press, 2009), p. 117.

16. See Jack M. Balkin, "The Footnote," *Faculty Scholarship Series* Paper 287 (1989), available at http://digitalcommons.law.yale.edu/fss_papers/287.

17. *U.S. v. Carolene Products*, 304 U.S. 144 (1938), 152, note 4.

18. Balkin, "The Footnote," Part III.

19. See also Michel de Certeau, *The Practice of Everyday Life* (Berkeley: University of California Press, 1984), on moving along the sidewalk.

20. Hannah Arendt, *The Human Condition* (Chicago: University of Chicago Press, 1958), pp. 8–9, 247. Arendt calls the speech and action that depends on speaking and acting with others "political" rather than social.

21. M. M. Bakhtin, *Speech Genres and Other Late Essays*, trans. Vern W. McGee (Austin TX: University of Texas Press, 1986); and M. M. Bakhtin, *The Dialogic Imagination: Four Essays*, trans. Caryl Emerson and Michael Holquist (Austin TX: University of Texas Press, 1981).

22. Elizabeth Mertz, *The Language of Law School: Learning to "Think Like a Lawyer."* (Oxford, UK, and New York: Oxford University Press, 2007).

23. Nice description in Fleur Johns, "Living in International Law," in *Reading Modern Law: Critical Methodologies and Sovereign Formations: Essays in Honour of Peter Fitzpatrick*, ed. Ruth Buchanan et al. (London: Routledge-Cavendish, 2010): 74–86.

24. Eugen Rosenstock-Huessy, "The Listener's Tract," in *Speech and Reality* (Norwich, VT: Argo, 1970), p. 149.

25. This is clear in German, where the (informal) imperative is formed by the root verb without the second-person ending. See also Dorothy Lee on "to be," in Dorothy Lee, *Valuing the Self: What We Can Learn from Other Cultures* (Englewood Cliffs, NJ: Prentice-Hall, 1976).

26. See also Louis Althusser, "Ideology and Ideological State Apparatuses," in *Lenin and Philosophy, and Other Essays* (New York: Monthly Review Press, 1972). On Althusser, see Judith Butler, "Gender Is Burning: Questions of Appropriation and Subversion," in *Bodies That Matter: On the Discursive Limits of "Sex"* (New York: Routledge, 1993).

27. Pierre Clastres compares the sovereign of a state who rules passive subjects to the chief of a society "against the state," whose role is to say how "we" have lived and will always live in "The Duty to Speak," *Society against the State:* (New York: Zone Books, 1987).

28. A related concept of recognition appears in Hegel and is richly discussed in contemporary scholarship. See, among others, Judith Butler, "Longing for Recognition," in *Hegel's Philosophy and Feminist Thought: Beyond Antigone?* ed. Kimberly Hutchings and Pulkkinen Tuija (New York: Palgrave Macmillan, 2010); Judith Butler, *Subjects of Desire: Hegelian Reflections in Twentieth-Century France* (New York: Columbia University Press, 2012); Jeffrey A. Gauthier, *Hegel and Feminist Social Criticism: Justice, Recognition, and the Feminine* (Albany: State University of New York Press, 1997); Paul Ricoeur, *The Course of Recognition* (Cambridge, MA: Harvard University Press, 2005); and Axel Honneth, *The I in We: Studies in the Theory of Recognition* (Malden, MA: Polity Press, 2012). See also Sarah K. Burgess, "Standing before the Law: Recognition, Power, and the Limits of Identity" (PhD dissertation, Rhetoric, University of California, Berkeley, 2007).

29. Rosenstock-Huessy argues that the conventional rules of Alexandrinian grammar suppress differences in emphases and attitudes crucial to proper speech. He uses the Latin *amo, amas, amat* (I love, you love, he loves) to show how each grammatical subject implies a different relation or attitude of speaker and listener to one another. *Amo* concerns self-revelation and raises issues of the wisdom of revealing oneself and the possibility of communion; *amas* involves an assertion of authority over the listener, whose freedom is at stake; *amat* raises problems of knowledge, observation and truth. "Grammar as Social Science," in *Speech and Reality*, pp. 98–114.

30. Plato, "Phaedrus," in *Euthyphro, Apology, Crito, Phaedo, Phaedrus*, trans. H. North Fowler, Loeb Classical Library (Cambridge, MA: Harvard University Press, 1990).

31. Jacques Derrida, *Of Grammatology*, trans. Gayatri Spivak (Baltimore: Johns Hopkins University Press, 1976).

32. Martin Heidegger, "The Thing," in *Poetry, Language, Thought*, trans. Albert Hofstadter (New York: Harper & Row, 1971).

33. Laurent Mayali, ed., *Of Strangers and Foreigners (Late Antiquity–Middle Ages)* (Berkeley: Regents of the University of California, 1993). See also discussion of associations in Michel Foucault, "The Discourse on Language (L'ordre du discourse)," *The Archaeology of Knowledge*, trans. A. M. Sheridan Smith (New York: Pantheon Books, 1970).

34. William L. F. Felstiner, Richard L. Abel, and Austin Sarat, "The Emergence and Transformation of Disputes: Naming, Blaming, Claiming," *Law & Society Review* Vol. 15, no. 3–4 (1980).

35. Or perhaps language is Kant's moral law? I do not pursue this question here. See Linda Meyer, *The Justice of Mercy* (Ann Arbor: University of Michigan Press, 2010).

36. Janet Ainsworth, "Silence, Speech, and the Paradox of the Right to Remain Silent in American Police Interrogation," in *Law and Language: Current Legal Issues*, eds. Michael Freeman and Fiona Smith, Vol. 15 (2011), pp. 371–385; Janet Ainsworth, "'You Have the Right to Remain Silent . . .' but Only if You Ask for It Just So: The Role of Linguistic Ideology in American Police Interrogation Law," *International Journal of Speech, Language and the Law* Vol. 15, no. 1 (2008). See also Janet Ainsworth, "The Meaning of Silence in the Right to Remain Silent," in *The Oxford Handbook of Language and Law*, ed. Peter Meijes Tiersma and Lawrence Solan (Oxford, UK, and New York: Oxford University Press, 2012).

37. Recall Ludwig Wittgenstein, *Philosophical Investigations*, trans. G. E. M. Anscombe (Oxford, UK: Blackwell, 1953), section 241, cited in Chapter One. The previous section 240 concerns where disputes break out. A more literal translation of section 241 is: "*What* human beings say is true or false; they agree in the speech (*der Sprache*). That is not agreement in meanings [about which human beings may dispute], but in lifeform."

38. On the one hand, Cavell distinguishes examples of judgments "from ordinary or civilian life" from those "announced by a judge from the bench." Of the latter he writes,

simplistically, that they "would perhaps . . . be condensed into a verdict plus an assign-
ment of penalty. This is not the context of a passionate utterance, which requires (so far)
exchange, not mediation or arbitration" (177). Moreover, he also differentiates the passionate utterance or exchange in which he is interested from "modes of discourse" that
are "characterized by different perlocutionary objectives"; these modes appear to include
other legal utterances. He distinguishes the passionate utterance, for instance, from types
of utterances in which I deny that I require particular standing to confront you or in
which my utterance claims authority to speak for an institution. He characterizes as "political oratory" utterances in which, rather than singling you out, I generalize from you
to a group (182). On the other hand, he also writes that he means to be following "one
of Austin's ambitious statements" of method, elucidating "the *only actual* phenomenon"
or "the total speech act in the total speech situation" (185, citing Austin 148), when he
describes the passionate utterance in a way that makes it sound very much like a dialogic
legal claim: "A mode of speech in or through which, by acknowledging my desire in confronting you, I declare my standing with you and single you out, demanding a response
in kind from you, and a response now, so making myself vulnerable to your rebuke, thus
staking our future" (185). Certainly the spirit of Cavell's pursuit of "some fragment of a
view of expression of [as?] recognizing language as everywhere revealing desire" in the
service of "a systematic recognition of speech as confrontation, as demanding, as owed"
is compatible with the claims of this book. If Cavell is "prepared to persist farther," as he
paradoxically puts it, than he is himself "perhaps [!] prepared to recognize, in regarding
cries of pain, or prolonged silences, or sobs, as 'preverbal' calls for help, or as traces of
rage, perhaps at oneself, or as reminders of comfort," then might not passionate utterances allow us to persist farther in the other direction, recognizing desire as an aspect of
legal claims that Cavell does not pursue (187)?

    39. Law functions as the state does for Winter, *A Clearing in the Forest: Law, Life, and
Mind* (Chicago: University of Chicago Press, 2001). He points out that

> the state is an imaginative social product over and above its personnel and other
> material manifestations . . . the state's identity remains contingent in two senses. First
> it is dependent on the unstable, inherently ambiguous character of its agents. . . . Sec-
> ond, . . . there is no determinate way in which to decide when it is a governmental
> entity that has acted: Just as the citizens can withhold their consent from an authority
> they view as illegitimate, a legal system can withhold its authorization from the acts
> of its officials. (167)

The point emerges in the context of the distinction in U.S. law between action done
"under color of law" and action done "by color of office." The latter signifies an act done
badly and duplicitously, with only the appearance or guise of official authority. Action
done "under color of law" by contrast is "conduct that is understood to be that of the state

and that, therefore, [when it goes wrong] has all the affective power of an act of betrayal by those upon whom one relies for protection," notes Winter (179).

40. Virgil, *Aeneid* (12, 950–953), emphasis added. Thanks to Juliana Stivanicevic for retranslating *dicens* and pointing out that it is a present active participle used for simultaneous action.

Chapter Four

1. From James Legge, *The Chinese Classics* (Hong Kong: Hong Kong University Press, 1960), pp. 263–264. Cited "with modification" in Deborah Cao, *Chinese Law: A Language Perspective* (Aldershot, UK, and Burlington, VT: Ashgate, 2004), pp. 185, note 1.

2. Shoshana Felman, *The Scandal of the Speaking Body: Don Juan with J. L. Austin, or Seduction in Two Languages* (Stanford, CA: Stanford University Press, 2003).

3. For English translation, I use Michael R. Halleran, *Euripides' Hippolytus: Translation with Notes, Introduction and Essay* (Newburyport, MA: Focus Publishing Company, 2001), except where noted. For Greek and for commentary on translation, I have consulted, among others, the following: Euripides II, *Children of Heracles; Hippolytus; Andromache; Hecuba*, ed. David Kovacs, Loeb Classical Library (Cambridge, MA: Harvard University Press, 1995). Euripides, *Hippolytus*, trans. Michael R. Halleran (Warminster, UK: Aris & Phillips, 1995). Euripides, *Hippolytos*, ed. William Spencer Barrett (Oxford, UK: Clarendon Press, 1978). Euripides wrote and presented two versions of the play; this is the second, in which he revised the story. Numbers in parentheses in the text refer to line numbers. I have found especially helpful Barbara E. Goff, *The Noose of Words: Readings of Desire, Violence, and Language in Euripides' Hippolytos* (Cambridge, UK, and New York: Cambridge University Press, 1990). See also Froma Zeitlin, "The Power of Aphrodite: Eros and the Boundaries of the Self in the *Hippolytus*," in *Directions in Euripidean Criticism: A Collection of Essays*, ed. Peter Burian (Durham, NC: Duke University Press, 1985), pp. 52–111, 189–208. I thank Chiara Ricciardone for her help with the Greek.

4. See Martin Heidegger, "The Way to Language," in *On the Way to Language*, trans. Peter D. Hertz (New York: Harper & Row, 1982). Heidegger suggests that speech is less a subject-centered activity than a mutual relation in which things show themselves to those who speak.

5. Cavell considers Austin's relation to Derrida (and to Felman) in several works, in which he also discusses Austin's relation to Hippolytus. See Cavell, "Counter-Philosophy and the Pawn of Voice," in *A Pitch of Philosophy: Autobiographical Exercises* (Cambridge, MA: Harvard University Press, 1994); "What Did Derrida Want of Austin?" in *Philosophical Passages: Wittgenstein, Emerson, Austin, Derrida* (Oxford, UK: Basil Blackwell, 1995).

6. Positive law can of course enact otherwise; see Adolf Reinach, "The A Priori Foundations of the Civil Law," in *Aletheia, Vol. 3, Philosophy of Law* (Irving, TX: International Academy of Philosophy Press, 1983), section 8.

7. George Washington apparently introduced the language of "So help me God" at the end of the constitutionally required oath. Chief Justice Roberts made "So help you God?" a question; Obama answered, "So help me God."

8. Frederic Maitland, *The Forms of Action at Common Law; A Course of Lectures by F. W. Maitland*, ed. A. H. Chaytor and W. J. Whittaker (Cambridge, UK: Cambridge University Press, 1936), pp. 15–16.

9. Austin uses *misfire* and *abuse* to refer to particular infelicities. Recall from Chapter One that "infelicity" refers in Austin's lectures to six ways that performative utterances as such can fail. (No convention may exist for doing the act. The particular situation may not fit the existing conventions. The act may be carried out by or on behalf of the wrong person, incorrectly or incompletely. Finally, relevant parties may not have the appropriate intentions or follow through.) The "unsatisfactoriness" or "unhappiness" of an act refers to the ways that an utterance can fail also as speech and as act.

10. The Greek *onoma*, like the English *name*, means both name and reputation/fame. *Eukleês*, the word Phaedra uses for reputation at 688, etymologically means well-called or well-named.

11. As the Chorus sings (in Kovacs's translation in Loeb), "Oh what a fine thing is chastity (*sôphron*) everywhere, and how splendid is the repute it gains among mortals" (431–432). (Halleran chooses to translate *sôphron* as moderation, equating it with its cousin *sôphrosune*, also a key theme of the play.)

12. Halleran's translation more literally gives, "Though precariously balanced in the scales, he still sees the light" (1162–1163).

13. Barbara E. Goff, *The Noose of Words: Readings of Desire, Violence, and Language in Euripides' Hippolytos* (Cambridge, UK, and New York: Cambridge University Press, 1990).

14. Ian Ayres, "Valuing Modern Contract Scholarship," *The Yale Law Journal* Vol. 112, no. 4 (2003): 881–901.

15. ALI website: "The Institute's charter stated its purpose to be 'to promote the clarification and simplification of the law and its better adaptation to social needs, to secure the better administration of justice, and to encourage and carry on scholarly and scientific legal work.'" American Law Institute, "The A.L.I. Annual Report: 2011–2012," available at www.ali.org/doc/thisIsALI.pdf.

16. Stewart Macaulay, John Kidwell, and William C. Whitford, *Contracts: Law in Action, The Concise Course* (Newark, NJ: LexisNexis, 2003); and Stewart Macaulay, "Noncontractual Relations in Business: A Preliminary Study," *American Sociological Review* Vol. 28 (1963): 55–68.

17. Morton J. Horwitz, "The Historical Foundations of Modern Contract Law," *Harvard Law Review* Vol. 87, no. 5 (1974); Roy Kreitner, *Calculating Promises: The Emergence of Modern American Contract Doctrine* (Stanford, CA: Stanford University Press, 2007);

A. W. B. Simpson, "The Horwitz Thesis and the History of Contracts," *The University of Chicago Law Review* Vol. 46, no. 3 (1979); and Frederic William Maitland, *The Forms of Action at Common Law; A Course of Lectures by F. W. Maitland*, ed. A. H. Chaytor and W. J. Whittaker. Cambridge, UK: Cambridge University Press, 1936.

18. Edward Allan Farnsworth, *Farnsworth on Contracts*, Vol. 1 (New York: Aspen, 1996), p. 74.

19. Farnsworth, *Farnsworth on Contracts*, Vol 1: 17–22; and. Maitland, *Common Law*, 68–70.

20. Farnsworth, *Farnsworth on Contracts*, Vol. 1: 74, citing Restatement Second.

21. *Hamer v. Sidway*, 124 N.Y. 538, 27 N.E. 256 (1891)

22. Douglas G. Baird, "Reconstructing Contracts: *Hamer v. Sidway*," in *Contracts Stories* (New York: Foundation Press, 2007).

23. Peter Meijes Tiersma, "Reassessing Unilateral Contracts: The Role of Offer Acceptance and Promise," *UC Davis Law Review* Vol. 26, no. 1 (1992): 1–86.

24. See Reinach, "The A Priori Foundations of the Civil Law," pp. 43–45. Reinach writes that "one can think away the possibility of any such harm, but that would not restrain the arising of the obligation." Further "one can imagine ever so much harm"—to others who themselves relied on B's getting the $100, for instance—"though no obligation results [to them] from the promise" (44). See also Duncan Kennedy, "From the Will Theory to the Principle of Autonomy: Lon Fuller's 'Consideration and Form,'" *Columbia Law Review* Vol. 100 (2000). He distinguishes in very different context and for different reasons, Corbin's justification of revocation due to reliance, the Restatement's making reliance equivalent to acceptance, and Lon Fuller's views on reliance (notes 162 and 215).

25. Farnsworth, *Farnsworth on Contracts*, Vol. 1: 75, note 11, citing M. Eisenberg, "The Responsive Model of Contract Law," *Stanford Law Review* (1984), 1107, at 1116–1117, and M. Kelman, *A Guide to Critical Legal Studies* (1987), p. 20. See also Macaulay, Kidwell, and Whitford, *Contracts, Law in Action : The Concise Course*. For an interesting case study of the "legislative revival" of unconscionability and its reentry into the courts, see Anne Fleming, "The Rise and Fall of Unconscionability as the 'Law of the Poor,'" retrieved on January 2, 2013, from: http://scholar.harvard.edu/files/afleming/files/fleming_rise_and_fall_of_unconscionability_draft_november_2013_glj.pdf.

26. Seana Valentine Shiffrin, "The Divergence of Contract and Promise," *Harvard Law Review* Vol. 120, no. 3 (2007): 708. But see Joseph Raz, "Promises in Morality and Law," *Harvard Law Review* Vol. 95, no. 4 (1982): 916–938.

27. Should the reader find this hard to conceive, see Alan E. Garfield, "Promises of Silence: Contract Law and Freedom of Speech," *Cornell Law Review* Vol. 83 (1994): 261–364.

28. John Rawls, *A Theory of Justice* (Cambridge, MA: Belknap Press of Harvard University Press, 1971). See also Bernard Williams, *Moral Luck: Philosophical Papers, 1973–1980* (Cambridge, UK, and New York: Cambridge University Press, 1981).

29. Nietzsche, *On the Genealogy of Morals*, in *Basic Writings of Nietzsche*, trans. Walter Kaufmann (New York: Modern Library, 1968) 2nd Essay, 6: "Revenge merely leads us back to the same problem: how can making suffer constitute a compensation?"

30. L. Fuller, *Legal Fictions* (Stanford CA: Stanford University Press, 1967).

31. Linda Meyer, "When Reasonable Minds Differ," *NYU Law Review* Vol. 71 (1996): 1467–1528 at 1479, n. 38, quoting George H. Smith, "Of the Certainty of the Law and the Uncertainty of Judicial Decisions" *American Law Review* Vol. 23 (1889) 699: 702–703.

32. Aristotle, *The Politics, and the Constitution of Athens*, ed. Stephen Everson, trans. Jonathan Barnes (Cambridge, UK, and New York: Cambridge University Press, 1996): Book I, Chap. 2, line 1253a10.

33. As Heidegger puts it, "Even deception is possible, and can be genuinely carried out only if one sees the truth." Martin Heidegger, *Plato's Sophist*, trans. Richard Rojcewicz and Andre Schuwer (Bloomington: Indiana University Press, 1997), p. 220.

Conclusion

1. Heidegger's term *Ereignis* is translated in various ways, by "event," "appropriation," "event of appropriation," and the neologism, "enowning."

2. Stanley Paulson, "Demystifying Reinach's Legal Theory," in *Speech Act and Sachverhalt: Reinach and the Foundations of Realist Phenomenology*, ed. Kevin Mulligan, 133–154 (Dordrecht: Martinus Nijhoff Publishers, 1987), at 152–153. See also Barry Smith, "On the Cognition of States of Affairs," 189–225 in the same volume.

3. See Jürgen Habermas, "Discourse Ethics: Notes on a Program of Philosophical Justification," *Moral Consciousness and Communicative Action*, trans. Christian Lenhart and Shierry Weber Nicholson, 43–115 (Cambridge, MA: MIT Press, 1990).

4. Giorgio Agamben, *The Sacrament of Language: An Archaeology of the Oath*, trans. Adam Kotsko (Stanford, CA: Stanford University Press, 2011), argues that "it is once more from *philosophy* that there can come, in the sober awareness of the extreme situation at which the living human being that has language has arrived in its history, the indication of a line of resistance and of change" (72, emphasis added).

5. See, for example, Susan Berk-Seligson, *The Bilingual Courtroom: Court Interpreters in the Judicial Process* (Chicago: University of Chicago Press, 1990); Susan Berk-Seligson, *Coerced Confessions: The Discourse of Bilingual Police Interrogations* (Berlin and New York: Mouton de Gruyter, 2009); Danielle S. Allen, *Talking to Strangers: Anxieties of Citizenship since* Brown v. Board of Education (Chicago: University of Chicago Press, 2004); and Danielle S. Allen, "The Art of Association," presented at General Aspects of Law, Kadish Center for Morality, Law, and Public Affairs, University of California, Berkeley, September 7, 2012.

6. Michel Foucault, *Discipline and Punish*, trans. Alan Sheridan (New York: Pantheon, 1977), pp. 297–298.

7. See Jonathan Simon, *Governing through Crime: How the War on Crime Transformed American Democracy and Created a Culture of Fear* (Oxford, UK: Oxford University Press, 2007).

8. Reid Hastie, "The Challenge to Produce Useful 'Legal Numbers,'" *Journal of Empirical Legal Studies* Vol. 8 (2011): 6–20, at 6.

9. Wendy Nelson Espeland and Mitchell L. Stevens, "Commensuration as a Social Process," *Annual Review of Sociology* Vol. 24 (1998): 313–338.

10. Marianne Constable, *Just Silences: The Limits and Possibilities of Modern Law* (Princeton, NJ: Princeton University Press, 2005). See also Constable, "Response," *PoLAR: Political and Legal Anthropology Review* Vol. 33 (2010): 148–151.

Bibliography

Cases Cited

A Book Named "John Cleland's Memoirs of a Woman of Pleasure" v. Attorney General of Massachusetts, 383 U.S. 413 (1966).

Crawford v. Washington, 541 U.S. 36 (2004).

Davis v. Washington, 547 U.S. 813 (2006).

Dickerson v. United States, 530 U.S. 428 (2000).

Duncan v. Walker, 533 U.S. 167 (2001).

Flores-Figueroa v. United States, 556 U.S. 646 (2009).

Garner v. Burr, 1 K.B. 31 (1951).

Hamer v Sidway, 124 N.Y. 538, 27 N.E. 256 (1891).

Hill v. Jones 725 P. 2d 1115 (1986).

Leocal v. Ashcroft, 543 U.S. 1 (2004).

McBoyle v. U.S., 283 U.S. 25 (1931).

Miranda v. Arizona, 384 U.S. 436 (1966).

Morissette v. United States, 342 U.S. 246 (1952).

Nix v. Heddon, 149 U.S. 304 (1893).

Ohio v. Roberts, 448 U.S. 56 (1980).

Palsgraf v. Long Island Railroad, 248 N.Y. 339 (1928).

Schenck v. United States, 249 U.S. 47 (1919).

Smith v. United States, 508 U.S. 223 (1993).

Tarasoff v. UC Regents, 17 Cal.3d. 425 (1976).

U.S. v. Carolene Products, 304 U.S. 144 (1938).

Other Legal Sources

U.S. Constitution
U.S. Federal Rules of Evidence
California Penal Code

Other Sources

Agamben, Giorgio. *The Sacrament of Language: An Archaeology of the Oath*, trans. Adam Kotsko. Stanford, CA: Stanford University Press, 2011.

Ainsworth, Janet. "'You Have the Right to Remain Silent . . .' but Only if You Ask for It Just So: The Role of Linguistic Ideology in American Police Interrogation Law." *International Journal of Speech, Language and the Law* Vol. 15, no. 1 (2008): 1–21.

———. "The Meaning of Silence in the Right to Remain Silent," in *The Oxford Handbook of Language and Law*, ed. Peter Meijes Tiersma and Lawrence Solan. Oxford, UK, and New York: Oxford University Press, 2012.

———. "Silence, Speech, and the Paradox of the Right to Remain Silent in American Police Interrogation," in *Law and Language: Current Legal Issues*, Vol. 15, 371-385, ed. Michael Freeman and Fiona Smith. Oxford, UK: Oxford University Press, 2013.

Allen, Danielle S. *Talking to Strangers: Anxieties of Citizenship since* Brown v. Board of Education. Chicago: The University of Chicago Press, 2004.

———. "The Art of Association," presented at General Aspects of Law, Kadish Center for Morality, Law, and Public Affairs, University of California, Berkeley, September 7, 2012.

Althusser, Louis. "Ideology and Ideological State Apparatuses." In *Lenin and Philosophy, and Other Essays*, 121–176. New York: Monthly Review Press, 1972.

American Law Institute. "The A.L.I. Annual Report: 2011–2012"; available at www.ali .org/doc/thisIsALI.pdf.

Arendt, Hannah. *The Human Condition*. Chicago: University of Chicago Press, 1958.

Aristotle. *The Politics, and the Constitution of Athens*, ed. Stephen Everson, trans. Jonathan Barnes. Cambridge, UK, and New York: Cambridge University Press, 1996.

Augustine. *On Free Choice of the Will*. Trans. Thomas Williams. Indianapolis: Hackett Publishing Company, 1993.

Austin, J. L. *How to Do Things with Words*. Cambridge, MA: Harvard University Press, 1962.

———. "Performatif-Constatif," in *Cahiers de Royaumont, Philosophie no. IV, La philosophie analytique* (Paris: Éditions de Minuit, 1962): 271–304.

———. *Philosophical Papers*, 3rd ed. Oxford, UK: Oxford University Press, 1979.

Austin, John. *The Province of Jurisprudence Determined*. 1832. Reprint, London: Wiedenfeld and Nicholson, 1954.

Ayres, Ian. "Valuing Modern Contract Scholarship." *The Yale Law Journal* Vol. 112, no. 4 (2003): 881–901.

"Baby Azaria's Mother Seeks Ruling That Dingo Killed Her." *BBC News Asia* (February 24, 2012).

Baird, Douglas G. *Contracts Stories*. New York: Foundation Press/Thomson/West, 2007.

Bakhtin, M. M. *The Dialogic Imagination: Four Essays*. Trans. Caryl Emerson and Michael Holquist. Austin, TX: University of Texas Press, 1981.

———. *Speech Genres and Other Late Essays*. Trans. Vern W. McGee. Austin, TX: University of Texas Press, 1986.

Balkin, Jack M. "The Footnote." *Faculty Scholarship Series* Paper 287, (1989); available at http://digitalcommons.law.yale.edu/fss_papers/287.

Berk-Seligson, Susan. *The Bilingual Courtroom: Court Interpreters in the Judicial Process*. Chicago: University of Chicago Press, 1990.

———. *Coerced Confessions: The Discourse of Bilingual Police Interrogations*. Berlin and New York: Mouton de Gruyter, 2009.

Bernal, Carlos L. "A Speech Act Analysis of Judicial Decisions." *European Journal of Legal Studies* Vol. 2, no. 1 (2007); available at http://www.ejls.eu/2/34UK.htm.

Bierbauer, Charles. "Its Goal More Widely Accepted Than Its Leader." *CNN.com* (October 17, 1995).

Blomquist, Robert F. "The Presidential Oath, the American National Interest and a Call for Presiprudence." *UMKC Law Review* Vol. 73, no. 1 (2004): 1–52.

Borrows, John. *Recovering Canada: The Resurgence of Indigenous Law*. Toronto: University of Toronto Press, 2002.

Brettler, Lucinda Ann Vandervort. "The Phenomenology of Adolph Reinach: Chapters in the Theory of Knowledge and Legal Philosophy." PhD dissertation, McGill University, 1973.

Burgess, Sarah K. "Standing before the Law: Recognition, Power, and the Limits of Identity." PhD dissertation, Rhetoric, University of California, Berkeley (2007).

Burkhardt, Armin, ed. *Speech Acts, Meaning, and Intentions: Critical Approaches to the Philosophy of John R. Searle*. Berlin and New York: W. de Gruyter, 1990.

Burns, Robert P. *A Theory of the Trial*. Princeton, NJ: Princeton University Press, 2001.

Butler, Judith. *Gender Trouble: Feminism and the Subversion of Identity*. New York: Routledge, 1990.

———. *Bodies That Matter: On the Discursive Limits of "Sex"*. New York: Routledge, 1993.

———. "Longing for Recognition." In *Hegel's Philosophy and Feminist Thought: Beyond Antigone?* ed. Kimberly Hutchings and Pulkkinen Tuija. New York: Palgrave Macmillan, 2010.

———. *Subjects of Desire: Hegelian Reflections in Twentieth-Century France*. New York: Columbia University Press, 2012.

Bybee, K. *All Judges Are Political—Except When They Are Not: Acceptable Hypocrisies and the Rule of Law*. Stanford, CA: Stanford University Press, 2010.

Calavita, Kitty. *Invitation to Law & Society: An Introduction to the Study of Real Law*. Chicago: University of Chicago Press, 2010.

Calvi, James V., and Susan Coleman, *American Law and Legal Systems*, 7th ed. Boston, MA: Longman, 2012.

Cao, Deborah. *Chinese Law: A Language Perspective* Aldershot, UK, and Burlington, VT: Ashgate, 2004.

――. "Illocutionary Acts of Chinese Legislative Language." *Journal of Pragmatics* Vol. 41, no. 7 (2009): 1329–1340.

Cardi, Jonathan W. "The Hidden Legacy of *Palsgraf*: Modern Duty Law in Microcosm." *Boston University Law Review, Forthcoming Wake Forest Univ. Legal Studies Paper No. 1851316* (2011).

Cavell, Stanley. *Must We Mean What We Say?* Cambridge, UK: Cambridge University Press, 1976.

――. *A Pitch of Philosophy: Autobiographical Exercises.* Cambridge, MA: Harvard University Press, 1994.

――. *Philosophical Passages: Wittgenstein, Emerson, Austin, Derrida.* Oxford, UK: Basil Blackwell, 1995.

――. *Philosophy the Day after Tomorrow.* Cambridge, MA: Belknap Press of Harvard University Press, 2005.

Chafee, Zechariah Jr. "Do Judges Make or Discover Law?" *Proceedings of the American Philosophical Society,* Vol. 91, no. 5 (Dec. 3, 1947): 405–420.

Charnock, Ross. "Hart as Contextualist? Theories of Interpretation in Language and the Law," in *Law and Language: Cambridge Legal Issues, Vol.15.* ed. Michael Freeman and Fiona Smith. Oxford, UK: Oxford University Press, 2013: 128–150.

――. "Overruling as a Speech Act: Performativity and Normative Discourse." *Journal of Pragmatics* Vol. 41, no. 3 (2009): 401–426.

Clastres, Pierre. "The Duty to Speak," in *Society Against the State: Essays in Political Anthropology.* New York: Zone Books, 1987.

Comaroff, John L., and Jean Comaroff. *Ethnicity, Inc.* Chicago: University of Chicago Press, 2009.

Conklin, W. E. *The Phenomenology of Modern Legal Discourse: The Juridical Production and the Disclosure of Suffering.* Alderport/Brookfield: Dartmouth/Ashgate, 1998.

Constable, Marianne. "Genealogy and Jurisprudence: Nietzsche, Nihilism, and the Social Scientification of Law." *Law & Social Inquiry* Vol. 19, no. 3 (1994): 551–590.

――. "Reflections on Law as a Profession of Words." In *Justice and Power in Sociolegal Studies,* ed. Bryant G. Garth and Austin Sarat. Evanston, IL: Northwestern University Press; American Bar Foundation, 1998.

――. "The Silence of the Laws: Justice in Cover's 'Field of Pain and Death,'" In *Law, Violence, and the Possibility of Justice,* ed. Austin Sarat (Princeton, NJ: Princeton University Press, 2001.

――. "On Not Leaving Law to the Lawyers." In *Law in the Liberal Arts,* ed. Austin Sarat. Ithaca, NY: Cornell University Press, 2004.

――. *Just Silences: The Limits and Possibilities of Modern Law.* Princeton, NJ: Princeton University Press, 2005.

——. "Response," *PoLAR: Political and Legal Anthropology Review* Vol. 33 (2010): 148–151.

——. "Speaking the Language of Law: A Juris-dictional Primer." *English Language Notes* Vol. 48, no. 2 (2010).

Cover, Robert. "Nomos and Narrative." *Harvard Law Review* Vol. 97, no. 4 (1983): 4-68.

——. "Violence and the Word," *Yale Law Journal* Vol. 95, no. 8 (1986): 1601–1629.

Crosby, John. "Adolf Reinach: Reinach's Discovery of the Social Act." In *Aletheia*, Vol. 3: *Philosophy of Law*. Irving, TX: International Academy of Philosophy Press, 1983.

"A Cry of Fire in a Crowded Theatre," *The New York Times*, September 25, 1884, 4.

Dayan, Colin. *The Law Is a White Dog: How Legal Rituals Make and Unmake Persons*. Princeton, NJ: Princeton University Press, 2011.

de Certeau, Michel. *The Practice of Everyday Life*. Berkeley: University of California Press, 1984.

Demaine, Linda J. "In Search of an Anti-Elephant: Confronting the Human Inability to Forget Inadmissible Evidence." *George Mason Law Review* Vol. 16 (Fall 2008): 99–140.

Derrida, Jacques. *Of Grammatology*, trans. Gayatri Spivak. Baltimore: Johns Hopkins University Press, 1976.

——. "Declarations of Independence." *New Political Science*, Vol. 7, no. 1 (1986): 7–15.

Deutscher, Guy. *Through the Language Glass: Why the World Looks Different in Other Languages*. Croydon, UK: Arrow Books, Random House, 2010.

"Dingo to Blame for Azaria's Death: Coroner." *The Age*, June 12, 2012; available at www.theage.com.au/national/dingo-to-blame-for-azarias-death-coroner-20120612-206wo.html.

Dreyfus, Hubert L. "The Current Relevance of Merleau-Ponty's Phenomenology of Embodiment." *Electronic Journal of Philosophy*, no. 4 (1996).

Dreyfus, Hubert L., and Stuart E. Dreyfus. "From Socrates to Expert Systems: The Limits of Calculative Rationality," *Technology in Society* Vol. 6 (1984): 217–233.

Dreyfus, Stuart E. "The Five-Stage Model of Adult Skill Acquisition." *Bulletin of Science, Technology & Society* Vol. 24, no. 3 (June 1, 2004): 177–181.

Dubois, James M. *Judgement and Sachverhalt: An Introduction to Adolf Reinach's Phenomenological Realism*. Dordrecht: Kluwer Academic Publishers, 1995.

Dunn, Pintip Hompluem. "How Judges Overrule: Speech Act Theory and the Doctrine of Stare Decisis." *Yale Law Journal* Vol. 113, no. 2 (2003): 493–531.

Edwards, Linda H. *Legal Writing and Analysis*, 2nd ed. New York: Aspen Publishers, 2007.

Esmeir, Samera. *Juridical Humanity: A Colonial History*. Stanford, CA: Stanford University Press, 2012.

Espeland, Wendy N., and Mitchell L. Stevens. "Commensuration as a Social Process," *Annual Review of Sociology* Vol. 24 (1998): 313–338.

Euripides. *Hippolytos*, ed. William Spencer Barrett. Oxford, UK: Clarendon Press, 1978.

———. *Euripides II*, ed. David Kovacs. Cambridge, MA: Loeb Classical Library, Harvard University Press, 1994.

———. *Hippolytus* [in Greek text and parallel English translation], trans. Michael R. Halleran. Warminster, UK: Aris & Phillips, 1995.

———. *Hippolytus*. trans. Michael R. Halleran. Newburyport, MA: Focus Classical Library, 2001.

Ewick, Patricia and Susan S. Silbey. *The Common Place of Law: Stories from Everyday Life*. Chicago: University of Chicago Press, 1998.

Farnsworth, Edward Allan. *Farnsworth on Contracts, Vol. 1*. New York: Aspen, 1996.

Farnsworth, Ward. *The Legal Analyst: A Toolkit for Thinking about the Law*. Chicago: University of Chicago Press, 2007.

Feeley, Malcolm. "Theoretical Issues and Methodological Problems: Three Voices of Socio-Legal Studies." *Israel Law Review* Vol. 35, no. 2 (2001): 175.

Felman, Shoshana. *The Scandal of the Speaking Body: Don Juan with J. L. Austin, or Seduction in Two Languages*. Stanford, CA: Stanford University Press, 2003.

Felstiner, William L. F., Richard L. Abel, and Austin Sarat. "The Emergence and Transformation of Disputes: Naming, Blaming, Claiming." *Law & Society Review* Vol. 15, no. 3/4 (1980): 631–654.

Fischweicher, Jessica. "Perjury." *American Criminal Law Review* Vol. 45, no. 2 (2008): 799-824.

Fitzpatrick, Peter. "Why the Law Is Also Nonviolent." In *Law, Violence, and the Possibility of Justice*, ed. Austin Sarat, pp. 142–174. Princeton, NJ: Princeton University Press, 2001.

Foucault, Michel. *The Archeology of Knowledge and the Discourse on Language*, trans. A. M. Sheridan Smith, New York: Pantheon Books, 1972.

———. *The Order of Things: An Archeology of the Human Sciences*. New York: Vintage Books, 1973.

———. *Discipline and Punish: The Birth of the Prison*. Trans. Alan Sheridan New York: Pantheon Books, 1977.

Friedman, Lawrence M. "The Law and Society Movement." *Stanford Law Review* Vol. 38, no. 3 (1986): 763–80.

Fuller, Lon L. "Positivism and Fidelity to Law—A Reply to Professor Hart." *Harvard Law Review* Vol. 71 (1958): 630–672.

———. *Legal Fictions*. Stanford CA: Stanford University Press, 1967.

Galanter, Marc. "Why the Haves Come Out Ahead: Speculations on the Limits of Legal Change." *Law & Society Review* Vol. 9, no. 1 (1974): 95–160.

Gammon, Robert. "Guns and the Code of Silence." *East Bay Express* August 17–23 (2011): 6.

Garfield, Alan E. "Promises of Silence: Contract Law and Freedom of Speech," *Cornell Law Review* Vol. 83 (1994): 261–364.

Garner, Bryan A. *The Elements of Legal Style*, 2nd ed. New York: Oxford University Press, 2002.

Gauthier, Jeffrey A. *Hegel and Feminist Social Criticism: Justice, Recognition, and the Feminine*. Albany: State University of New York Press, 1997.

Ginsburg, Jane C. *Introduction to Law and Legal Reasoning*, 3rd ed. New York: Foundation Press, 2003.

Givelber, Daniel J., William J. Bowers, and Carolyn L. Blitch. "Tarasoff, Myth and Reality: An Empirical Study of Private Law in Action," originally published in *Wisconsin Law Review* Vol. 443 (1984); reprinted in "Social Impact: The Importance of Communication Networks," in *Law & Society: Readings on the Social Study of Law*, ed. Stewart Macaulay, Lawrence M. Friedman, and John Stookey. pp. 627–658 New York: W. W. Norton & Company, 1995.

Glazebrook, P. R. "Misprision of Felony; Shadow or Phantom?" *American Journal of Legal History* Vol. 8 (1964): 189–208 and 293–302.

Goehr, Lydia. *The Imaginary Museum of Musical Works: An Essay in the Philosophy of Music*. Oxford, UK: Oxford University Press, 2007.

Goff, Barbara E. *The Noose of Words: Readings of Desire, Violence, and Language in Euripides' Hippolytos*. Cambridge, UK, and New York: Cambridge University Press, 1990.

Goodrich, Peter. *Oedipus Lex: Psychoanalysis, History, Law*. Berkeley: University of California Press, 1995.

Habermas, Jürgen. "Discourse Ethics: Notes on a Program of Philosophical Justification," in *Moral Consciousness and Communicative Action*, trans. Christian Lenhart and Shierry Weber Nicholson, 43–115. Cambridge, MA: MIT Press, 1990.

Halleran, Michael R. *Euripides' Hippolytus: Translation with Notes, Introduction and Essay*. Focus Classical Library. Newburyport, MA: Focus Publishing Company, 2001.

Hart, H. L. A. "Positivism and the Separation of Law and Morals." *Harvard Law Review* Vol. 71 (1958): 593–629.

———. *The Concept of Law*. Oxford, UK: Clarendon Press, 1961.

———. "The Ascription of Responsibility and Rights." In *Logic and Language*, ed. Antony Flew, 151-174. Garden City, NY: Anchor, Doubleday, 1965.

Hastie, Reid. "The Challenge to Produce Useful 'Legal Numbers.'" *Journal of Empirical Legal Studies* Vol. 8 (2011): 6–20.

Heidegger, Martin. *Poetry, Language, Thought*, trans. Albert Hofstadter. New York: Harper & Row, 1971.

———. *Basic Writings: From Being and Time (1927) to the Task of Thinking (1964)*, ed. David Farrell Krell, New York: Harper & Row, 1977.

———. *On the Way to Language*, trans. Peter D. Hertz. New York: Harper & Row, 1982.

———. *Plato's Sophist*, trans. Richard Rojcewicz and Andre Schuwer. Bloomington: Indiana University Press, 1997.

Hewett, Martin A. "Hearsay at Guantanamo: A 'Fundamental Value' Determination." *Georgetown Law Journal* Vol. 96 (2008): 1375–1409.

Hibbits, Bernard J. "Making Sense of Metaphors: Visuality, Aurality, and the Reconfiguration of American Legal Discourse." *Cardozo Law Review* Vol. 16 (1994–1995): 229–356.

Ho, H. L. "What Does a Verdict Do? A Speech Act Analysis of Giving a Verdict." *International Commentary on Evidence* Vol. 4, no. 2 (2002): Article 1.

Hoebel, E. Adamson. *The Law of Primitive Man.* Harvard, MA: Atheneum, 1954.

Hoebel, E. Adamson, and Karl N. Llewellyn. *The Cheyenne Way.* Norman, OK: University of Oklahoma Press, 1941.

Honig, B. "Declarations of Independence: Arendt and Derrida on the Problem of Founding a Republic." *The American Political Science Review* Vol. 85, no. 1 (1991): 97–113.

Honneth, Axel. *The I in We: Studies in the Theory of Recognition.* Cambridge, UK, and Malden, MA: Polity Press, 2012.

Horwitz, Morton J. "The Historical Foundations of Modern Contract Law." *Harvard Law Review* Vol. 87, no. 5 (1974): 917–956.

"I Really Do Swear, Faithfully: Obama and Roberts Try Again." *The New York Times*, January 21 2009. Available at www.nytimes.com/2009/01/22/us/politics/22oath.html?_r=0.

Johns, Fleur. "Living in International Law," in *Reading Modern Law: Critical Methodologies and Sovereign Formations: Essays in Honour of Peter Fitzpatrick*, ed. Ruth Buchanan, Stewart Motha, and Sundhya Pahuja. London: Routledge-Cavendish, 2010: 74–86.

Jordan, June. "Nobody Mean More to Me than You and the Future Life of Willie Jordan." *Harvard Educational Review* Vol. 58, no. 3 (1988): 363–375.

Kadish, Sanford H., Stephen J. Schulhofer, Carol S. Steiker, and Rachel E. Barkow. *Criminal Law and Its Processes: Cases and Materials*, 9th ed. New York: Aspen Publishers, 2012.

Kagan, Robert A., Bliss Cartwright, Lawrence M. Friedman, and Stanton Wheeler. "The Evolution of State Supreme Courts." *Michigan Law Review* Vol. 76, no. 6 (1978): 961–1005.

Kalman, Laura. *Legal Realism at Yale, 1927–1960.* Chapel Hill: University of North Carolina Press, 1986.

Kassin, Saul M., and Samuel R. Sommers. "Inadmissible Testimony, Instructions to Disregard, and the Jury: Substantive Versus Procedural Considerations." *Personality and Social Psychology Bulletin* Vol. 23, no. 10 (1997): 1046–1054.

Kazanijan, David. *The Colonizing Trick: National Culture and Imperial Citizenship in Early America.* Minneapolis: University of Minnesota Press, 2003.

Kelly, John M. "Audi Alteram Partem," *Natural Law Forum* Vol. 9, no. 103 (1964): 103–110.

Kendall, Sara. "Contested Jurisdictions: Legitimacy and Governance at the Special Court for Sierra Leone." PhD dissertation, Rhetoric, University of California, Berkeley (2009).

Kennedy, D. "From the Will Theory to the Principle of Private Autonomy: Lon Fuller's 'Consideration and Form.'" *Columbia Law Review* Vol. 100 (2000): 94–175.

Knop, Karen, Ralf Michaels, and Annelise Riles, eds. *Transdisciplinary Conflict of Laws*, in *Law & Contemporary Problems*, Vol. 71, no. 3 (2008).

Koskenniemi, Martti. *The Politics of International Law*. Oxford, UK: Hart Publishing, 2011.

Kreitner, Roy. *Calculating Promises: The Emergence of Modern American Contract Doctrine*. Stanford, CA: Stanford University Press, 2007.

Krygier, Martin. "Law as Tradition." *Law and Philosophy* Vol. 5, no. 2 (1986): 237–262.

———. "Thinking Like a Lawyer," in *Ethical Dimensions of Legal Theory*, Poznan Studies in the Philosophy of the Sciences and Humanities, ed. Wojciech Sadurski. Amsterdam: B. R. Grüner Publishing Company, 1991.

———. "Public Values," in *Civil Passions: Selected Writings*. Melbourne: Black Inc., 2005.

Lacey, Nicola. *A Life of H. L. A. Hart : The Nightmare and the Noble Dream*. Oxford, UK: Oxford University Press, 2004.

Latour, Bruno, writing as Jim Johnson. "Mixing Humans and Nonhumans Together: The Sociology of a Door-Closer." *Social Problems* Vol. 35, no. 3 (1988): 298–310.

Laugier, Sandra. "Performativité, Normativité et Droit." *Archives de Philosophie* Vol. 67, no. 4 (2004): 607–627.

———. "Actes de Langage et États de Choses: Austin et Reinach." *Les Études philosophiques*, no. 1 (2005): 73–97.

Law Commission of Canada, "Justice Within: Indigenous Legal Traditions," Discussion Paper (2006), available as http://dalspace.library.dal.ca/bitstream/handle/10222/10229/ILT%20Discussion%20Paper%20EN.pdf?sequence=1as at www/lcc/gc.ca.

Lee, Dorothy. *Freedom and Culture*. Englewood Cliffs, NJ: Prentice-Hall, 1959.

———. *Valuing the Self: What We Can Learn from Other Cultures*. Englewood Cliffs, NJ: Prentice-Hall, 1976.

Lee, Grace Soyon. "Our Word (or the Lack Thereof) Is Our Bond," in *Speech and Silence in American Law*, ed. Austin Sarat. New York: Cambridge University Press, 2010: 39-47.

Legge, James. *The Chinese Classics*. Hong Kong: Hong Kong University Press, 1960.

Lemons, Katherine. "At the Margins of Law: Adjudicating Muslim Families in Contemporary Delhi." PhD dissertation, Anthropology, University of California Berkeley (2010).

Liptak, Adam. "Justices Are Long on Words but Short on Guidance." *The New York Times*, November 17, 2010.

Liptak, Adam, and Julia Preston. "Justices Limit Use of Identity Theft Law in Immigration Cases." *The New York Times*, May 5, 2009.

Macaulay, Stewart. "Noncontractual Relations in Business: A Preliminary Study," *American Sociological Review* Vol. 28 (1963): 55–68.

Macaulay, Stewart, John Kidwell, and William C. Whitford. *Contracts: Law in Action, The Concise Course.* Newark, NJ: LexisNexis, 2003.

Maitland, Frederic William. *The Forms of Action at Common Law; A Course of Lectures by F. W. Maitland,* ed. A. H. Chaytor and W. J. Whittaker. Cambridge, UK: Cambridge University Press, 1936.

Manderson, Desmond. *Songs without Music: Aesthetic Dimensions of Law and Justice.* Berkeley: University of California Press, 2000.

Mayali, Laurent. *Of Strangers and Foreigners (Late Antiquity–Middle Ages).* Berkeley: Regents of the University of California, 1993.

Mellinkoff, David. *The Language of the Law.* Boston: Little, Brown and Co., 1963.

Mertz, Elizabeth. *The Language of Law School: Learning to "Think Like a Lawyer."* Oxford, UK, and New York: Oxford University Press, 2007.

Meyer, Jeffrey A. "Authentically Innocent: Juries and Federal Regulatory Crimes." *Hastings Law Journal* Vol. 59 (2007): 137-194.

Meyer, Linda. "When Reasonable Minds Differ." *NYU Law Review* Vol. 71 (1996): 1467–1528.

———. *The Justice of Mercy.* Ann Arbor: University of Michigan Press, 2010.

Mnookin, Robert, and Lewis Kornhauser. "Bargaining in the Shadow of the Law: The Case of Divorce." In *Law & Society: Readings on the Social Study of Law,* ed. Stewart Macaulay, Lawrence M. Friedman, and John A. Stookey. New York: W. W. Norton & Co., 1995.

Mulligan, Kevin, ed. *Speech Act and* Sachverhalt: *Reinach and the Foundations of Realist Phenomenology.* Dordrecht, Boston, and Hingham, MA: M. Nijhoff, Kluwer Academic Publishers, 1987.

Murphy, Jeffrie G., ed. *Punishment and Rehabilitation,* 3rd ed. Belmont, CA: Wadsworth Publishing Company, 1994.

Neumann, Richard K. *Legal Reasoning and Legal Writing: Structure, Strategy, and Style,* 4th ed. Gaithersburg, MD: Aspen Law & Business, 2001.

Nietzsche, Friedrich. *Twilight of the Idols,* trans. R. J. Hollingdale. London: Penguin, 1968.

———. *On the Genealogy of Morals,* in *Basic Writings of Nietzsche,* trans. Walter Kaufmann. New York: Modern Library, 1968.

———. *Beyond Good and Evil: Prelude to a Philosophy of the Future,* trans. Walter Kaufmann. New York: Vintage Books, 1989.

Noonan, John. *Persons and Masks of the Law.* Berkeley, CA: University of California Press, 2002; Chapter 4.

Oakley, John B, Edgar Bodenheimer, and Jean C. Love. *Introduction to the Anglo-American Legal System,* 4th ed. (St. Paul, MN: Thomson/West, 2004).

Parker, James. "The Soundscape of Justice," *Griffith Law Review* Vol. 20, no. 4 (2011): 962–993.

Paulson, Stanley. "Demystifying Reinach's Legal Theory" in *Speech Act and* Sachverhalt: *Reinach and the Foundations of Realist Phenomenology*, ed. Kevin Mulligan, 133–154. Dordrecht: Martinus Nijhoff Publishers, 1987.

Pether, Penelope. "Inequitable Injunctions: The Scandal of Private Judging in the U.S. Courts." *Stanford Law Review* Vol. 56 (2004): 1435–1580.

Plato. "Phaedrus," trans. Harold North Fowler. In *Euthyphro, Apology, Crito, Phaedo, Phaedrus*. Loeb Classical Library. Cambridge, MA: Harvard University Press, 1990.

Post, Robert C. "Defending the Lifeworld: Substantive Due Process in the Taft Court Era." *Faculty Scholarship Series* Paper 193 (1998): 1489–1647. *Boston University Law Review* Vol. 78 (1998): 1489–1546.

———. "The Supreme Court Opinion as Institutional Practice: Dissent, Legal Scholarship, and Decisionmaking in the Taft Court." *Faculty Scholarship Series* Paper 186 (2001). *Minnesota Law Review* Vol. 85 (2000–2001): 1267–1390.

Pound, Roscoe. "Law in Books and Law in Action." *American law Review* Vol. 44 (1910): 12–36.

Prosser, William L., John W. Wade, Victor E. Schwartz, Kathryn Kelly, and David F. Partlett. *Torts: Cases and Materials*, 12th ed. New York: Foundation Press, 2010.

Rawls, John. *A Theory of Justice*. Cambridge, MA: Belknap Press of Harvard University Press, 1971.

Raz, Joseph. "Promises in Morality and Law." *Harvard Law Review* Vol. 95, no. 4 (1982): 916–938.

Reinach, Adolf. "Die Apriorischen Grundlagen Des Bürgerlichen Rechtes," in *Jahrbuch Für Philosophie Und Phänomenologische Forschung*. Halle: Max Niemeyer, 1913.

———. "The A Priori Foundations of Civil Law," trans. John Crosby. In *Aletheia*, Vol. 3: *Philosophy of Law*. Irving, TX: International Academy of Philosophy Press, 1983.

Resnik, Judith, and Dennis E. Curtis. *Representing Justice: Invention, Controversy, and Rights in City-States and Democratic Courtrooms*. New Haven, CT: Yale University Press, 2011.

Richland, Justin B. *Arguing with Tradition: The Language of Law in Hopi Tribal Court*. Chicago: University of Chicago Press, 2008.

———. "Jurisdiction: Grounding Law in Language." *Annual Review of Anthropology* Vol. 42 (2013): 209–226.

Ricoeur, Paul. *The Course of Recognition*. Cambridge, MA: Harvard University Press, 2005.

Riles, Annelise. "Cultural Conflicts," in *Law and Anthropology*, ed. Michael Freeman and David Napier. Oxford, UK: Oxford University Press, 2009.

Rosenstock-Huessy, Eugen. *Speech and Reality*. Norwich, VT: Argo Books, 1970.

Roy, Christopher. "Marriage in Connecticut: A Guide to Resources in the Law Library," in *Connecticut Judicial Branch Law Series*. New Britain, CT: Judicial Branch, State of Connecticut, 2012.

Rubenfeld, Jed. *Freedom and Time: A Theory of Constitutional Self-Government.* New Haven, CT: Yale University Press, 2001.

Salyer, Lucy. "'You Never Loved Me': Allegiance and the Loss of Citizenship in Wartime America," paper presented at American Historical Association meeting, Washington, D.C., January 2006.

Salzwedel, Matthew. "Scrubbing Adverbs from Legal Writing," September 12, 2012. Available at http://lawyerist.com/scrubbing-adverbs-from-legal-writing/.

Sammons, Jack. "Origin of the Opinion as a Work of Art," paper presented at Association for the Study of Law, Culture and the Humanities, Annual Meeting, March 2012.

Sarat, Austin. Ed. *Speech and Silence in American Law.* New York: Cambridge University Press, 2010.

Sarat, Austin, Marianne Constable, David Engel, Valerie Hans and Susan Lawrence, Eds. *Everyday Practices and Trouble Cases.* Evanston, IL: Northwestern University Press, 2009

Scheb, John M. *An Introduction to the American Legal System*, 3d ed. New York: Aspen Publishers, 2012.

Scheppele, Kim. *Legal Secrets: Equality and Efficiency in the Common Law.* Chicago: University of Chicago Press, 1988.

Searle, John R. *Speech Acts: An Essay in the Philosophy of Language.* London: Cambridge University Press, 1969.

Seifert, Josef. "Is Reinach's 'Apriorische Rechtslerhre' More Important for Positive Law Than Reinach Himself Thinks?" In *Aletheia*, Vol. 3: *Philosophy of Law.* Irving, TX: International Academy of Philosophy Press, 1983.

Selznick, Philip. *The Moral Commonwealth.* Berkeley, CA: University of California Press, 1994.

Shapiro, Barbara J. "Oaths, Credibility and the Legal Process in Early Modern England: Part One." *Law and Humanities* Vol. 6, no. 2 (December 2012) 145–178 and "Oaths, Credibility and the Legal Process in Early Modern England: Part Two," Vol. 7, no. 1 (2013) 19–54.

Sherwin, Richard K. *Visualizing Law in the Age of the Digital Baroque: Arabesques and Entanglements.* London: Routledge, 2011.

Shiffrin, Seana Valentine. "The Divergence of Contract and Promise." *Harvard Law Review* Vol. 120, no. 3 (2007): 708–753.

Shuy, Roger W. *Language Crimes: The Use and Abuse of Language Evidence in the Courtroom.* Cambridge, MA: Blackwell, 1993.

Silbey, Susan. "J. Locke, op. cit.: Invocations of Law on Snowy Streets." *Journal of Comparative Law* Vol 5, no. 2 (2010): 66–91.

Silving, Helen. "The Oath: I." *Yale Law Journal* Vol. 68, no. 7 (June 1959): 1329–1390.

Simon, Jonathan. *Governing through Crime: How the War on Crime Transformed American Democracy and Created a Culture of Fear* (Oxford, UK: Oxford University Press, 2007).

Simpson, A. W. B. "The Horwitz Thesis and the History of Contracts." *The University of Chicago Law Review* Vol. 46, no. 3 (1979): 533–601.

Sklansky, David Alan. *Evidence: Cases, Commentary and Problems*, 2d ed. (Austin, TX: Aspen Casebooks/Wolters Kluwer, 2008).

Smith, Barry. "On the Cognition of States of Affairs," in *Speech Act and* Sachverhalt: *Reinach and the Foundations of Realist Phenomenology*, ed. Kevin Mulligan, 189–225. Dordrecht: Martinus Nijhoff Publishers, 1987.

———. "Towards a history of speech act theory," in *Speech Acts, Meaning, and Intentions; Critical Approaches to the Philosophy of John R. Searle*, ed. Armin Burkhard. Berlin and New York: W. de Gruyter, 1990.

Smith, George H. "Of the Certainty of the Law and the Uncertainty of Judicial Decisions," *American Law Review* Vol. 23 (1889): 699–718.

Solan, Lawrence. *The Language of Statutes: Laws and Their Interpretation.* Chicago and London: The University of Chicago Press, 2010.

Solan, Lawrence, and Peter Meijes Tiersma. *Speaking of Crime: The Language of Criminal Justice.* Chicago: University of Chicago Press, 2005.

Strunk, William Jr., and E. B. White. *The Elements of Style.* 4th ed. New York: Macmillan, 1999.

Thomas, George C. III, and Richard A. Leo. "The Effects of *Miranda v. Arizona*: Embedded in Our National Culture?" *Crime and Justice* Vol. 29 (2002): 203–271.

Tiersma, Peter Meijes. "Reassessing Unilateral Contracts: The Role of Offer, Acceptance and Promise." *UC Davis Law Review* Vol. 26, no. 1 (1992): 1–86.

———. The Plain English Movement; retrieved on May 30, 2013, from www.language andlaw.org/PlainEnglish.htm.

Tiersma, Peter Meijes, and Lawrence Solan. *The Oxford Handbook of Language and Law.* Oxford, UK, and New York: Oxford University Press, 2012.

Tomlins, Christopher. "Law and History," in *Oxford Handbook of Law and Politics*, ed. Keith E. Whittington, R. Daniel Keleman, and Gregory A. Caldeira. Oxford, UK and New York: Oxford University Press, 2010: 723–735.

———. "'Law as . . .': Theory and Practice in Legal History," *UC Irvine Law Journal* Vol. 1, no. 3 (2011): 1039–1079.

———. "Memo Prepared as Background Reading for Panel on Social Science and Legal Scholarship," in *Berkeley-NSF Workshop, The Interplay between Social Science and Law Schools.* Berkeley: UC Berkeley School of Law, May 2012.

Tomlins, Christopher L., and Bruce H. Mann, eds. *The Many Legalities of Early America.* Chapel Hill: University of North Carolina Press, 2001.

Tomlins, Sir Thomas Edlyne. "Quakers." In *The Law-dictionary, Explaining the Rise, Progress, and Present State of the British Law: Defining and Interpreting the Terms or Words of Art, and Comprising Also Copious Information on the Subjects of Trade and Government*, Volume 2. London: J. and W. T. Clarke; Longman, Rees, Orme, Brown, Green, and Longman: 1835.

Toobin, Jeffrey. *The Oath: The Obama White House and the Supreme Court*. New York: Doubleday, 2012.

Tsai, Robert. "Fire, Metaphor, and Constitutional Myth-Making." *Georgetown Law Review* Vol. 93 (2004–2005): 181–240.

Virgil, *The Aeneid*, trans. W. F. Jackson Knight. London: Penguin Classics, 1956.

Webber, Jeremy. "The Grammar of Customary Law." *McGill Law Journal* Vol. 54 (2009): 579–626.

Weston, Nancy. "The Metaphysics of Modern Tort Theory," *Valparaiso University Law Review* Vol. 28, no. 3 (1994): 919–1006.

White, Edward G. *Tort Law in America: An Intellectual History*. Oxford, UK: Oxford University Press, 2003.

White, James Boyd. *Heracles' Bow: Essays on the Rhetoric and Poetics of Law*. Madison: University of Wisconsin Press, 1985.

———. *The Legal Imagination*, abridged ed. Chicago: University of Chicago Press, 1985.

———. *Justice as Translation: An Essay in Cultural and Legal Criticism*. Chicago: University of Chicago Press, 1990.

———. *Living Speech Resisting the Empire of Force*. Princeton, NJ: Princeton University Press, 2006.

Williams, Bernard. *Moral Luck: Philosophical Papers, 1973–1980*. Cambridge, UK, and New York: Cambridge University Press, 1981.

Winter, Steven L. *A Clearing in the Forest: Law, Life, and Mind*. Chicago: University of Chicago Press, 2001.

Witmore, Michael. *Culture of Accidents: Unexpected Knowledges in Early Modern England*. Stanford, CA: Stanford University Press, 2001.

Wittgenstein, Ludwig. *Philosophical Investigations*, trans. G. E. M. Anscombe. Oxford, UK: Blackwell, 1958.

Wydick, Richard C. *Plain English for Lawyers*, 5th ed. Durham, NC: Carolina Academic Press, 2005.

Zeitlin, Froma. "The Power of Aphrodite: Eros and the Boundaries of the Self in the Hippolytus," in *Directions in Euripidean Criticism: A Collection of Essays*, ed. Peter Burian, 52–111, 189–208. Durham, NC: Duke University Press, 1985.

Index

THE CULTURAL LIVES OF LAW

Austin Sarat, Editor

The Cultural Lives of Law series brings insights and approaches from cultural studies to law and tries to secure for law a place in cultural analysis. Books in the series focus on the production, interpretation, consumption, and circulation of legal meanings. They take up the challenges posed as boundaries collapse between as well as within cultures, and as the circulation of legal meanings becomes more fluid. They also attend to the ways law's power in cultural production is renewed and resisted.

The Street Politics of Abortion: Speech, Violence, and America's Culture Wars
Joshua C. Wilson
2013

Better Left Unsaid: Victorian Novels, Hays Code Films, and the Benefits of Censorship
Nora Gilbert
2012

Zooland: The Institution of Captivity
Irus Braverman
2012

After Secular Law
Edited by Winnifred Fallers Sullivan, Robert A. Yelle, and Mateo Taussig-Rubbo
2011

All Judges Are Political—Except When They Are Not: Acceptable Hypocrisies and the Rule of Law
Keith J. Bybee
2010

Riding the Black Ram: Law, Literature, and Gender
Susan Sage Heinzelman
2010

Tort, Custom, and Karma: Globalization and Legal Consciousness in Thailand
David M. Engel and Jaruwan S. Engel
2010

Law in Crisis: The Ecstatic Subject of Natural Disaster
Ruth A. Miller
2009

The Affective Life of Law: Legal Modernism and the Literary Imagination
Ravit Reichman
2009

Fault Lines: Tort Law as Cultural Practice
Edited by David M. Engel and Michael McCann
2008

Lex Populi: The Jurisprudence of Popular Culture
William P. MacNeil
2007

The Cultural Lives of Capital Punishment: Comparative Perspectives
Edited by Austin Sarat and Christian Boulanger
2005